ROUTLEDGE LIBRARY EDITIONS:
GERMAN HISTORY

Volume 31

T0298448

THE NUREMBERG DOCUMENTS

THE NUREMBERG DOCUMENTS
Some Aspects of German War Policy
1939–45

PETER DE MENDELSSOHN

Routledge
Taylor & Francis Group

NEW YORK AND LONDON

First published in 1946 by George Allen & Unwin Ltd

This edition first published in 2020
by Routledge
52 Vanderbilt Avenue, New York, NY 10017

and by Routledge
2 Park Square, Milton Park, Abingdon, Oxon OX14 4RN

Routledge is an imprint of the Taylor & Francis Group, an informa business

© 1946 Peter de Mendelssohn

British Library Cataloguing in Publication Data
A catalogue record for this book is available from the British Library

ISBN: 978-0-367-02813-8 (Set)
ISBN: 978-0-429-27806-8 (Set) (ebk)
ISBN: 978-0-367-24742-3 (Volume 31) (hbk)
ISBN: 978-0-367-24749-2 (Volume 31) (pbk)
ISBN: 978-0-429-28415-1 (Volume 31) (ebk)

Publisher's Note
The publisher has gone to great lengths to ensure the quality of this reprint but points out that some imperfections in the original copies may be apparent.

Disclaimer
The publisher has made every effort to trace copyright holders and would welcome correspondence from those they have been unable to trace.

PETER DE MENDELSSOHN

THE NUREMBERG DOCUMENTS

Some Aspects
of German War Policy
1939-45

LONDON
GEORGE ALLEN & UNWIN LTD

FIRST PUBLISHED IN 1946

PRINTED IN GREAT BRITAIN
in 11-pt. Baskerville type
BY WILLMER BROS. & CO. LTD., BIRKENHEAD

To
Kingsley Martin

INTRODUCTORY NOTES

During the first four weeks of the Nuremberg Trial alone the British and American delegations to the prosecution submitted in evidence more than five thousand documents taken from captured enemy files and archives. These represented approximately one-tenth of a total considered relevant to the charges and sifted and scrutinised for this purpose at Nuremberg. But even that larger mass constituted only a fraction of the total haul. What this amounts to, in the British and American zones alone, we have yet to learn, but we know that it must run into at least several hundred thousand individual papers, some of them of considerable length. To these must be added, of course, the archives which fell into Soviet and French hands as well as the material seized and now held by the governments of the liberated countries.

This is an event without precedent or parallel in history. There was, of course, never such a national collapse as that of the Nazi State. Nor has ever before a disintegrating big power, in surrendering, yielded practically all its state secrets, military, political and economic, and many private secrets into the bargain, from confidential speeches of its leaders down to their secret diaries, private correspondence, and even telephone conversations. After the discoveries at Flensburg, Fechenheim, Berchtesgaden and scores of other minor hiding places, it seems unlikely that any of the important events and developments of the twelve years of Hitler's régime will now remain obscure or open to conflicting interpretation. We know or shall know in due course, the whole inside story of this period, and for the first time it will be the contemporaries and not the historians of future generations who will be able to present the full and authentic record without having to rely, more often than not, on shrewd guess-work, indiscretions or documents of doubtful origin. This time it is all here for everyone to see and read. Or at least, it should be.

We have no reason to doubt that eventually and in their own good time those among the United Nations who, by right of conquest, are the possessors of this material, will join in the task of preparing a full and integral official publication, amply and expertly commented, in as many languages as necessary. Such a publication must needs run into many stout folio volumes and is likely to take several years to prepare. When it appears it· may prove far too costly for the average reader to acquire and too voluminous and intricate for him to study with profit. The present series of studies, based on some of this captured material, is an attempt, not to anticipate the official publication of the full records, but to place before the general reader, condensed to their essentials and arranged in their proper sequence and context, those documents which are meanwhile available and which are of immediate interest. It is not claimed that this first survey supplies a complete picture or answers all the questions the common man has been asking himself during the past twelve years. But it is felt that with the help of this compilation the picture may become a little less obscure than it has been so far, and that at least some of the questions find a provisional answer. If these studies do not provide the whole truth—and no such claim is made for them—they may at least give an indication in which direction to look for what is missing.

The great lesson in contemporary history which the·full range of these documents contains, could not be learned at Nuremberg. There we had a court house and not a school house. It was perhaps both fortunate and unfortunate that these documents were made public in the course of the proceedings of the International Military Tribunal—fortunate because in this way the world was allowed at least a series of brief, though often disconnected glimpses into the secrets of German war policy under the Hitler regime ; unfortunate because these glimpses had to remain glimpses and could not broaden into a wide and comprehensive panorama. That was and remains most tantalizing to the student of contemporary history. But it was not the task of the Tribunal to present to the world an authentic, fully documented running account of the last twelve years, revealing in full light the pattern and texture of this period. Had it attempted this the trial would have digressed from its original purpose and it would have lasted many years. Its task was to judge and sentence twenty war criminals, and the prosecution which was in the hands of lawyers and not historians—but lawyers called upon to judge on history and some of its makers—made use of these documents which happened to be in Allied hands, only where and when they helped to substantiate particular points in the charges.

The publication of part of the secret German state archives at Nuremberg was therefore purely incidental. If no captured

German files had been available, the prosecution would have had to look elsewhere for evidence, but the trial would not therefore have been held up or rendered impossible. On the other hand, had there been no Nuremberg Trial even less or possibly nothing might have been made public for several years. As it was, much came to light, but by no means all and not necessarily what is most interesting or most important and urgent for us to know. To make matters even more complicated, even those documents that were used by the prosecution, were seldom issued in full and often only in such disconnected extracts as happened to bear out specific points in the indictment. This is the material on which these preliminary studies are based, and the author offers them with all possible reserve and conscious of their inadequacy.

History, it will be argued, is not presented in this entirely accidental or incidental manner, and the author is the last person to argue that it is. But it does speak for the untold wealth of information contained in these archives that even under these restrictive and selective circumstances these documents enable one, by careful cross-checking and piecing together, to form an idea of at least some aspects and episodes of the war period which contain new and entirely unexpected angles. On whatever spot in this pile of documents one plays the flash-light of inquiry, some intriguing detail invariably shines up. The author has attempted no more than to disentangle and isolate them from the mass of secondary information in which they are embedded, to place them in what seemed to him their proper relation to each other, and to add here and there a paragraph of connecting comment. If mistakes or errors occurred, only the publication of further documents can correct them. If gaps were left and question-marks remained, only what is still withheld can provide the answer. If the reader is tantalized now and then by an incongruousness, so is the author. No one is looking forward with greater impatience to the publication of the full records than he, and no one, therefore, is more conscious of the shortcomings of this first effort to piece together the inside story of the monstrous twelve years through which we have passed.

The author had the choice of presenting all the material in his possession in one straight, consecutive narrative following a chronological order, or of dividing it up under a number of main headings indicating certain selected phases and periods or particular military operations. The first method had the advan-

tage of providing a broad panorama, but there was a danger of
the picture becoming so crammed with detail that the
pattern itself would be lost to view and chronological order
difficult to maintain. The second method had the obvious advantage of concentrating on specific aspects and dealing with them
in as much detail as was available, but a certain number of
cross-references and the duplication and even triplication of
certain key quotations which were of significance in more than
one connection, became unavoidable.

The author has attempted to combine the two methods.
In the opening chapter he has endeavoured to outline the broad,
general direction of German political and military planning
from about 1938 until the invasion of the Low Countries. The
documents themselves recommended this method since, as
the reader will perceive, almost invariably each new step or
action followed from the preceding one and their sum total
presented a well thought-out whole. In the succeeding chapters
certain specific aspects of German war planning on which a
particular wealth of documentary evidence was available, are
treated by themselves, although not in full isolation. Thus one
chapter presents documents relative to German-Italian relations
before and during the war, while another assembles what
material there is relating to the planned invasion of Great
Britain. A brief study is devoted to German-Spanish relations
and the final part is an attempt to present, in chronological
order, a mass of documents bearing on German Soviet relations
from August, 1939, until the German invasion of the Soviet
Union and such information as has become available on the
actual planning, military and political, of this invasion. The
chapters are not necessarily interdependent and may be read
in isolation, but the reader will no doubt gain a better and
more complete view if he reads them in the order in which they
are presented.

The author is not responsible for the English translations of
the German documents quoted, often at length, in these studies.
These translations were made by British and American officials,
mostly military, of the Military Tribunal at Nuremberg, and
the author is aware that frequently they leave a good deal to
be desired in regard both to smoothness and clarity. Many of
these translations were made in great haste, in order to have them
ready for the opening of the trial, and many of them, the author
is certain, offered formidable difficulties even to experienced

translators owing to the peculiarly involved and prolix style affected by Nazi officials including Hitler himself. Apart from correcting here and there an obvious error or smoothing out what could only be due to haste or carelessness, the author has not attempted to improve on these translations. He felt that they presented official texts officially submitted to the Tribunal and, no matter how inadequate, had to be accepted as such.

The author is indebted to the Editor of the *New Statesman and Nation* for permitting him to incorporate in these studies material previously published in that journal.

Berlin, May, 1946.

CONTENTS

The Best Way to Start a War

Phases of German political and military planning,
1937-40

In his " Political Testament " which was discovered by the Allied authorities in Germany and published in January, 1946, Hitler writes :

" It is untrue that I or anybody else in Germany wanted the war in 1939. It was willed and instigated exclusively by those international statesmen who were either of Jewish origin or were working on behalf of Jewish interests. I have made too many offers of restriction and limitation of armaments which posterity will not be able to dispute forever, to be charged with the responsibility for the outbreak of this war. Furthermore I never desired, after the unfortunate first world war, to see another conflict arise with Great Britain or even the United States."

Shortly after this had been written, the archives of the Supreme Command of the German Armed Forces (OKW), were captured by the Allies at Flensburg. Among these files there was the text of a speech which Hitler made at a secret briefing meeting of all Commanders-in-Chief, on November 23rd, 1939, shortly after the conclusion of the campaign in Poland. In this he says :

" One might accuse me of wanting to fight and fight again. In struggle I see the fate of all beings. I did not organize the armed forces in order not to strike. The decision to strike was always in me. Time is working for our adversary. I shall strike and not capitulate ! "

It is not the purpose of these studies to prove that Hitler was a liar. The world knows that. Nor is it intended to demonstrate, with the aid of these documents, that Hitler and his associates deliberately and wilfully started the war, knowing full well at every stage what they were doing and what the consequences of their actions were likely to be. That proof has been given, a hundred times over, before the Nuremberg Tribunal. The purpose of the present analysis is to inquire into Hitler's technique of starting the war ; to follow as far as possible the various phases and stages of his political and military planning as it lead up to and into the war ; and to form an idea of the overall conception which dominated this planning.

We know that Hitler wanted the war. But how did he go about arranging for it? It is on this question that the Nuremberg Documents help to throw a good deal of fresh, and sometimes glaring, light.

If War Broke out Tomorrow

When did Hitler start to plan for war? The answer, without much fear of exaggeration, is : on the day he came to power.

Already in 1934, eighteen months after the establishment of the National Socialist régime, Schacht submitted to Hitler a " Report on the state of preparation for war-economic mobilization." It is dated September 30th, 1934, and in it Schacht states :

" The Reich Ministry of Economy has been charged with the economic preparation for war, a task considered important in view of the lessons of the first World War. The work can be divided into two parts. The theoretical part includes the legal and organizationial preparation, such as laws and directives. Practical preparation includes building up of stocks, new construction of facilities to produce scarce goods, re-deployment of industry to safe areas and influence over fiscal and trade policies. Preparations had to be made for two contingencies— the sudden outbreak of war in the immediate future, and a future goal of active mobilization. The first goal was to be reached through mostly negative measures (restrictions), the second needs active measures and directives. The task of building up stocks is hampered by the lack of foreign currency. The need for secrecy and camouflage is also a retarding influence."

Schacht then describes the intricate organization of his department, gives a list of Laws and Directives he wishes to see enacted to facilitate his work, and concludes with this remark :

" The aim of the proposed directives is the establishment of strict economy. The uncertainty of conditions under which a future war may be fought, together with the lack of raw materials and foreign currency, requires this forthwith. Therefore strict control of all economic activity is required, with special attention paid to the use of scarce materials, *i.e.*, rationing and priority systems."

Two years later we find the planners in the thick of it, surrounded by all the difficulties Schacht had pointed out. 1936 was a year of frantic planning. Conscription had been introduced the year before, and the demilitarized zone of the Rhineland occupied. The rapidly expanding armed forces had to be equipped and money and raw materials found for this purpose. We possess a number of documents relating to this period and showing, in a series of glimpses, how under the direction of Goering supreme efforts were made to surmount forbidding obstacles and to adapt the entire German national economy to the huge priority claims of the armed forces.

On May 3rd, 1935, Schacht in another memorandum to Hitler on the Financing of Armament," had said : " The following explanations take as their premise the fact that the execution of the armament programme is, by its speed and extent, *the mission of German policy* and that everything else therefore must be subordinated to this purpose, unless the neglect of other aspects endangers the main goal. Even after March 16th, 1935, the difficulty continues to exist, that to expose the German nation to propaganda for the purpose of winning its support for armament cannot be undertaken without imperilling our position internationally. The financing of the armament programme, already almost impossible, is being made especially difficult by that."

On May 27th, 1936 a conference of the Council of Ministers is held under Goering's chairmanship, in which the question of substituting raw materials is discussed. Schacht has many objections. Goering brushes them aside with the words : " All measures are to be considered from the standpoint of an assured waging of war." On August 31st, 1936, Blomberg, then War Minister and Supreme Commander of the Armed Forces, sends a long letter to Goering in which he asks him to take care of the finances of the armed forces. He explains that the 1936 Budget is inadequate, and that the sum of about 10 milliard Reichsmarks which was provided for the Wehrmacht for 1936, is not sufficient.

"Additional expenditure for the Army is required chiefly owing to the remilitarization of the Rhineland, the fortification of the Rhineland, the setting up of all the 36 divisions already by October 1st, 1936, the speeding up of motorization, particularly the establishment of 4 fully motorized infantry divisions " etc. In the Navy " the required faster increase of personnel, the building of a 4th entry to Wilhelmshaven, and the refortification of Heligoland are causing additional expenses." Finally " according to an order of the Führer, the setting up of all planned air force units has to be completed by April 1st, 1937. Therefore considerable expenditure is required for 1936 which at the time when the budget for 1936 was made, was envisaged for later years only."

B

A further Council of Ministers is held on September 4th, 1936, again under Goering's chairmanship, with Schacht, Blomberg, Schwerin-Krosigk and others present. Goering announces that he has received from Hitler a memorandum containing general instructions for the execution of the armament programme. Goering adds : " It starts from the basic thought that the showdown with Russia is inevitable. What Russia has done in the field of reconstruction, we too can do. Just what sort of risk is it our industry is afraid of, compared to the risks in the sphere of foreign affairs which the Fuhrer runs so continuously ? If war should break out tomorrow, we would be forced to take measures from which we might possibly shrink at the present moment. They are, therefore, to be taken. All measures have to be taken just as if we were actually in the stage of imminent danger of war. The execution of the order of the Führer is an absolute command."

The Blomberg Directive 1937-38

What kind of war did they envisage ? What was the political and strategic concept underlying this planning ?

The earliest document released at Nuremberg and allowing some insight into the ideas of the planners, is the " Directive for Unified Preparation for War of the Armed Forces," issued by Blomberg, then Reich Minister for War and Commander-in-Chief of the Armed Forces, on June 24th, 1937. It is not the first of its kind, for in its covering letter reference is made to " Directives for the Unified Preparation of a possible war by Army, Navy, and Air Force, issued on June 26th, 1936 " which Blomberg asks all commands to return to him upon receipt of the new Directive. This new Directive, of which we possess the full text, was valid from July 1st, 1937, until presumably September 30th, 1938, when the Directive for "Case Green," the invasion of Czechoslovakia, came into force.

It is a lengthy and instructive document, and is divided into three parts : general guiding principles, likely warlike eventualities, and special preparations.

Part One (general guiding principles) opens with this statement :

" The general political situation justifies the assumption that Germany need not consider an attack from any side. Chief grounds for this are, in addition to the lack of desire for war in almost all nations, particularly the Western Powers, the deficiencies in the preparedness for war of a number of states, and of Russia in particular.

" The intention to unleash a European War is held just as little by Germany. Nevertheless the politically fluid world situation, which does not preclude surprising incidents, demands a continuous preparedness for war of the German Armed Forces, in order (a) to counter attack at any time ; (b) to enable the military exploitation of politically favourable opportunities should they occur. Preparations of the Armed Forces for a possible war in the Mobilization Period 1937–38 must be made with this in mind."

These general preparations comprise " the permanent preparedness for mobilization of the German Armed Forces, even before the completion of the rearmament and full preparedness for war ; further work on ' Mobilization without Public Announcement ' in order to put the Armed Forces in a position to begin a war suddenly and by surprise both as regards strength and time ; work on the transport of the bulk of the regular army from East Prussia to the Reich ; preparatory measures in case German territory is violated suddenly by a foreign power with hostile intent. In the latter event armed resistance will be offered without special orders. The services will therefore empower the competent frontier or coastal territory commanders to take in such cases all necessary counter-measures against hostile attacks, irrespective of whether a legal basis exists for any individual measure or not. Under no circumstances, however, may the German frontier be crossed or flown over or foreign territory be violated without my approval. German territory is not deemed to be violated in the case of individual sentries or patrols crossing our frontiers accidentally or not deliberately, or as a result of the excessive zeal of a junior commander ; nor is territory deemed to be violated if flown over owing to faulty navigation or if German territorial waters are entered by warships with obviously non-hostile intentions."

So far so good. Such precautionary measures against violations of national territory by a foreign power are normal, and form part of the natural routine work of any General Staff in any country in the world. It is interesting, however, that the Directive expressly empowers commanders not to trouble about the legal basis of their measures. But the catch is at the beginning. Germany does not believe anybody, least of all the Western Powers, has the intention of attacking her. But should a " politically favourable opportunity " occur, everything must be ready to " enable its military exploitation." In other words : we shall attack if it seems profitable for us to do so, and if there is a chance of doing so with impunity." The pattern for Austria and Czechoslovakia is set.

The next paragraphs in the Directive make this quite clear. They deal with " the probable warlike eventualities for which concentration plans will be drafted." These are

    I. War on two fronts with the focal point in the West.
          (Concentration ' Red ')
   II. War on two fronts with the focal point in the South-East.
          (Concentration ' Green ')

Furthermore, special preparations are to be made for the following eventualities :

    I. Armed intervention against Austria.
          (Special Case ' Otto ')
   II. Warlike entanglements with Red Spain.
          (Special Case ' Richard ')
  III. Britain, Poland, Lithuania, take part in a war against us.
          (Special case ' Extension Red–Green ')

The Directive adds : " Although we can in all probability reckon, as matters stand at present, on one or more allies in particular, individual circumstances, all elaborations and plans are to be based on the fundamental assumption that we stand alone for the time being.

" The Directive for the conduct of the war itself, and the definition of the objects of the war which depend on the general political as well as the military and economic situation at the beginning of a war, will be issued through me by the Führer and Supreme Commander."

The time is June, 1937. The thinking of the German High Command clearly centres round Austria, Czechoslovakia, and France. That is where sooner or later they intend to strike. Part Two of the " Blomberg Directive " shows the details of these plans.

Concentration " Red "

" War on Two fronts with focal point in the West " (Concentration ' Red ') is based on the following assumptions :

" In the West, France is the opponent. Belgium may side

with France, either at once, or later, or not at all. It is also possible that France may violate Belgium's neutrality if the latter is neutral ; she will certainly violate that of Luxembourg.

"In the East we shall in all probability have to reckon with the hostile attitude of Russia and Czechoslovakia. One can assume that Poland and Lithuania will remain neutral for the time being.

"From Austria, Italy, Hungary and Yugoslavia at least, benevolent neutrality is expected. Britain's attitude will be uncertain.

"The outbreak of war will presumably take the form of a surprise attack by the French army and air force against Germany with the participation of the French fleet. In the east, Czechoslovakia can be counted upon to stay out for the time being, as long as political pressure by Russia does not force her to act prematurely, mainly with her air force, reinforced by Russia. Operations by Russian naval forces are probable."

It is, looking back on it, a strange picture. France is credited by Hitler with extraordinary aggressiveness and initiative—he obviously visualizes her pouncing upon him out of the blue sky for no particular reason that one is able to discern—whereas in the East he assumes a close understanding between the Soviet Union and Czechoslovakia, and he obviously bases his calculations on the assumption that nothing can prevent the mutual assistance pacts between France, the Soviet Union, and Czechoslovakia from coming automatically into force. He sees no way out of a two-front war, and accepts it. What, in this event, would his actions be ?

The Directive says : "It is the task of the German armed forces to make their preparations in such a manner that the bulk of the armed forces can be employed against France, and that our action in the east is at first limited to defence—and that with the employment of the smallest possible forces." On this basis the following tasks are allotted to the three Services :

For the Army the chief emphasis lies in the West. "It will be the first task of the army, by commencing the battle as near as possible to the frontier, to prevent the enemy from advancing towards and across the Rhine and the Black Forest, and to defend the area to the west of the Rhine and the north of the Moselle as long as possible. If Belgium is neutral it is particularly important to hold the Eifel as a position in the flank of, and a base for action against, the northern French wing. Every favourable opportunity for effective minor blows against the French army is to be made use of. The defence of the eastern and southern frontiers of the Reich can be left to the frontier guards and reserve divisions for the time being. East Prussia is to be defended. But according to the political situation, transport of part of, or all the active forces to the Reich by sea must be allowed for."

The Navy will have its main duties either in the Baltic or in the North Sea, according to the naval situation. " The strategic task of the navy is to secure our sea-communications in the Baltic, the North Sea, and the oceans of the world ; in particular communications with East Prussia are to be safeguarded. The operational execution of this task depends on the ratio of strength at sea-and it is to be striven for through eliminating the enemy's naval forces. At the same time as defending and guiding our own sea communications, enemy traffic in the North Sea and Baltic is to be made impossible and that in the Atlantic, Mediterranean and, as occasion arises, in other seas, is to be interfered with by suitable naval forces. Prevention and delay of French troop transports from Africa can considerably ease our own war on land. In all these preparations the political necessity is to be taken into account that at the beginning of a war we ensure for ourselves the neutrality of non-belligerent countries by a painstaking observance of their rights."

The Air Force, finally, is also concentrated in the West. " The first tasks of the air force here will in all probability be (a) the battle against the air forces of the western enemies and their ground organization as well as against the main armament centres of the enemy's aircraft industry ; (b) participation in the battles on land, and at a later date possibly also the delaying of the enemy's deployment if that is the only way to prevent larger initial successes by the enemy army which it might not be possible, under certain circumstances, to catch up with later ; (c) protection of the German sources of production, and in particular of Berlin, the Ruhr, and the Central German industrial area ; (d) attacks on targets of mainly political importance, such as Paris, need my special consent in every case."

Concentration " Green "

" War on two fronts with focal point in the Southeast " (Concentration " Green ") is the alternative plan, and in the light of history reads as considerably more real than its counterpart. It is based on this assumption :

" To parry the imminent attack of a superior enemy coalition, the war in the East may begin with a German surprise operation against Czechoslovakia. The conditions for such a stroke in the fields of politics and international law must be created beforehand. It is to be expected that Poland and Lithuania will probably take a neutral or at least a temporizing attitude, while Austria, Italy and Yugoslavia will be at least benevolent neutrals. Hungary will sooner or later perhaps join Germany in her action against Czechoslovakia ; France and Russia will most probably open hostilities against Germany, Russia at first with her naval and air forces only. The leaders of German policy will endeavour with all possible means to assure the neutrality of Britain, which is to be regarded as an absolutely essential prerequisite for ' Case Green,' and also of all other countries not so far mentioned but capable of conducting military operations against Germany."

We can see that the planning has left the sphere of the vague and somewhat nebulously hypothetical and has entered an area which we recognize as familiar. It is noteworthy to what extent purely propagandist phrases penetrate even the argument of these highly technical military calculations. Why should Blomberg want to talk about " the imminent attack of a superior enemy coalition " when, at the outset of his Directive, he states explicitly that no one is likely to attack Germany, and that the Western Powers in particular have no desire whatever for war ? What, then, v. ould there be to parry ? Nothing except that these military planners feel that they must lie even to themselves in order to have a clear conscience. That they intend to pick a deliberate quarrel with Czechoslovakia is clear from the statement that political conditions for such an invasion must be created beforehand by the political leaders, as was actually done.

How is the operation to be carried out ?

" The task of the German Armed Forces," says the Blomberg Directive, " is to prepare in such a way that the main body of all forces can break into Czechoslovakia quickly, by surprise and with the greatest possible weight, while in the West the smallest possible force is provided to cover the rear of this attack. The aim and object of this surprise attack by the German Armed Forces should be to destroy the hostile armed forces and to occupy Bohemia and Moravia and thus eliminate completely, for the duration of the war, the threat by Czechoslovakia to the rear of the operations in the West, and to take from the Russian Air Force the most substantial portion of its operational base in Czecho-slovakia.''

It is useful to remind oneself, from time to time, that this was written in June, 1937, long before Munich and nine months before the invasion of Austria.

The tasks of the three services are then outlined.

" The largest part of the Army will be used for an attack on Czechoslovakia. The short-term planning of this operation will depend on the strength and operational readiness of the German Army at the time, on the state of preparations, and also on the attitude of Poland. The possibility that German troops will be deployed on Austrian territory should be taken into consideration in the long-term preparations, since 'it can be assumed that the necessary conditions for this will be created by the political leaders. The beginning of military operations must be fully synchronized with air force operations and I therefore reserve the right to determine the exact time for the attack.

"The aim is a strategic pounce on Czechoslovakia, systematically planned in peace-time, which will overrun her fortifications by a surprise attack, pin down and destroy her armed forces whilst still being mobilized, and conquer Czechoslovakia in a short time by making use of her racial disintegration. The military prerequisite for this surprise attack can only be attained if the tank formations are fully equipped and completely ready for employment.

" The troops covering the rear in the West must be reduced both in number and in quality to the utmost degree, having regard to the state of fortifications existing at that time. The limit of this reduction is to be determined only by the necessity to hold the industrial areas in the Rhineland and Westphalia, and to maintain communications between Northern and Southern Germany. East Prussia will be defended but according to the political situation the transport away of some or all of the operational forces by the sea route to the Reich must be reckoned with.''

It is June, 1937, and already it is all as we know it. Some noteworthy points stand out. It is assumed as possible that German troops will be able to operate against Czechoslovakia from Austria. The High Command is aware that Hitler is planning the incorporation of Austria in the Reich, but it is not certain how and when it will come about. There is, however, the possibility of its being accomplished before action is taken against Czechoslovakia. No decision seems as yet to have been taken. That the troops which are at Blomberg's disposal are not really sufficient in number or quality to cover adequately both fronts, is clear from his remark about the West, and it is remarkable to what extraordinary lengths he is prepared to go in thinning the line in the West, in order to assure adequate striking power in the Southeast. Maintenance of communications between Northern and Southern Germany as a minimum objective for the defence, strikes one as grotesquely hazardous. Yet Blomberg was apparently willing to run this perilous risk. On the other hand, he seems to be fairly certain that his troops in East Prussia will not be able to hold out and will have to be evacuated by sea.

As regards the Air Force, practically the whole of it is to be employed against Czechoslovakia, and only a minimum strength is to be provided for the West. The first tasks of the Air Force will be :

" The paralyzing of the Czechoslovak mobilization, especially combating the Czech air force and its ground organizations, also of the mobilization centres, and the most important communication centres. The intention is effectively to disintegrate the Czechoslovak State, and thus to facilitate the army's task of taking possession. With regard to the assignment of targets, all industries and plants to be used by us later on should nevertheless be preserved in our own future interest as far as military considerations permit.

" Protection of the sources of German production, with special reference to Berlin, the Central German industrial area and the Ruhr area.

" The beginning of operations of the Air Force against Czechoslovakia must be completely synchronized with the beginning of operations by the Army. I therefore reserve for myself the fixing of zero hour."

Special Case " Otto "

Part Three of the " Blomberg Directive " mentions three " special cases " which the High Commands of the Services are requested to consider. The first is " Special Case ' Otto ' " which is defined as " armed intervention in Austria in the event of her restoring the monarchy." This sub-chapter throws some useful light on the co-ordination of the various plans as they stood at that time.

" The object of this operation," says the Directive, " will be to compel Austria by armed force to renounce a restoration. Making use of the domestic political divisions in Austria, the march-in will be made in the general direction of Vienna and all resistance will be broken. Parts of the German Air Force are to be employed in direct support of the Army. Any further employment of Air Force units will be decided only by me. The question whether formations of the National Socialist Party will be employed over and above the Armed Forces, rests with the Supreme Commander of the Armed Forces."

The Directive orders that " Case Otto " be planned, "(a) as an isolated action without simultaneous concentration on other fronts ; (b) as part of concentration ' Red.' Special case ' Otto ' will *not* be planned as an operation simultaneous with concentration ' Green.' Should the political prerequisites for both cases arise simultaneously, special case ' Otto ' will be deferred until the conclusion of concentration ' Green.' The possibility of concentration ' Green ' developing out of special case ' Otto ' must be taken into account, and this possibility must be included in the planning."

The picture emerges in clearer outlines. Translated into non-military language, this means : the invasions of Austria and Czechoslovakia must on no account be mixed up and conducted as a single operation. Should conditions arise in which both could be carried out, Czechoslovakia must have preference, and Austria must wait. While Blomberg would obviously prefer to annex Austria without being engaged at the same time on other fronts, he does foresee that a war with its main emphasis against France, and only rear-guard defence against Czechoslovakia, might make it necessary to take Austria quickly in order the better to safeguard his rear. He also foresees that the invasion of Austria might embroil him in a conflict with Czechoslovakia, but this he would prefer to avoid. Finally, in invading Austria, he foresees resistance and orders it to be crushed. There is no talk here of the union of two brother nations. The country is to be conquered in a straightforward military campaign.

The second special case which has the code-word " Richard " and covers " warlike entanglements with Red Spain " is discussed in detail in another chapter of these studies. (Chapter IV, Felix and Isabella). The third, finally, called " Extension Red–Green " envisages that the military and political basis for operations " Red " and " Green " would run into difficulties

" if either Britain, Poland or Lithuania, or all three, join the side of our opponents from the very beginning of the war," and not in its later course. This is a situation which horrifies the planners.

" Our military position would be worsened to an unbearable, even hopeless extent. The political leaders will therefore do everything to keep these countries neutral, above all Britain and Poland. Nevertheless, supplementary plans are to be worked out for plans " Red " and " Green " for the event of the political leadership failing to achieve this aim. The following conditions are to be the basis for discussion :

(a) Britain will employ all her available economic and military means against us. She will at first support France with naval and air forces, and for the latter she will try to win Belgium, and eventually Holland as bases.

(b) That Poland should take part in the opening phases of hostilities against us, possibly on the side of Russia, is, in the present political situation, more than improbable. Should it nevertheless come to this, Poland's concentration on land against Germany would take place in a form which is, in its essence, known to us, in order to gain first East Prussia and thereafter, in co-operation with Czechoslovakia, Silesia.

(c) Lithuania will, above all, serve the Russian Air Force as an advanced base. An attack on land need only be reckoned with in combination with Poland or after the arrival of Russian Army forces in Lithuania."

So much for the purely military plan which emerges from the " Blomberg Directive." What is the larger political conception of which this is but the technical expression in terms of military strategy ? In other words : what is it that Hitler is after at this time ?

The Hossbach Minutes

The answer is contained in a secret speech which Hitler made four months later. On November 5th, 1937, he called six men to the Reich Chancellery in Berlin. They were the Minister for War, Blomberg, the Commander-in-Chief of the Army, Fritsch, the Commander-in-Chief of the Navy, Raeder, the Commander-in-Chief of the Air Force, Goering, the Reich Minister for Foreign Affairs, Neurath, and Hitler's aide-de-camp, Colonel Hossbach. Hitler spoke to them for over four hours. He told them that what he was going to say was of the highest importance, and the result of detailed deliberations and of the experiences of his 4½ years in government. He desired to explain to those present his fundamental ideas on the possibilities and necessities of expanding German foreign policy and " in the interests of a far-sighted policy he requested that his statements be looked upon, in the case of his death, as his Last Will and Testament." The minutes of this meeting were taken by Colonel Hossbach, and this record, the complete text of which is available, has since become known as the " Hossbach Minutes." It is indeed a most important document.

Hitler began by stating that the aim of German policy was the security and the preservation of the nation and its propagation. This was a problem of space.

" The German nation comprises 85 million people who, because of the number of individuals and the compactness of habitation, form a homogeneous European racial body which cannot be found in any other country. On the other hand it justifies the demand for larger living space more than for any other nation. If no political body exists in the living space which corresponds to the German racial body, this is the consequence of several centuries of historical development, and should this political condition continue to exist, it will represent the greatest danger to the preservation of the German nation at its present high level. An arrest of the deterioration of the German element in Austria and Czechoslovakia is just as little possible as the preservation of the present state in Germany itself. Instead of growth, sterility will appear, and as a consequence tensions of a social nature will make themselves felt after a number of years, because political and philosophical ideas are of a permanent nature only as long as they are able to produce the basis for the realization of the actual claim to existence of a nation. The German future depends, therefore, exclusively on the solution of the need for living space. Such a solution can be sought naturally only for a limited period, about 1—3 generations."

How can this problem be tackled ? Before going into the question of more living space, Hitler examines two other possible ways of attaining a prosperous future for the German people, " either by way of autarky, or by way of an increased share in world trade and industry." What are the chances ?

Autarky not possible

Autarky, Hitler explains, can be carried out only on the basis of a strict National Socialist state policy. Assuming that this could be achieved, the results would be as follows :

" In the field of raw materials, only limited but not total autarky can be attained. Wherever coal can be used for the extraction of raw materials, autarky is feasible. In the case of ores the position is much more difficult. Requirements in iron and light metals can be covered by ourselves. Copper and tin, however, cannot. Cellulose materials can be covered by ourselves as long as sufficient wood supplies exist. A permanent solution is not possible. Regarding edible fats, self-sufficiency is possible.

" With regards to foodstuffs, the question of autarky must be answered with a definite ' No.' The general increase in the standard of living as compared with 30 or 40 years ago, has brought about a simultaneous increase in demand, an increase in personal consumption even among the producers, the farmers, themselves. The proceeds from the production increase in agriculture have been used to cover the increase in demand, therefore they represent no absolute increase in production. A further increase in production by making greater demands on the soil is not possible because the soil already shows signs of deterioration owing to the use of artificial fertilizers, and it is therefore certain that, even with the greatest possible increase in production, participation in the world market could not be avoided."

" The considerable expenditure of foreign exchange to secure food by import, even in periods when our own harvests are good, increases catastrophically when our own harvest is really poor. The possibility of such a catastrophe grows in proportion to the increase in population, and the annual excess of 560,000 births over deaths would result in an increased consumption of bread since the child is a greater bread-eater than the adult."

" Permanently to counter the difficulties of food supplies by lowering the standard of living and by rationalization is impossible on a continent which has developed an approximately equalized standard of living. As the solution of the unemployed problem has resulted in maximum consumption capacity, some small corrections in our agricultural home production will be possible, but not a wholesale alteration of the standard of food consumption. Consequently autarky becomes impossible, especially in the sphere of food supplies, as well as generally."

Self-sufficiency, then, is out. What of the other possibility ?

Participation in world economy too risky

Hitler sees no future in Germany attempting to take its full
share in world economy. " There are limits to our participation
which we are unable to transgress. Market fluctuations would be
an obstacle to a secure foundation of the German position.
International commercial agreements do not offer any guarantees
for practical execution. It must be borne in mind, as a matter
of fact, that since the World War (1914–18) industrialization has
taken place in countries which formerly exported food. We live
in an age of economic empires in which the tendency to colonize
once again approaches the condition which originally motivated
colonization. In Japan and Italy economic motives are the basis
of their will to expand. The economic need will also drive
Germany to it. Countries outside the great economic empires
have special difficulties in expanding economically.

" The upward tendency which we observe in world economy
and which is due to armament competition, can never form a
permanent basis for an economic settlement, and the latter is
also hampered by the economic disruption caused by Bolshevism.
It is a pronounced military weakness of those states who base
their existence on export. As our exports and imports are carried
over those sea lanes which are ruled by Britain, it is more a
question of security of transport than of foreign currency, and this
explains the great weakness in our food situation in wartime.

" The only way out, and one which may appear imaginary,
is to secure greater living space, an endeavour which at all times
has been the cause of the formation of states and of movement of
nations."

These views of Hitler's are not reproduced here in order to
demonstrate their correctness or invalidity. It is obvious that they
contain a few indisputably true observations among swarms of
uninformed, half-baked, and at times deliberately misleading
speculations. Hitler rejects in particular the second solution not
because it is unworkable but because he wants to reject it. His
mind is set on something else. His arguments are quoted here
only in order to show the general trend of his thought. This may
be summarized as follows : I want to pull all the Germans living
in Europe together into one compact body, physically and
geographically. Unless I do this, the Austrians will develop more
and more along their own lines and away from the Reich, the
Germans in Czechoslovakia and elsewhere will be absorbed
by these countries and assimilated, and German national

conscience will " deteriorate " in favour of a greater integration in the general European body. But if I pull them all together how can I feed them ? I cannot maintain them on the same standard of living as the rest of Europe under a system of self-sufficiency. I shall always have to buy the balance of our food requirements abroad, and I am unable and unwilling to spend foreign exchange on this. Besides, I am unwilling to participate in world economy and give and take my share in world markets as I undoubtedly could, because I am unwilling to be dependent on anybody, and participation in world economy would put restraints on my foreign policy which I am unwilling to accept. Besides, what is the use of extensive foreign trade if you are unable to protect that trade in times of war ? Therefore I prefer to take the food-producing areas I need by force and pull all my Germans together at the same time.

That, in fact, is the policy Hitler prescribes to the six men listening to him.

Greatest Conquest at Lowest Cost

" It is understandable," Hitler continues, " that this tendency (of securing greater living space) meets with no interest in Geneva and the satisfied states. If the security of our food position is to be our foremost thought, it follows that the space required for this can only be sought in Europe. We shall not copy liberal capitalist policies which rely on exploiting colonies. It is not a case of conquering people, but of conquering agriculturally useful space. It would also be more to the purpose to seek raw material producing territory in Europe directly adjoining the Reich, and not overseas, and this solution would have to be achieved in one or two generations. What would be required at a later date over and above this, must be left to subsequent generations. The development of great world-wide national bodies is naturally a slow process, and the German people, with its strong racial root, has for this purpose the most favourable foundation in the heart of the European continent.

" The history of all times—Roman Empire, British Empire—has proved that every space expansion can be effected only by breaking resistance and taking risks. Even setbacks are unavoidable. Neither in former times nor today has space been found without an owner. The attacker always comes up against the proprietor. The question for Germany is where the greatest possible conquest can be made at lowest cost."

Two Hateful Enemies

" German policy," Hitler points out, " must reckon with its two hateful enemies, Britain and France, to whom a strong German colossus in the centre of Europe would be intolerable. Both these states would oppose a further strengthening of Germany, in Europe as well as overseas, and in this opposition they would have the support of all parties. Both countries would view the building of German military strong-points overseas as a threat to their overseas communications, as a security measure for German commerce, and in the long run as a strengthening of the German position in Europe.

" Britain is not in a position to cede to us any of her colonial possessions, owing to the resistance which she experiences in the Dominions. After the loss of prestige which Britain suffered with the transfer of Abyssinia to Italian ownership, a return of East Africa can no longer be expected. Any resistance on Britain's part would, at best, consist in her readiness to satisfy our colonial claims by taking away colonies which at the present moment are not in British hands, for instance, Angola. French favours would probably be of the same nature."

We may note in passing the curious notion Hitler has of British political practices. He recognizes quite rightly that neither Britain nor the Dominions would feel safe in handing back to National Socialist Germany former German colonies. But he assumes as wholly natural that Britain would not hesitate to give to Hitler something that does not belong to her, in this case Portuguese Angola. It is one of his outstanding characteristics that he invariably judges others, and particularly his actual or potential opponents, by his own standards. He credits them with precisely the same perfidy and double-crossing which he, himself, never hesitates to adopt. If he sees nothing unusual in Britain taking Angola away from the Portuguese in order to give it to the Germans, it is because he himself, eventually, thinks nothing of taking something away from Rumania and giving it to Hungary or vice versa, if that eases his position. If these are the methods of the gangster, they are, however, not those of a very superior kind of gangster. It is the primitive gangster who assumes all his enemies also think and act like gangsters ; the refined gangster knows that they think and act differently, and plays his cards accordingly. Hitler is rarely capable of this.

He has his own ideas of Britain and the Empire, and develops them.

" A serious discussion regarding the return of colonies to us could be considered only at a time when Britain is in a state of emergency and the German Reich is strong and well-armed. The Führer does not share the opinion that the Empire is unshakeable. Resistance against the Empire is to be found less in conquered territories than amongst its competitors. The British Empire and the Roman Empire cannot be compared with one another in regard to durability ; after the Punic Wars the latter never had a serious political enemy. Only the dissolving effects which originated in Christianity, and the signs of old age which creep into all states, made it possible for the Ancient Germans to subjugate Ancient Rome.

" Alongside the British Empire there exist today a number of states which are stronger than it. The British mother country is able to defend its colonial possessions only if allied to other states, and not with its own power. How could Britain alone, for example, defend Canada against an attack from the United States, or its Far Eastern interests against an attack by Japan ? The singling out of the British Crown as the bearer of Empire unity is in itself an admission that the universal empire cannot be maintained permanently by power politics."

He draws an interesting conclusion :

" We can state in conclusion that the British Empire cannot be held together permanently by the power politics of 45 million Britons, in spite of all the solidity of its ideals. The proportion of the populations in the Empire, compared with that of the mother country, is 9:1, and this should be a warning to us that if we expand in space, we must not allow the level of our population to sink too low."

The position of France he considers more favourable than that of Britain. " The French Empire is better placed geographically. The population of its colonial possessions represents a potential military increase. But France is faced with difficulties of internal politics. At the present time in the life of the nations parliamentary government obtains only in 10 per cent. of them, whereas 90 per cent. of them have totalitarian governments. Nevertheless we have to take the following into our political considerations as power-factors : Britain, France, Russia and the adjoining smaller states."

What is the conclusion ?

" The German question can be solved only by way of force, and this is never without risk. The battles of Frederick the

C

Great for Silesia, and Bismarck's wars against Austria and France carried tremendous risks, and the speed of the Prussian action in 1870 prevented Austria from participating in the war. If we base ourselves on the decision to apply force with risk, we are left to reply to the questions of ' when ' and ' how '."

He explains that there are three possibilities.

When and How

The first possibility is to strike during the period between 1943 and 1945, that is, from six to eight years hence. It is, Hitler believes, the latest possible date.

" After this we can only expect a change for the worse. The re-arming of the Army, Navy, and Air Force as well as the formation of the Officers' Corps, are practically concluded." (In November, 1937 !) " Our material equipment and armaments are modern, with further delay the danger of their becoming out-of-date will increase. In particular the secrecy of ' special weapons ' cannot always be safeguarded. Enlistment of reserves would be limited to the current recruiting age groups and an addition from older untrained groups would be no longer available.

" By comparison with the rearmament which will have been carried out at that time by the other nations, we shall decrease in relative power. Should we not act until 1943–45, in view of the absence of reserves, any year could bring about the food crisis for the countering of which we do not possess the necessary foreign exchange. This must be considered as a point of weakness in the régime. Over and above that, the world will anticipate our action and year by year increase its counter-measures. Whilst other nations isolate themselves we should be forced on the offensive. What the actual position would be in the years 1943–45 no one knows today. It is certain, however, that we can wait no longer. On the one hand the large armed forces with the necessity of securing their upkeep, the ageing of the National Socialist movement and of its leaders, and on the other hand the prospect of a lowering of the standard of living and a drop in the birth-rate—all this leaves us no choice but to act. If the Führer is still alive, it will be his irrevocable decision to solve the German space problem not later than 1943–45."

But, he goes on to say, we may be compelled to act before 1943–45, if either Possibility Number Two or Three arises.

Case Number Two foresees that " the social tensions in France lead to an internal political crisis of such dimensions that it absorbs the French Army and thus renders it incapable for employment in war against Germany. In that case the time for action against Czechoslovakia has come."

Under Case Number Three "it would be equally possible to act against Czechoslovakia if France should be so tied up by a war against another state that she cannot 'proceed' against Germany."

But, whichever case arises, "for the improvement of our military-political position it must be our first aim, in every case of entanglement by war, to conquer Czechoslovakia and Austria simultaneously, in order to remove any threat from the flanks in case of a possible advance westward. In the case of a conflict with France it would hardly be necessary to assume that Czechoslovakia would declare war on the same day as France. However, Czechoslovakia's desire to participate in the war will increase proportionally as we are being weakened. Her actual participation could make itself felt by an attack on Silesia, either towards the North or the West. Once Czechoslovakia is conquered—and a common frontier between Germany and Hungary obtained—a neutral attitude by Poland in a German-French conflict could more surely be relied upon. Our agreements with Poland remain valid only as long as Germany's strength remains unshakeable ; should Germany have any setbacks, an attack by Poland against East Prussia, perhaps also against Pomerania and Silesia, must be taken into account."

It is the familiar picture as we know it from the " Blomberg Directive " with one important difference. Whereas the " Blomberg Directive " lays it down that on no account must Austria and Czechoslovakia be attacked and absorbed simultaneously, Hitler reverses the order and directs that "it must be our first aim to conquer Czechoslovakia and Austria simultaneously." This change in strategy we do not find explained anywhere in the documents, and as things turned out, it was not followed. When the time for action came, the two countries were tackled separately and Austria was given priority. Nevertheless, throughout this planning, the emphasis is on Czechoslovakia as the richer prize.

Next, Hitler analyses the "development of the situation which would lead to a planned attack on our part in the years 1943–45," and comes to the conclusion that "the attitude of France, Poland, and Russia would probably have to be judged in the following manner :

" The Führer believes personally that in all probability Britain and perhaps also France have already written off Czechoslovakia, and that they have accustomed themselves to the idea that this question would one day be cleaned up by Germany. The difficulties in the British Empire and the prospect of being entangled in another long-drawn-out European war, were factors decisive for the non-participation of Britain in a war against Germany. The British attitude would certainly not remain without influence on the attitude of France. An attack by France without British support is hardly probable since it must be assumed that a French offensive would stagnate along our Western fortifications. Without British support it would also not be necessary to take into consideration a French march through Belgium and Holland, nor would we have to reckon with it in case of a conflict with France as in every case it would have as a consequence the enmity of Britain.

"Naturally, we should in every case have to bar our frontier during our operations against Czechoslovakia and Austria. It must be taken into consideration here that Czechoslovakia's defence measures will increase in strength from year to year, and that a consolidation of the inner values of the Austrian army will also be effected in the course of the years. Although Czechoslovakia is not thinly populated, the incorporation of Czechoslovakia and Austria would nevertheless constitute the conquest of food for 5 to 6 million people, assuming that a compulsory emigration of 2 million from Czechoslovakia and 1 million from Austria can be carried out. The annexation of the two states to Germany would mean, militarily and politically, a considerable relief, owing to shorter and better frontiers, the freeing of fighting personnel for other purposes and the possibility of re-constituting new armies up to a strength of about 12 divisions, representing a new division per each million population."

Apart from his curious obsession with the difficulties inside the British Empire which all through clouds his judgment of the world situation, Hitler now calls a spade a spade and tells his six listeners precisely what he is after. He intends to drive out or exterminate 3 million people in Austria and Czechoslovakia, and capture food for 5 or 6 million of his own folk. In addition he intends to raise in the newly won territories 12 new divisions, and he will have his hands free for " other purposes." The drive for living space, to be sure, is only just beginning.

What opposition does he anticipate ?

" No opposition to the removal of Czechoslovakia is expected on the part of Italy. However, it cannot be judged today what would be her attitude in the Austrian question since it would depend largely on whether the Duce were alive at the time or not. The measure and speed of our action would decide Poland's attitude. Poland will have little inclination to enter the war against a victorious Germany, with Russia in her rear. Military participation by Russia must be countered by the speed of our operations. It is a question whether this need be taken into consideration at all in view of Japan's attitude. Should Case Two occur—paralysis of France by a civil war—the situation should be exploited at any time for operations against Czechoslovakia, as Germany's most dangerous enemy would be eliminated."

But curiously, it is Case Three which fascinates Hitler most at this time, although it is an oddly unreal scheme. " The Führer sees Case Three looming nearer," the record says. " It could develop from the existing tensions in the Mediterranean, and should it occur he has firmly decided to make use of it at any time, perhaps even as early as 1938." What he foresees is that Italy, owing to her participation in the Spanish Civil War and her occupation of the Balearic Isles, will get herself involved in a war with both France and Britain which will set the entire Mediterranean ablaze, keep France fully occupied and engage all Britain's attention as well. This scheme is discussed more fully elsewhere in these studies. (Chapter II, Otto to Alaric, and Chapter IV, Felix and Isabella).

" If Germany profits from this (Mediterranean) war," continues Hitler, " by disposing of the Czechoslovak and Austrian questions, it can be assumed as probable that Britain, being at war with Italy, would decide against commencing hostilities against Germany. Without British support a warlike action by France against Germany is not to be anticipated. The date of our attack on Czechoslovakia and Austria must be made dependent on the course of the Italian-British-French war, and would not be simultaneous with the initiation of military agreements with Italy. Rather would the Führer act in full independence and, by exploiting this uniquely favourable opportunity, begin to carry out operations against Czechoslovakia. The attack on Czechoslovakia would have to take place with the ' speed of lightning '."

That ends Hitler's exposé. The " Hossbach Minutes "

record that, after he had finished speaking, Blomberg, Fritsch, and Neurath raised a number of objections. Blomberg pointed out that " the war with Italy would not tie down the French army to such an extent as to make it impossible for it to commence operations on our Western frontier with superior forces." Fritsch believed that " the French would attempt to advance into the Rhineland. We should consider the lead which France possesses in mobilization, and quite apart from the very small value of our then existing fortifications, the four motorised divisions which had been earmarked for the West would be more or less incapable of movement." With regard to the offensive in a south-easterly direction, Blomberg " drew special attention to the strength of the Czechoslovak fortifications the building of which has assumed the character of a Maginot Line, and which would present extreme difficulties to our attack." Neurath remarks that " a British-Italian conflict would not seem to be so near as the Führer appeared to assume." But Hitler states that " the date which appeared to him a possibility was the summer of 1938." (See also Chapter II, Otto to Alaric). He " repeated his previous statements and said that he was convinced of Britain's non-participation, and that consequently, he did not believe in military action by France against Germany. Should the Mediterranean conflict already mentioned lead to a general mobilization in Europe, we should have to commence operations against Czechoslovakia at once. If, however, the powers who are not participating in the war should declare their disinterestedness, Germany would, for the time being, have to side with this attitude."

Ribbentrop on Britain

What strikes one, time and again, in these calculations of Hitler's, is the curiously unreal notion he harbours of British policy, and more precisely, of the frame of mind of the British people, and the stubbornness with which he adheres to it despite the doubts voiced by experienced advisers like Neurath. Whence did he derive these extraordinary ideas, which, in the end, turned out to be the hidden rock on which his carefully rigged ship foundered ? We possess, among the Nuremberg Documents, a paper which provides at least part of the answer.

It is a " Memorandum for the Führer," marked " Very Confidential " and " Personal Only " and contains " Deductions on the report ' German Embassy London A5522 ' " regarding the future of Anglo-German relations. The German Ambassador in London at that time was Ribbentrop, and the document which is dated January 2nd, 1938, is obviously an abstract made in the Berlin Foreign Office of one of Ribbentrop's reports. It was found on a micro-film, among the archives of the German Foreign Office. Only extracts from the document were released at Nuremberg (the middle part is missing), but these are here quoted in full.

" With the realization that Germany will not tie herself to a *status quo* in Central Europe, and that sooner or later a military conflict in Europe is possible, the hope of an agreement will slowly disappear amongst Germanophile British politicians, in so far as they are not merely playing a part that has been assigned to them. Thus the fateful question arises—will Germany and Britain eventually be forced to drift into separate camps, and will they, one day, march against each other ? In order to answer this question, one must realise the following :

" A change of the *status quo* in the East in the German sense can only be carried out by force. As long as France knows that Britain, who, so to speak, has taken on a guarantee to aid her against Germany, is on her side, it is probable (and in any case always possible) that France will fight for her eastern allies, and therefore there is always a possibility, if not a probability, of war between Britain and Germany. This would apply even if Britain did not want war, because, believing that she must defend her frontier on the Rhine, Britain would be dragged in automatically by France. In other words, peace or war between Britain and Germany rests solely in the hands of France, who could bring about such a war between Germany and Britain by way of a conflict between Germany and France. It follows therefore, that war between Germany and Britain on account of France can be prevented only if France knows from the start that Britain's forces would not be sufficient to guarantee their common victory. Such a situation might force Britain, and thereby France, to accept a great many things which a strong Anglo-French coalition would never tolerate. This position would arise, for instance, if Britain, through insufficient armament, or as a result of threats to her Empire by a superior coalition of powers (such as Germany-Italy-Japan), which would tie down her military forces elsewhere, were unable to assure France of sufficient support in Europe.

" Regarding the question of the coalition of powers, this depends on further developments, on our own policy of alliances, and on the future of Anglo-American relations. It would be unfavourable for Britain should she, not yet sufficiently armed, stand opposed to the above-mentioned coalition all on her own. However, this coalition would have to be firmly welded, and there must be no doubt in either Britain or France about the fact that Italy and Japan are firmly on our side, and that if necessary the combined forces of the coalition would be employed at one stroke. Italy's and Japan's interests in a strong Germany are as great as ours in a strong Italy and Japan.

" The existence of the new Germany has been of great advantage to both of them in their efforts to expand during the last few years. With reference to this and to common aims in the future, it should be possible to get these two powers to announce their solidarity with us at the right time. Given such a situation it may be possible that Britain would prevent France from interfering, in the event of a war by Germany against one of France's allies in the east, so as to localise the conflict. Britain, in that case, would not be compelled, through France's interference, to fight for her Empire under unfavourable conditions possibly in three theatres, the Far East, the Mediterranean, and Europe. Even if it meant a considerable strengthening of Germany, Britain, in my opinion, would not risk fighting for her Empire under unfavourable conditions for the sake of a local Central European conflict. In such a case France, without Britain, would hardly be willing to run against the German fortifications in the West all by herself. It appears to me that the decisive factor in this connection is the speed with which such a Central European war could be victoriously decided. In the event of a lightning success I am convinced that the West would not interfere. A lengthy campaign, however, might give our enemies the idea that they had overrated Germany's strength, and with this the moment of intervention by the Western Powers would definitely approach.

" In conclusion I should like to summarize my ideas under the following headings :

(1) Britain is behindhand with her armaments and therefore is playing for time.

(2) Britain believes that in a conflict with Germany time is on her side (utilization of her greater economic possibilities

for her armaments, time for the extension of her treaties, *e.g.*, the U.S.A.).

(3) The Halifax visit is therefore to be regarded as a reconnaissance and screening move ; Germanophiles in Britain are for the most part only playing the parts they have had assigned to them.

(4) In my opinion Britain and her Prime Minister do not see in Halifax's visit the possibility of the basis of an agreement with Germany. They have as much faith in National Socialist Germany as we have in Britain. Therefore they fear that one day they may be forced by a strong Germany to accept a solution which is not agreeable to them. To counter this Britain is preparing herself in any case militarily and politically for war with Germany.

(5) Therefore conclusions to be drawn by us :

    (*a*) Outwardly further understanding with Britain in regard to the protection of the interests of our friends.

    (*b*) Formation, under great secrecy but with wholehearted tenacity, of a coalition against Britain, *i.e.*, tightening of our friendship with Italy and Japan, also winning over of all other nations whose interests conform with ours directly or indirectly, and close and confidential co-operation of the diplomats of the three great powers towards this purpose.

" Only in this way can we confront Britain, be it in a settlement or in war."

Prepare Case Otto

The story of the National Socialist conspiracy which brought about the collapse of the independent Austrian state and its incorporation in the German Reich is known to the world in its broad outlines and in many of its details. Where obscurities remain—and a number of intriguing gaps still have to be filled in before the contemporary historian can feel satisfied that he is in possession of all the facts—the Nuremberg Documents contribute little towards their clarification. The chief question that remains unanswered is, at what point did Hitler decide to " tackle " Austria after all in an isolated operation ? On November 5th, 1937, he had reversed the strategy laid down in the " Blomberg Directive " and ruled that " it must be our first aim to conquer Czechoslovakia and Austria simultaneously." On March 11th, 1938, he reversed his own reversal and marched into Austria without apparently paying much attention to the Czechoslovak question, although in all his earlier planning Czechoslovakia had always been given priority over Austria. What had made him change his mind, and why?

It is true that between the two critical dates internal disruption work had made good progress in Austria, and that the situation, thanks mainly to Papen, was "maturing" perhaps rather faster than had been anticipated; but it is also true that in the face of the growing National Socialist agitation, Austrian monarchist tendencies were asserting themselves more strongly as an alternative solution, and this was the one solution Hitler was determined not to tolerate. All this must have caused Hitler to think again between November 5th, 1937 and March 11th, 1938 or, to be more precise, February 11th, 1938, the day Schuschnigg had his fateful interview with Hitler at Berchtesgaden. But it will be useful to remember that during this same period some important and deep-reaching changes occurred in Hitler's own government. Between January 25th and February 4th, 1938, German affairs were thoroughly and drastically refashioned. The three men who had voiced doubts about Hitler's plans during the meeting of November 5th, 1937—Blomberg, Fritsch, and Neurath—found themselves removed from office. Hitler became his own War Minister and new names appeared at the head of the Army—Brauchitsch, Keitel, List, Reichenau. Ribbentrop, recalled from London, became Foreign Minister in Neurath's place, and Papen, the ambassador to Vienna, lost his job. His last act was to hand Schuschnigg, on February 7th, 1938, Hitler's invitation to come to see him at Berchtesgaden.

Some insight into what went on in the inner councils of the German Army during these critical days is afforded by a number of entries in the Diary of General Jodl, sections of which were made available at Nuremberg. They contribute nothing essentially new but illustrate, in a number of flashes, the prevailing atmosphere.

Jodl's entry for February 11th, 1938 reads: "In the evening and on February 12th, General K. (Keitel) with General Reichenau and Sperrle at Obersalzberg. Schuschnigg together with G. Schmidt are again being put under heaviest political and military pressure. At 23.00 hours Schuschnigg signs protocol." On February 13th, 1938 he notes: "In the afternoon, General K. (Keitel) asks Admiral C. (Canaris, Chief of German Counter-Intelligence) to come to his apartment. He tells us that the Führer's order is to the effect that military pressure by shamming military action should be kept up until February 15th. Proposals for these deceptive manoeuvres are drafted and submitted to the Führer by telephone for approval."

These proposals, discovered independently from Jodl's Diary, are in our possession. They are signed by Keitel and read as follows:.

" Orders will be given immediately, after the detailed numbers and letters have been released by the Führer, for accomplishment.

(1) To take no real preparatory measures in the Army or Luftwaffe. No troop movements or deployments.

(2) Spread false but credible news which may lead to the conclusion that military preparations against Austria are in progress.

    (*a*)   through V-men in Austria.

    (*b*)   through our customs personnel at the frontier.

    (*c*)   through travelling agents.

(3) Such news could be :

    (*a*)   Army leave is supposed to have been cancelled in the Sector of the VII A.K.

    (*b*)   Rolling stock is being assembled in Munich, Augsburg, and Regensburg.

    (*c*)   Major-General Muff, the Military Attaché in Vienna, has been called for a conference to Berlin. (As a matter of fact, this is the case).

    (*d*)   Police stations located at the Austrian frontier have called up reinforcements.

    (*e*)   Customs officials report imminent manoeuvres of the Mountain Brigade in the region of Freilassing, Reichenhall, and Berchtesgaden.

(4) Order a very active make-believe wireless exchange in Wehrkreis VII and between Berlin and Munich.

(5) Real manoeuvres, training flights, and winter manoeuvres of the mountain troops near the frontier.

(6) Admiral Canaris has to be ready beginning on February 14th in the Service Command Headquarters in order to carry out measures given by order of the Chief of the Supreme Command, Armed Forces.

(7) An answer is requested to General Keitel through the Reich Chancellery."

Jodl notes on February 14th, 1938 : "At 02.40 hours the agreement of the Führer arrives. Canaris goes to Munich to the Counter-Intelligence office VII and initiates the various measures. The effect is quick and strong. In Austria the impression is created that Germany is undertaking serious military preparations." During the next few days everything goes according to plan. On February 15th " an official communiqué about the positive results of the Obersalzberg conference is issued." On February 16th " changes in the Austrian Government and general political amnesty " are noted. On March 3rd, however, Jodl records that " the Austrian question is becoming critical. One hundred officers are to be despatched there. The Führer wants to see them personally. Their task is not to ensure that the Austrian Armed Forces will fight better against us, but rather that they do not fight at all."

A week later the fat is in the fire. On March 10th, 1938, Jodl notes : " By surprise and without consulting his ministers, Schuschnigg ordered a plebiscite for Sunday, March 13th, 1938, which should bring a strong majority for the Legitimists in the absence of a plan or preparations. The Führer is determined not to tolerate it. The same night, March 9th–10th, he calls for Goering. General Reichenau is called back from the Cairo Olympic Committee. Gen. v. Schubert is ordered to attend, as well as Minister Glaise-Horstenau who is with Gauleiter Buerckel in the Palatinate. Gen. Keitel communicates the facts at 01.45 hours. He drives to the Reich Chancellery at 10.00 hours. I follow at 10.15 hours, according to the wish of Gen. v. Viebahn, to give him the old draft. ' Prepare Case Otto '."

Jodl's Diary continues :

" 13.00 hours : Gen. Keitel informs Chief of Operational Staff and Admiral Canaris. Ribbentrop is being detained in London. Neurath takes over Foreign Office. Führer wants to transmit ultimatum to the Austrian Cabinet. A personal letter is dispatched to Mussolini, and the reasons are developed which force the Führer to take action. 18.30 hours: mobilization order is given to the Command of the 8th Army (Corps Area 3), 7th and 13th Army Corps ; without Reserve Army. Air puts 300 Junkers 52 in readiness for dropping of propaganda pamphlets. In addition, one Pursuit Squadron, three bomber groups, and two companies as airborne troops with transport planes are held ready at civilian airports in Bavaria."

The following day, March 11th, 1938, Jodl notes :

" Directive No. 1 of the Führer is given out on March 11th, 1938, at 02.00 hours without signature ; at 13.00 hours with his signature."

This Directive is in our possession.

Directive Number One

Directive No. 1, stamped " Top Secret," dated March 11th, 1938, and bearing the reference " Operation Otto," is signed by Hitler and initialled by Jodl, Keitel, and a third person whose initials are indecipherable.   The copy in our possession is the one issued to the Supreme Command of the Navy.   It reads as follows :

(1) If other measures prove unsuccessful, I intend to invade Austria with armed forces to establish constitutional conditions there and to prevent further outrages against the pro-German population.

(2) The whole operation will be directed by myself.

According to my instructions :

The Supreme Commander of the Army will direct the land operations with the 8th Army in the formation and strength suggested to me, and with the attachments of the Air Force, the SS, and police.

The Supreme Commander of the Air Force will direct the air operations with the forces suggested to me.

(3) Operational duties :

(a) Army.   The invasion of Austria must be carried out in the manner explained by me.   The Army's first target is the occupation of Upper Austria, Salzburg, Lower Austria, Tyrol, the speedy occupation of Vienna and the securing of the Austro-Czech frontier.

(b) Air Force.   The Air Force must demonstrate and drop propaganda material, occupy Austrian aerodromes for the use of further possible reinforcements, assist the Army upon demand as necessary, and apart from this, hold bomber units in readiness for special tasks.

(4) The forces of the Army and Air Force detailed for this operation must be ready for invasion and/or ready for action from March 12th, 1938, onwards, at the latest at 12.00 hours.

I reserve the right to give permission for crossing and flying over the frontier, and to decide the actual moment for invasion.

(5) The behaviour of the troops must give the impression that we do not wish to wage war against our brother nation. It is in our interest that the whole operation shall be carried out without any violence but in the form of a peaceful entry welcomed by the population.   Therefore, any provocation is to be avoided.   If, however, resistance is offered it must be broken ruthlessly by force of arms.

(6) On the remaining German frontiers no security measures are to be taken for the time being."

Under the same date, March 11th, 1938, the entries in Jodl's Diary continue :

" The Army is joined by the SS Military Units by regiments, 40,000 men of the police and the Death's Head Unit Upper Bavaria as second wave. 17.00 hours : the Navy has ordered all ships back. 18.00 hours : Schuschnigg has resigned ; Seyss-Inquart is Chancellor. SA and SS perform duty in uniform. Own movements have commenced. Frontier will not be crossed at the moment. Air Force plans large-scale propaganda flights for tomorrow. The police force will be needed in any case, and will be mixed with the troops. 20.30 hours : briefing received from Gen. Viebahn that the situation has changed once more. The occupation will take place."

Directive Number Two

What change had occurred ?

Fifteen minutes after Jodl's last entry, Hitler issued " Directive No. 2 " regarding " Operation Otto." It is dated Berlin, March 11th, 1938, 20.45 hours. Again we possess the Navy's copy. It is signed by Hitler and initialled by Jodl, and states :

" (1) The demands of the German ultimatum to the Austrian Government have not been fulfilled.

(2) The Austrian Armed Forces have been ordered to withdraw in front of the entry of the German troops and to avoid fighting.

The Austrian Government has ceased to function of its own accord.

(3) To avoid further bloodshed in Austrian towns, the entry of the German Armed Forces into Austria will commence, according to Directive No. 1, at daybreak on March 12th, 1938.

I expect the set objectives to be reached, by exerting all forces to the full, as quickly as possible."

On the same day, March 11th, 1938, and apparently simultaneously with Directive No. 2, " Special Instructions No. 1 " for " policy towards Czechoslovak and Italian troops or militia units on Austrian soil " were issued. They are signed by Jodl and order :

" (1) If Czechoslovak troops or militia units are encountered in Austria, they are to be regarded as hostile. (2) The Italians are everywhere to be treated as friends, especially as Mussolini has declared himself disinterested in the solution of the Austrian question."

A number of interesting points can be noted in connection with these documents.

The first is Jodl's reference to the Schuschnigg plebiscite. He states that the plebiscite " should bring a strong majority for the Legitimists," that is, the supporters of the Habsburg Restoration, and adds that " the Führer is determined not to tolerate it." The implication here is that the question to be decided by the plebiscite was whether or not there was to be a restoration of the monarchy. But this was never the issue, and Jodl knew very well that it wasn't. The question put to the Austrian people was, " Are you for a free and German, independent and social, Christian and united Austria, for peace and work, for the equality of all those who declare themselves for the people and the fatherland ? " In other words : Are you for an independent Austria, or are you for an Anschluss ? Naturally, the monarchists would have voted " Yes " to Schuschnigg's question, but so would a great many other people. Hitler knew that the National Socialist pro-anschluss party would find itself in a minority, and would be defeated at the polls. It was this he was " determined not to tolerate," and not an alleged " strong majority for the Legitimists," although one is left to speculate whether Schuschnigg, had he been able to carry through the plebiscite and had he won it (as he would have done), would not have made a strong bid to put Otto of Habsburg back on the Austrian throne. It is probable that he would have made the attempt. " Case Otto " might then have looked very different.

The second point is the clear and unequivocal admission, in Directive No. 2, that an ultimatum had been handed to the Austrian Government by the German Government.

The third is that Ribbentrop, the newly appointed Foreign Minister, was not at his post but away in London, presumably clearing his desk. We now know why he was there, during these critical days, and what he was doing.

The final point is that Hitler struck against Austria on the day when France, in the throes of another ministerial crisis, had no government. It was his old, favourite scheme. With the British Government " covered " by Ribbentrop, and no French Government in office, Schuschnigg's envoys in London and Paris were unable to make even representations, and Austria was effectively isolated.

The Goering Telephone Conversations

One of the most interesting documents issued at Nuremberg is the record of a series of telephone conversations which Goering conducted on March 11th, 1938, with Seyss-Inquart and a number of German representatives in Vienna, and of one exceedingly long telephone conversation which he had with Ribbentrop in London on March 13th, 1938. These records which were kept at Goering's request by an official of the Air Ministry, are voluminous documents, and only a few relevant passages can be quoted here.

Goering did a great deal of telephoning with Vienna on March 11th, 1938. Things were not proceeding too smoothly in Vienna, and in particular it did not look as if Seyss-Inquart had a very firm grip on the situation. At 14.45 hours Goering rang up Seyss-Inquart to find out what was happening and was told that Schuschnigg had cancelled the plebiscite for the coming Sunday, but this had put Seyss-Inquart and his friends in a difficult position. Goering replied that Schuschnigg's measures were unsatisfactory in all respects. The Führer would take a clear stand very shortly, but in Goering's opinion the cancellation of the plebiscite merely postponed, but did not change, the situation created by Schuschnigg's breach of the Berchtesgaden agreement. Goering thereupon consulted Hitler, and ten minutes later telephoned Seyss-Inquart again. Schuschnigg, he declared, no longer enjoyed the confidence of the German Government because he had broken the Berchtesgaden agreement. Therefore, Seyss-Inquart and his pro-German colleagues in the Cabinet were requested immediately to hand their resignation to Schuschnigg whom they should request to resign as well. The German Government insisted, of course, that at the same time Seyss-Inquart should be commissioned by the Austrian President to form a new Cabinet, and they expected definite word in Berlin by 17.30 hours.

But matters turned out to be rather difficult. At 17.00 hours Goering telephoned the German Legation in Vienna, where he was told by an official named Dombrowski that Seyss-Inquart had talked to Schuschnigg, but that Schuschnigg could not dissolve his cabinet by 17.30 hours as demanded since it was technically impossible. Goering insists. " By 1930 the Cabinet must be formed. I want to know what is going on. Did he tell you that he is now Chancellor ? " Dombrowski apparently gets flustered and splutters out " Yes." Goering replies " Good. By what time can he form the Cabinet " ? Dombrowski suggests

21.15 hours. But Goering insists on 19.30 hours and tells him that Keppler, one of Hitler's personal envoys, is on his way, to discuss with him the "kind of plebiscite that is to be" in lieu of that cancelled by Schuschnigg. He then dictates to Dombrowski over the telephone a list of names which are to be included as ministers in Seyss-Inquart's cabinet. They include Kaltenbrunner for the Security Ministry, and Goering's brother-in-law for the Ministry of Justice.

Dombrowski, however, has misinformed Goering. At 17.26 hours Goering speaks to Seyss-Inquart on the telephone and is told that the President has accepted Schuschnigg's resignation but is not inclined to appoint Seyss-Inquart. Goering bursts forth "Well, that won't do. Under no circumstances! The matter is in progress now; therefore the President has to be informed immediately that he has to turn the powers of the Chancellor over to you and to accept the cabinet as it was arranged." He orders Seyss-Inquart immediately to go with General Muff, the German Military Attaché in Vienna, and tell the President that if the conditions are not accepted at once the troops already stationed at the frontier will march in that night and that Austria will cease to exist. "Tell Miklas there is no time for jokes. The situation is now that tonight the invasion will begin from all the corners of Austria. The invasion will be stopped and the troops held at the frontier only if we are informed by 19.30 hours that Miklas has entrusted you with the Chancellorship. If Miklas could not understand it in four hours, we shall make him understand it now in four minutes."

But the Muff action misfires. At 18.34 hours Goering speaks with Keppler who answers the telephone instead of Muff and tells him that the President "refuses to agree." Goering answers, "Well, in that case Seyss-Inquart has to dismiss him (the President); just go upstairs again and tell him plainly that Seyss-Inquart will call on the National Socialist guards, and in five minutes the troops will march in by my order." Confusion ensues. The line is interrupted, suddenly Muff is on the telephone instead of Keppler, then both vanish and a burlesque interlude follows in which Goering, trying desperately to speak to someone, gets hold of one unfortunate Fehsemeier who claims to be the adjutant of someone whose name Goering fails to catch, but before Fehsemeier is enabled to make his position clear, Seyss-Inquart appears and takes the telephone. He is plainly in utter confusion. "Well," asks Goering, "how do we stand"? Seyss-

D

Inquart mutters an incoherent " Please, Field Marshal, yes."—
" What is going on ? " Goering wants to know. Seyss-Inquart :
" Yes, well, the President sticks to his old point of view. Now
So-and-So (the name is not understandable on the telephone)
went to see Schuschnigg in order to change his mind. He himself
uses all his influence but no decision has yet been made." The
conversation no longer makes sense. Goering asks " But do you
think it possible that we shall come to a decision in the next
few minutes ? " Seyss-Inquart : " Well, the conversation cannot
take longer than 5 or 10 minutes, it won't take any longer, I
shouldn't think." Goering insists on being called back
immediately.

Yet the next telephone conversation between the two men
doesn't take place until 19.57 hours. Seyss-Inquart tells his
master in Berlin that Schuschnigg is going to announce over the
radio that Germany has sent an ultimatum. The government
itself has abdicated. General Schiwaski is in command of the
military forces and he will withdraw the troops. " The
gentlemen pointed out that they are waiting for the troops to
march in."—" Well," asks Goering, " were they appointed by
you ? " No, answers Seyss-Inquart, they weren't. " Did you
dismiss them from their office ? " No, answers Seyss-Inquart.
" No one was dismissed from his office, but the government
itself has pulled back and let matters take their course." It
now dawns on Goering that Seyss-Inquart has bungled it again.
" And you were not commissioned ? " he asks. " It was refused ?"
Seyss-Inquart has to admit that this is so. " They expect that
they are taking a chance with the invasion, and that, if it actually
takes place, the executive power will be transferred to other
people." That is enough for Goering. " Very well. I shall
give the order to march in, and then you make sure that you
get the power. Notify the leading people about the following
which I shall tell you now : everyone who offers resistance or
organizes resistance, will immediately be subjected to our court
martial, the court martial of the invading troops. Is that clear ?
Including leading personalities, it doesn't make any difference."
" Yes," answers Seyss-Inquart intimidated, " they have given
orders not to offer any resistance." " It doesn't matter," Goering
goes on. " The President did not entrust you with the government, and that also can be considered as resistance." Seyss-
Inquart answers " Yes." Goering : "Well, now you are
officially authorized. Good luck, Heil Hitler."

At 20.48 hours, however, Keppler, Hitler's special envoy in Vienna, rings up Goering to tell him what has actually happened. His account is slightly more orderly than that of the utterly confused Seyss-Inquart. He tells Goering : " President Miklas has refused to do anything. Nevertheless the Government has ceased to function. I spoke to Schuschnigg who said they had laid down their functions, and it was now up to us to act. The old Government has ordered the Army not to put up any resistance. Therefore, shooting is not allowed." Goering interrupts : " I don't give a damn. Listen : the main thing is that Seyss-Inquart takes over all powers of the Government, that he keeps the radio stations occupied——" Keppler : " Well, we represent the Government now." Goering : " Yes, that's right. You are the Government. Now listen carefully. The following telegram should be sent here by Seyss-Inquart. Take notes." And he dictates :

" The Provisional Austrian Government which after the dismissal of the Schuschnigg Government considers it its task to establish peace and order in Austria, sends to the German Government the urgent request to support it in its task and to help it to prevent bloodshed. For this purpose it asks the German Government to send German troops as soon as possible."

Keppler, it appears, does not immediately grasp it. He declares that SA and SS are marching through the streets, but that everything is quiet. But Goering continues with his instructions. Seyss-Inquart is to guard the frontiers so that " they " cannot disappear with their fortunes. He is to take over the Austrian Foreign Office and inform the Austrian missions abroad that he has formed the provisional Government of Austria. " He should call on the people we have recommended to him. It is totally unimportant what the President may have to say. And he should send the telegram as soon as possible." Suddenly, Goering has an even better idea. " Show him the text of the telegram," he tells Keppler, " and tell him that we are asking him——well, he doesn't even have to send the telegram. All he needs to do is to say : Agreed."

At last, at 21.54 hours when Dr. Dietrich in Berlin rings up Keppler in Vienna, things are straightened out. Dietrich complains that he needs the telegram urgently. Keppler answers : " Tell the Field Marshal that Seyss-Inquart agrees." The outrageous farce has come to an end.

Two days later, on March 13th, 1938, when all was over

bar the shouting, Goering had a forty minute telephone conversation with Ribbentrop in London. The record of this
conversation is possibly the most extraordinary among the
many extraordinary documents issued at Nuremberg. The
conversation was plainly made in order to be overheard in
London, it being readily assumed in Berlin that all diplomatic
telephone calls were tapped by the British as a matter of course.
The purpose, then, was clearly, to lay down a smoke-screen for
world opinion about events in Austria.

Goering's chief anxiety is the ultimatum. " This story,"
he tells Ribbentrop, " that we had given an ultimatum is just
quatsch (utter rubbish)." It was Schuschnigg who had attempted
to provoke civil war, and anyway it was Seyss-Inquart, taking
over the government, who had asked them to march in. In
reality 80 per cent. of the Fatherland Front (Schuschnigg's
organization) were Nazis, and events surpassed all expectations.
Ribbentrop : " So it seems all Austria is on our side." Goering :
" Well, let me tell you, if there were an election tomorrow—I
have already told Seyss-Inquart that he should invite representatives of the democratic powers—we should have 90 per
cent. of the votes in our favour." This is not quite what Hitler
proclaimed in his " Directive No. 2 " about the ultimatum,
nor what Gen. Jodl noted in his Diary about the " Strong
majority of the Legitimists," but it isn't meant to be.

Goering rambles on. " The Austrian people have only been
freed now. I would just suggest to Halifax or some really
serious people whom he trusts to send them over here, so they
may get a picture of what is going on here. Yesterday, you
know, they were saying the most serious things, war and so on,
it made me laugh because where would one find such an
unscrupulous statesman who would send again millions of
people to death only because two German brother nations—
what state in the world will get hurt by our union ? Do we
take anything away from any other state ? Therefore, it is
ridiculous, if France——" He goes on to tell Ribbentrop
that the Czechoslovak Minister had seen him yesterday and
explained that the rumour of a Czechoslovak mobilization
was taken out of thin air, and that they would be satisfied with
one word from him (Goering) that he would not undertake the
slightest thing against Czechoslovakia. " Thereupon I said the
following : ' The German troops are supposed to stay at a
distance of 15 to 20 kilometres from the frontier, on their march

through Austria, and north of the Danube in the whole sector only one dissolved battalion was to march so that these villages can share in the joy and pleasure.' "

Ribbentrop who had planned to fly back to Berlin that afternoon—it would look strange, he said, if he stayed in London—remarks that he has " already spoken very openly with Halifax and Chamberlain." Goering insists that he should inform people in London of what is really going on. " Above all, it is absolutely wrong to think Germany had given an ultimatum. Tell the following to Halifax and Chamberlain : it is not correct that Germany has given any ultimatum. This is a lie by Schuschnigg, because the ultimatum was presented to him by Seyss-Inquart, Glaise-Horstenau and Jury. Furthermore, it is not true that we have presented an ultimatum to the President, but this also was given by the others, and as far as I know just a military attaché came along, asked by Seyss-Inquart, because of a technical question. He was supposed to ask whether in case Seyss-Inquart were to ask for the support of German troops, Germany would grant this request. Furthermore I want to state that Seyss-Inquart asked us expressly bv telephone and by telegram to send troops——"

Next, Goering is anxious for London to know that the coming plebiscite in Austria—for or against incorporation in the Reich—is going to be a free and secret election and not a put up show à la Schuschnigg. " We shall respect the decision Austria is going to make in every respect. And, in case she decides for union—of which we have no doubt—no power on earth will be able to separate us. It may be that a world league of all states may overpower Germany, but we shall not tolerate being separated again if Austria decides to go together with Germany. And this is no threat to any state whatsoever. I want to make that clear. In no respect are we threatening Czechoslovakia, but Czechoslovakia has now the chance of coming to a friendly and reasonable agreement with us. Everything on condition that France remains sensible and does not take any steps. Naturally, if France now organizes a big mobilization close to the border, it will not be so funny."

Ribbentrop, who has listened patiently to this harangue, now puts in his part. " I had a long conversation with Halifax, and I told him our basic conception also in respect of a German-British understanding." Goering interrupts him : " You know yourself, Ribbentrop, that I always was in favour of an Anglo-

German understanding. No one would be happier than I
if the British really wanted it seriously. and if they also recognized
that we too are a proud and free nation. After all, we also
represent two brother nations." Ribbentrop takes it up again.
" I can tell you one thing, Herr Goering. The other day I
spoke to Chamberlain after that breakfast, and I had a very good
impression of him. I do not want to speak about it over the
telephone, but I have the impression that Chamberlain also
is very serious about an understanding. I told him in this
conversation that once the Austrian problem had been settled,
the understanding between Germany and Britain would be
much less complicated than before. I believe he realised that.
I also pointed out that we got rid of a situation which always
caused much trouble. Even if there was some excitement at this
moment, in the long run the basis for an Anglo-German understanding could only be strengthened by it. I also said to Halifax
at the end of our conversation that we honestly wish to come to
an understanding, and he replied that his only worry was
Czechoslovakia." " No, no," interjects Goering from Berlin,
" that is out of the question." " I told him then," Ribbentrop
continues, " that we were not interested, and we did not intend
to do anything there. On the contrary, if our fellow-Germans
were treated in a sensible way, we should come to an agreement
there too." Goering : " Yes, I am also convinced that Halifax
is an absolutely reasonable man." And Ribbentrop again :
" I got the best impression of Halifax as well as Chamberlain.
I must say, though, that from my last conversation with Halifax,
I have the impression that he did not react to the arguments I
gave him, but in the end, he said I could be convinced that he
also was favouring an Anglo-German understanding." And
Goering : " So more or less everything is in wonderful peace——"
    And so the chatter goes on. Whom did it deceive?
    As has been said at the beginning of this chapter, it is not the
purpose of this study to demonstrate that Hitler and his
associates were liars. But one cannot help noticing, all the same,
how on almost every turn their public utterances stand in
glaring contradiction to what we now know they were saying
and planning among themselves behind their closed doors.

Case Green

    In his secret Munich speech of November 7th, 1943, Gen.
Jodl says :

" The Austrian *Anschluss*, in its turn, brought with it not only the fulfilment of an old national aim, but also had the effect both of reinforcing our fighting strength and of materially improving our strategic position. Whereas up till then the territory of Czechoslovakia had projected in a most menacing way right into Germany—a wasp waist in the direction of France and an air base for the Allies, in particular Russia—Czechoslovakia herself was now enclosed by pincers. Her own strategic position had now become so unfavourable that she was bound to fall a victim to any attack pressed home with vigour before effective aid from the West could be expected to arrive."

In an undated entry in his Diary which would seem to have been made on or about May 21st, 1938, Jodl states further :

" After the annexation of Austria, the Führer mentioned that there was no hurry to solve the Czech question because Austria has to be digested first. Nevertheless preparations for ' Case Green ' will have to be carried forward energetically. They will have to be newly drawn up on the basis of the changed strategic position because of the annexation of Austria. The state of preparations was reported to the Führer on April 21st. The intention of the Führer not to touch the Czech problem as yet is, however, changed because of the Czechoslovak troop concentrations of May 21st which occur without any German threat and without the slightest cause for it. Because of Germany's self-restraint, its consequences lead to a loss of prestige for the Führer which he is not willing to face a second time. Therefore, the new order is issued for ' Green ' on May 30th, 1938."

Thus, whatever the reasons which prompted Hitler to deviate from his original plan and give Austria priority over Czechoslovakia, he has by no means forgotten that country, and, as we can see, proceeds with his plans and preparations even before Austria has been " digested." The Nuremberg Documents enable us to follow this planning in considerable detail. Major (later Colonel) Schmundt, Hitler's adjutant at that time, had the good sense to collect a great many of the official papers relating to the planned invasion of Czechoslovakia, if not all of them, in one file, presumably for his personal reference, and this file, which was captured intact, was issued at Nuremberg and is available.

On April 21st, 1938, just over five weeks after the annexation
of Austria, Hitler had a discussion with Keitel on the basis on
which " Case Green " (the code-name for the invasion of Czechoslovakia) could be carried into effect. The minutes of this
discussion state :

" A. Political Aspect.

  (1) Strategic surprise attack out of a clear sky without
      any cause or possibility of justification has been turned
      down, as the result would be : hostile world opinion
      which can lead to a critical situation. Such a measure
      is justified only for the elimination of the *last* opponent
      on the mainland.

  (2) Action after a time of diplomatic clashes, which
      gradually come to a crisis and lead to war.

  (3) Lightning-swift action as the result of an incident
      (e.g. assassination of German Ambassador in connection
      with anti-German demonstrations).

B. Military Conclusions.

  (1) Preparations are to be made for political possibilities
      (2) and (3). Case (2) is the undesired one since ' Green '
      will have taken security measures.

  (2) The loss of time caused by transporting the bulk of the
      divisions by rail, which is unavoidable but should be
      cut down as far as possible, must not impede a lightning-
      swift blow at the time of action.

  (3) ' Separate thrusts ' are to be carried out immediately
      with a view to penetrating the enemy fortification
      lines at numerous points and in a strategically favourable
      direction. The thrusts are to be worked out to the
      smallest detail (knowledge of roads, of targets, com-
      position of columns according to their individual
      tasks). Simultaneous attacks by the Army and Air
      Force. The Air Force is to support the individual
      columns, e.g. dive-bombers, sealing-off installations at
      penetration points, hampering the bringing up of
      reserves, destroying signals, communications traffic,
      thereby isolating the garrisons.

  (4) Politically, the first 4 days of military action are decisive.
      If there are no effective military successes, a European
      crisis will certainly arise. Accomplished facts must
      prove the senselessness of foreign military intervention,
      draw Allies into the scheme (division of spoils !), and

demoralise ' Green.' Therefore : bridging the time gap between the first penetration and the employment of the forces to be brought up, by a determined and ruthless thrust by a motorised army, e.g. via Pilsen past Prague.

(5) If possible, separation of transport movement ' Red ' from ' Green.' A simultaneous strategic concentration ' Red ' might induce ' Red ' to take undesirable measures. On the other hand, it must be possible to put ' Case Red ' into operation at any time.

C. Propaganda.

(1) Leaflets on the conduct of Germans in ' Greenland ' (Czechoslovakia).

(2) Leaflets with threats for intimidation of the ' Greens ' (Czechs)."

Once this was firmly laid down, everybody set to work. Hitler, through Schmundt, sent questionnaire after questionnaire to the Army General Staff, demanding information on a host of technical questions connected with the planned invasion. Thus, on May 16th, 1938, he wishes to know from Zeitzler, then a Lieutenant-Colonel on the General Staff, " which divisions on the ' Green ' frontiers are ready to march within 12 hours, in case of mobilization," and Zeitzler sends the answer via " most secret " teleprinter, that there are 12 armoured and mountain divisions in readiness in garrisons. Hitler is not satisfied and wants to know the division numbers. Zeitzler sends the numerals.

Next day, May 17th, 1938, Hitler, through Schmundt, requests information regarding Czechoslovak fortifications. Zeitzler reports back : "Fortified construction consists of fairly large number of steel and concrete fortifications as well as light, medium, and heavy machine-gun emplacements to close gaps between fortifications. Number of steel and concrete fortifications varies from one to nine per kilometre. Positions constructed consist of light, medium, and heavy machine-gun emplacements and an occasional steel and concrete fortification in between. Number of machine-gun emplacements varies from two to nine per kilometre. Block construction consists of light, sometimes medium and heavy machine-gun emplacements at main roads and thoroughfares. Defensive potentialities : steel and concrete fortifications bullet-proof against all known calibres. Light machine-gun emplacements bullet-proof against all calibres up to 10.5 centimetres, medium machine-gun emplacements

bullet-proof against calibres up to 10.5 centimetres, heavy
machine-gun emplacements bullet-proof against calibres up to
21.00 centimetres, sometimes against the largest calibres."

The New Directive " Green "

On May 20th, 1938, Keitel submits to Hitler the " Draft for
the New Directive ' Green ' " which is based on their conversation
of April 21st, 1938. Addressing Hitler as " My Führer," Keitel
writes in his covering letter :

" Effective October 1st, 1938 (beginning of the new mobilization year for the army), new strategic directives must be issued for
which you, my Führer, intend yourself to lay down the political
basis and stipulations. For the meantime, however, it is
necessary that the ' Green ' section of the strategic directives be
replaced by a new version which takes into account the situation
which has arisen as a result of the incorporation of Austria into
the Reich, and the newly-suspected intentions of the Czech
General Staff."

The draft which is attached, repeats in broad outlines the
conclusions reached on April 21st, 1938. In particular it states
under the heading " Political Possibilities for the Commencement
of the Action " :

" An invasion without suitable obvious cause and without
sufficient political justification cannot be considered with
reference to the possible consequences of such an action in the
present situation. Rather will the action be initiated either,
(a) after a period of increasing diplomatic clashes and tension,
which is coupled with military preparations and is made use of
to saddle the enemy with the war guilt. Even such a period
of tension preceding the war will, however, terminate in a
sudden military action on our part, which must come with all
possible surprise as to time and extent, or (b) by lightning-swift
action as a result of a serious incident through which Germany
is provoked in an unbearable way, and for which at least part of
world opinion will grant the moral justification of military
action. Case (b) is militarily and politically the more favourable."

Under " Conclusions for the Preparation of ' Case Green ' "
it is then stated :

" For armed war it is essential to create already in the first
four days a military situation which plainly proves to hostile
nations eager to intervene, the hopelessness of the Czechoslovak
military situation, and gives the nations with territorial claims

against Czechoslovakia an incentive to immediate intervention against that state. In such a case the intervention of Poland and Hungary against Czechoslovakia can be expected, especially if France, owing to Italy's clearly pro-German attitude, fears, or at least hesitates, to unleash a European war by her intervention against Germany. It is very probable that attempts by Russia to give military support to Czechoslovakia are to be expected. If concrete successes are not achieved as a result of the ground operations during the first few days, a European crisis will certainly arise."

On May 22nd, 1938, Jodl notes in his Diary that there has been a "fundamental conference between the Führer and Konrad Henlein." The next day, May 23rd, 1938, he records that "Major Schmundt reports ideas of the Führer" and notes that "further conferences which gradually reveal the exact intentions of the Führer" are to take place with the Chief of the Supreme Command of the Armed Forces, who is Keitel. On the same day Schmundt informs Keitel that "the Führer is going into 'Green' in detail. Basic ideas not changed. Surprise element to be emphasised more." In a second message to Keitel and Brauchitsch, Schmundt tells them that Hitler suggests manoeuvres to be held to practise the taking of fortification by surprise attack, but that he disagrees with the plan of the Commander-in-Chief of the Army to hold training exercises in September. "The Führer thinks that moment too late." Finally the Führer "repeatedly emphasised the necessity of pressing forward greatly the fortification work in the West." Still on the same day, Zeitzler answers another of Hitler's lengthy questionnaires. This time Hitler wishes to know the peace-time strength of divisions prepared for march readiness, the strength of mobile divisions, the composition of the 2nd Armoured Division in the case of mobilization, the strength, possibilities and composition of a motorised division to be used for an independent thrust, how soon the field units can be equipped with 15-centimetre mortars, and what calibres and how large a number of artillery pieces are available for combating fortifications such as fortresses. Zeitzler provides the answer with a wealth of technical detail. The extent to which Hitler dominates the General Staff with directives, appreciations, and questions becomes abundantly clear.

On May 30th, 1938, the new Directive is ready. Jodl notes in his Diary : " The Führer signs Directive ' Green ' where he states his final decision to destroy Czechoslovakia soon, and thereby initiates military preparation all along the line. The previous intentions of the Army must be changed considerably in the direction of an immediate break-through into Czechoslovakia right on D-Day, combined with aerial penetration by the Air Force. Further details are derived from directive for strategic concentration of the army. The whole contrast becomes acute once more between the Führer's intuition that we *must* do it this year, and the opinion of the Army that we cannot do it as yet, as most certainly the Western Powers will intervene, and we are not as yet equal to them."

Thus the Army's old fear that non-intervention on the part of Britain and France in case of an invasion of Czechoslovakia could not be relied upon, which had manifested itself on earlier occasions, still overhangs the scene. But Hitler is certain that the Western Powers will not move. He relies on his intuition and signs the Directive.

Keitel's covering letter to the new Directive which is dated May 30th, 1938, explains that it replaces Part 2, Section II of the Blomberg Directive of June 24th, 1937 ("Two-front war with main effort in the South-East—strategic concentration 'Green'"), and states that its execution "must be assured as from October 1st, 1938, at the latest." We thus get for the first time an indication of the date Hitler had set himself for the liquidation of Czechoslovakia. The campaign set forth in the directive was never fought. But its objective was reached—on September 29th, 1938.

The Directive opens with a paragraph entitled "Political Prerequisites." This reads :

"It is my unalterable decision to smash Czechoslovakia by military action in the near future. It is the task of the political leaders to await or bring about the politically and militarily suitable moment. An inevitable development of conditions inside Czechoslovakia or other political events in Europe creating a surprisingly favourable opportunity, and one which may never occur again, may cause me to take early action. The proper choice and determined and full utilisation of a favourable moment is the surest guarantee of success. Accordingly preparations are to be made at once."

The Directive then outlines "Political Possibilities for the Commencement of the Action" and "Conclusions for the Preparation of ' Case Green ' " which are identical with the corresponding chapters in the draft submitted by Keitel on May 20th, 1938. Continuing, it states the " Tasks of the Armed Forces " :

" Armed Forces Preparations are to be made on the following basis :

(a) The mass of all forces must be employed against Czecho-slovakia.

(b) For the West, a minimum of forces is to be provided as rear cover which may be required ; the other frontiers in the East against Poland and Lithuania are merely to be protected ; the Southern frontiers to be watched.

(c) The sections of the army which can be rapidly employed must force the frontier fortifications with speed and decision, and must break into Czechoslovakia with the greatest daring in the certain knowledge that the bulk of the mobile army will follow them with the utmost speed. Preparations for this are to be made and timed in such a way that those sections of the army which can be rapidly employed, cross the frontier at the appointed time, simultaneously with the penetration by the Air Force before the enemy can become aware of our mobilization. For this, a time-table between Army and Air Force is to be worked out in conjunction with the Supreme Command and submitted to me for approval."

Next, the " Missions for the Branches of the Armed Forces " are stated in detail.

" (a) *Army* : The basic principle of the surprise attack against Czechoslovakia must not be endangered by the inevitable time required for transporting the bulk of the field forces by rail or the initiative of the Air Force be wasted. Therefore, it is first of all essential to the army that as many assault columns as possible be employed at the same time as the surprise attack by the Air Force. These assault columns—the composition of each according to their tasks at that time—must be formed from troops which can be employed rapidly owing to their proximity to the frontier, or to motorisation and to special measures of readiness. It must be the purpose of these thrusts to break into the Czechoslovak fortification lines at numerous points and in a strategically favourable direction, to achieve a break-through or to break them down from the rear. For the success of this operation, co-operation with the Sudeten German frontier population, with deserters from the Czechoslovak army, with parachutists or airborne troops and with units of the sabotage service, will be of importance. The bulk of the army has the task of frustrating the Czechoslovak plan of defence, of preventing the Czechoslovak army from escaping into Slovakia, of forcing a battle, of beating the Czechoslovak army, and of speedily occupying Bohemia and Moravia. To this end a thrust into the heart of Czechoslovakia must be made with the strongest possible motorised and armoured units, using to the full the first success of the assault columns and the effects of the Air Force operations.

The rear cover provided for the West must be limited in numbers and quality to the extent commensurate with the present state of fortifications. Whether the units assigned to this will be transported to the Western frontier immediately or held back for the time being, will be decided in my special order. Preparations must, however, be made to enable security detachments to be brought up to the Western frontier even during the strategic concentration 'Green'. Independent of this, a first security garrison must be improvised from the engineers at present employed in constructing fortifications, and from formations of the Labour Corps. The remaining frontiers as well as East Prussia are to be thinly protected. But, always depending on the political situation, the transfer by sea of a part or even the bulk of the active forces in East Prussia into the Reich, must be taken into account.

(b) *Air Force* : While leaving a minimum of defensive forces in the West, the Air Force is to be employed in bulk in a surprise attack against Czechoslovakia. The frontier is to be flown over at the same time as it is crossed by the first section of the army. The most important task of the Air Force is the destruction of the Czechoslovak Air Force and their supply bases within the shortest possible time, in order to eliminate the possibility of its employment as well as that of Russian and French air forces, should the occasion arise, against the strategic concentration and penetration of the German army and against the German 'lebensraum'. Next to this the crippling of enemy mobilization, of the direction of the government and armed forces, as well as the delaying of the strategic concentration of the Czechoslovak Army by attacks on communication installations, mobilization and government centres, can be of considerable importance to the initial successes of the army.

At points in the frontier area where strong sections of the Czechoslovak Army or the depth of the defensive system might make the success of the sudden breakthrough of the German land attack questionable, the employment of adequate bomber forces must be assured. Czechoslovak industrial installations are to be spared as far as the course of operations permits. Retaliatory attacks against the population will be carried out only with my permission. Centres of air defence are to be created throughout Berlin, the Central German industrial area and the Ruhr area, and gradually prepared even now in an inconspicuous manner.

(c) *Navy* : The Navy will assist the army operations by employing the Danube flotilla. For this purpose the flotilla will be under the orders of the Commander-in-Chief of the Army. As regards the conduct of naval warfare, at first only those measures are to be taken which appear to be necessary for the careful protection of the North Sea and the Baltic against a sudden intervention in the conflict by other states. These measures must be confined to the absolutely necessary extent. Their inconspicuousness must be guaranteed. It is of decisive importance that all actions which might influence the political attitude of the European Great Powers unfavourably, be avoided."

Finally, the Directive deals with sabotage, insurrection, and war economy. Regarding the former, it states that " all preparations for sabotage and insurrection will be made by the Supreme Command of the Armed Forces. They will be made in agreement with and according to the requirements of the branches of the Armed Forces so that their effects accord with the operations of Army and Air Force."

Regarding the " Tasks of the War Economy," the Directive orders :

" In war economy it is essential that in the field of the armament industry a maximum employment of forces is made possible through increased supplies. In the course of operations, it is of value that a contribution be made to the reinforcement of the total war-economic strength by rapidly reconnoitring and restarting important factories. For this reason the sparing of Czechoslovak industrial and works installations, in so far as military operations permit, can be of decisive importance to us."

The Air Force Looks West

Meanwhile, it is noteworthy that the German Air Force, despite the heavy commitments placed on it under " Case Green " keeps its eyes fixed firmly on the West. Here too, it seems, Hitler's firm conviction that the Western Powers would not intervene in a conflict between Germany and Czechoslovakia, was not fully shared. Like the General Staff of the Army, it remained preoccupied with " Case Red," a war with the West as a result of the war with Czechoslovakia, and the German *Luftwaffe* prepared extensive plans in order to cope with such a situation. As has already been seen, measures to keep the Czechoslovak Air Force at arm's length from Berlin and the Ruhr, and the establishment of anti-air defence centres, particularly in the Central German industrial area, were provided for in the Directive for " Case Green." Two other documents in our possession go considerably further. They are a " Plan Study 1938 " containing " Instruction for Deployment and Combat during ' Case Red '," issued by the Supreme Command of the Air Force on June 2nd, 1938, and an " Air Force General Staff Memorandum " on the subject of " Extended Case Green," issued on August 25th, 1938.

The first document is based on the assumption that " if war threatens between France and Germany, hostilities will be started by France." France will then " either intervene in the struggle between the Reich and Czechoslovakia in the course of ' Case Green ', or start hostilities simultaneously with Czechoslovakia, or, as is possible but not likely, France will begin the fight while Czechoslovakia still remains aloof." Further assumptions are : " France will begin the war with her Air Force, probably without a declaration of war. Britain's entry into the war and the employment of the British Air Forces, even from continental bases, must be reckoned with. Belgium's participation is uncertain. It is doubtful whether France and Britain will respect a possible Belgian neutrality. It is unlikely that France will respect the neutrality of Luxembourg. German formations will not fly over Belgian or Luxembourg territory until they receive specific orders from the Supreme Command of the Air Force."

There follows speculation as to the probable deployment and strategic plan of the French Air Force, and in a later paragraph " the entire area of France " is declared a potential combat area for the German Air Force. Intentions of the German Air Command are then stated. " Regardless of whether France enters the war as a result of ' Case Green ' or whether she makes the opening move of the war simultaneously with Czechoslovakia, in any case the mass of the German offensive formations will, in conjunction with the Army, first deliver the decisive blow against Czechoslovakia. Until the main forces employed in the Southeast become available, it will be the task of Air Force Group III to prevent France from obtaining complete freedom of action in the air. For this purpose, attacks will be carried out continuously, in varying strength and in irregular sequence ; air defence will be mobile and will be concentrated on focal points. In addition it may be necessary in exceptional cases to relieve Army Group West through concentrated use of the air force at threatened points of the front, or through attacks against the deploying French armies, the deployment routes and the supply service. It is intended to use parachute sabotage troops which will be assigned by the Supreme Command of the Air Force as the situation may require, for the purpose of destroying suitable targets against which bombing raids cannot guarantee decisive success."

This reads like a very considerable effort, seeing that it is planned, at any rate in the opening stages, as a subsidiary operation. But Goering is aware that he will have to do a good deal of bluffing. " By means of simulated activities on as many peacetime aerodromes as possible, and on other aerodromes known to the enemy, further, by installing new dummy aerodromes, and by distributing our own forces in small units over a wide area, we intend to create a deceptive impression of great fighting strength and so split up the enemy's combat forces." At a later stage, " when stronger forces are assigned in the course of operations," the main task will be : " to break up the French

E

flying formations on their aerodromes, to destroy their supply depots and vital installations on the aerodromes. In addition, preparations will be made for attacks against power and transformer stations which are indispensable for the supply of power to armament industries in and around Paris ; attacks against the French fuel supply, especially the refineries and oil depots ; attacks on the unloading of troops and cargoes in the French Mediterranean ports."

Finally, "preparatory measures for employment against the West of further offensive air forces freed from service in the Southeast " are outlined. " As the enterprise against Czechoslovakia progresses, offensive air forces freed from service in the Southeast will, in the event of ' Case Red ', be transferred to the West, and employed against France with as much sudden hitting-power as possible. Depending on the development of the situation in the Southeast, the transfer of reinforcements to the West may become possible already a few days after the start of ' Case Red.' The strength of these forces cannot be determined exactly beforehand. The following are the maximum forces which may be counted upon, in addition to the forces already employed in the West under Air Force Group III : 3 Air Division Commands with an average of 2. combat squadrons, 1 dive-bomber group and 1 reconnaissance group each. Total strength therefore, approximately 30 combat and dive-bomber groups."

This, then, in addition to the 5 divisions behind the unfinished Western fortification line, was what France would have had to face—had there been no Munich.

The second Air Force Directive, issued eleven weeks later, is definitely based on the assumption that France will declare war during " Case Green", but only if military assistance from Britain is assured. It is also assumed that the Soviet Union will side immediately with the Western Powers. The Dutch-Belgian area now " assumes much more importance for the prevention of the war in Western Europe than during the World War." It is further assumed that the actual beginning of hostilities will take place only after the French armed forces have been tactically deployed. " That means within the fourth to eighteenth day." The war aim of the Entente Powers, as the Directive calls them, is seen as the " overcoming of Germany through attacking its war economy. In other words, through a long war " Two possible methods of operation are anticipated for the French army : (a) to man and hold the Maginot Line ; (b) to march into Belgium and the Netherlands at the very beginning of the war with the aim of occupying the Ruhr territory. " All suppositions support the first alternative," says the Directive—correctly.

" The French Air Force," continues the Directive, " will probably attack both German economic and air force targets as well as military and communication objectives. Thus no concentrated effect will be achieved at any one place. The British Air Force is assumed to be committed from British bases against the Rhine-Westphalia industrial area and the North Sea ports. Sooner or later Belgian-Dutch neutrality will be violated. A camouflaged aircraft-reporting network in Belgium and the Netherlands has to be taken into account from the first day of the war. No transfer to France on the part of the British Air Force need be expected at the beginning of the war. Equally it is held to be out of the question for any large parts of the British armed forces to be transferred to France. Provision seems to have been made for the use of Northern French ground organizations during the course of the war at least by part of the attacking British Air Force. The existence of a relatively large number of civilian airfields in Belgium and the Netherlands seems to indicate the intention of moving advanced elements of the air defences of London (light fighters and reconnaissance aircraft) into this area, at a later stage."

Immediate attacks by the British and French air forces were thus expected, and the German aim, based on having two air forces available in the West at the beginning of hostilities and five of them after three or four weeks, was " to bring about a decision by the defeat of the Western Powers."

This document contains some interesting speculations on the probable strength of the British and French air forces at that time. It estimates that by October 1st, 1938, France would have a first-line strength of 640 aircraft, and Britain some 850 aircraft, only 350 of which could be regarded as modern. The majority of the British front-line aircraft could be described as only conditionally serviceable in the face of modern defences. " Owing to their inadequate range the present British formations are not in a position to carry on a vigorous air war from their home bases without violating sovereign Dutch or Belgian territory. Even if Dutch and Belgian neutrality were ignored, only the modern

British aircraft need be taken into account as a serious threat to the Ruhr. A transfer of British air forces to Northern France is to be expected at the earliest after several weeks of war."

Finally, the document has a note on British and French aircraft production. " The first aircraft put into mass production as a result of the expansion of France's military aircraft industry during the years 1934 to 1938, are at present rolling off the assembly lines. At the moment the aero-engine factories are lagging behind with deliveries. In August 1938, 40 single-engined and 30 twin-engined military aircraft were delivered to the French air force. It must be assumed that these figures will be increased during the coming months to 100 aircraft a month, 50 single-engined and 50 twin-engined. A further moderate increase in production is possible, and to be expected from spring 1939 onwards. In Great Britain, existing plants have been extended since 1936, and the effect will begin to make itself felt increasingly from 1939 onwards. If present plans are adhered to, the programme will be completely carried out by 1941. Present production (August 1938) is estimated at some 200 aircraft of all types (commercial and military) a month. It must be noted that it is intended to import training aircraft and long-range reconnaissance aircraft from the United States and Canada."

The document ends with an elaborate discussion of bombing plans for the German Air Force, to which reference is made elsewhere in these studies (Chapter III, Operation Sea-Lion). It closes with this remark :

" Belgium and the Netherlands would, in German hands, represent an extraordinary advantage in the prosecution of the air war against Britain as well as against France. Therefore, it is held to be essential to obtain the opinion of the Army, as to the conditions under which an occupation of this area could be carried out, and how long it would take. In this case it would be necessary to reassess the commitments against Great Britain."

The air force planners are casting their shadows ahead, and they are long shadows. It will be seen that they found themselves in no disagreement with the Army.

Czech Army Up to Date

Planning went ahead steadily, with a constant stream of new directives and instructions issuing from Hitler's office, and new questionnaires for the General Staff almost daily. On June 9th, 1938, Zeitzler submitted a detailed survey of the armament of the Czech Army, from heavy artillery to infantry guns, mortars, machine-guns down to small arms. On the same day, he sends detailed answers to a questionnaire referring to the same subject. He states that " arming and equipping of the Czech Army with new weapons of war is progressing, thanks to the excellent production capacity of the Czech armament industry. The armament was built up from the weapons of the old Austrian army. It is slowly and steadily being modernised." He points out that in medium artillery modern armament predominates, that heavy infantry weapons like howitzers and mortars are modern. The same is true of tanks. Reserve stocks of weapons and ammunition seem to be guaranteed. He comes to the conclusion that " the Czechoslovak Army must be considered up-to-date as far as armament and equipment are concerned."

Hitler is also worrying about the West. He wants to know how many battalions are employed in the West for the construction of artillery emplacements, and what the frontier protection is like. He is told that the strength of the Frontier Guard on the Western frontier is 15,200 men with 1,250 light machine-guns.

On June 18, 1938, Hitler has the draft ready for yet a new Directive. It falls into three parts, of which the first contains some new and interesting observations. Under " General Guiding Principles " Hitler says :

" There is no danger of a preventive war by foreign states against Germany. Germany has not committed herself to any military alliance which would automatically force her into a warlike conflict with foreign powers. The immediate aim is a solution of the Czech problem by my own, free decision ; this stands in the foreground of my political intentions. I am determined to use to the full every favourable political opportunity to realize this aim. Thereby friends, interested parties and enemies can be called upon to take part in this scheme, and other powers can remain indifferent, even though they could not be previously placed with absolute certainty in one of these categories. However, I shall decide to take action against Czechoslovakia only if I am firmly convinced, as in the case of the occupation of the demilitarised zone and the entry into Austria, that France will not march, and therefore Britain will not intervene."

In the second part, under " Strategic Concentrations " he confirms most of what had been laid down in earlier directives, but adds this, in respect of " Case Red " :

" Since even a war against us started by the Western Powers *must*, in view of the present situation, begin with the destruction of Czechoslovakia, the preparation of strategic concentrations for a war with the main effort by Army and Air Force against the West, is no longer of primary importance. The preparations made to date for ' Case Red ' remain, however, in force. They contribute, as far as the Army is concerned, toward camouflaging and screening the other strategic concentration and serve, in the case of the Air Force, as a preparation for the shifting of the main effort from the East to the West, which may, under certain circumstances, suddenly become necessary. They also serve as preliminary work for future possibilities of war in the West."

The third part considers what is to happen after " Case Green." It appears to have been drafted later, and is dated July 7th, 1938.

" How the political situation will develop during the execution or after the conclusion of ' Green ' cannot be predicted. Therefore, the Armed Forces will confine themselves to the preparations of ' Case Green ' and ' Case Red '. However, it seems expedient to make at least theoretical considerations and calculations for several possible eventualities to avoid being mentally unprepared. These considerations would have to cover (1) what would have to be done if other nations intervened against us during the execution of ' Green,' contrary to our expectations ; (2) what should be done after the conclusion of ' Green '."

Regarding the first eventuality, Hitler says : " If, during the execution of ' Green', France intervenes against us, the measures provided in ' Case Green ' come into force. The primary essential in this connection is to hold the Western fortifications until the execution of the action ' Green ' permits forces to be freed. Should France be supported by Britain, this will at first have small effect on the land war. It is the duty of the Air Force, the Navy, and the Supreme Command (War Economy Staff, Defence, Armed Forces Communications), to carry out farsighted deliberations in their respective spheres. Among the Eastern powers, Russia is the most likely to intervene. This, in the beginning at any rate, will probably consist of reinforcing the Czech Air Force and armament. However, the decision must not be neglected concerning what measures are to be taken if Russia were to come to the point of starting a naval and air war against us, or even wishing to penetrate into East Prussia through the border states. In the case of a penetration by Poland, we must hold the Eastern fortifications and East Prussia, using the Frontier Guard and other formations, until the conclusion of ' Green ' once more gives us freedom of movement."

Regarding the second eventuality, Hitler observes : " If ' Green ' takes place still during this mobilization year, we must be in a position, after the conclusion of ' Green ', to put a provisional strategic concentration quickly into force. In connection with the latter, it is of primary importance to safeguard the German frontiers, including the new addition by the armed forces, and still have the bulk of the field forces and the Air Force at our disposal. It would have to be possible to put such a future strategic concentration, " Frontier Protection," into force separately for the various frontiers."

This Directive seems significant, above all, for one fact. Although Hitler continues to be emphatic in his belief that Britain and France will not intervene on behalf of Czechoslovakia—it would be " contrary to our expectations "—he seems less sure of himself than earlier, and certainly shows a growing concern with the state of affairs on Germany's Western frontiers. It is almost as if he knew that his assumption was wrong, or at least very dangerous, but he refuses to admit it and in order to fortify himself, goes as far as saying in his preliminary remarks that he will " decide to take action against Czechoslovakia only if I am firmly convinced that France will not march, and therefore Britain will not intervene." He knows that with the help of his intuition he can " convince " himself of almost anything he wishes. But it seems that a point has been reached where he is beginning to be afraid fully to face the facts as he knows them. Gen. Jodl bears this out.

Three Weeks or Three Years ?

On August 10th, 1938, Gen. Jodl notes in his Diary, the Army chiefs and the commanders of the Air Force groups as well as Col. Jeschonnek and Jodl himself, were ordered to the Berghof, Hitler's residence at Berchtesgaden. After dinner, Hitler made a speech lasting for almost three hours, in which he developed his political thoughts. The text of this speech, unfortunately, is not in our possession. But Jodl records carefully what happened after Hitler had finished.

"The subsequent attempts to draw the Führer's attention to the defects of our preparation, which are undertaken by some of the Army generals, are rather unfortunate," he writes. "This applies especially to the remark made by General Wietersheim which, to crown it all, he claims to quote from General Adams— namely, that the western fortifications can only be held for three weeks. The Führer becomes very indignant and flares up, bursting into the remark that in such a case the whole army would not be good for anything. 'I assure you, General, the position will not only be held for three weeks, but for three years !' This despondent view which, unfortunately, is held very widely among the Army General Staff, is based on a variety of reasons. First of all, the General Staff is restrained by old memories ; political considerations play a part as well, instead of obeying and executing its military mission. That is certainly done with traditional devotion, but the vigour of the soul is lacking, because at bottom they do not believe in the genius of the Führer. And one does perhaps compare him with Charles XII. And since water flows downhill, this defeatism may not only possibly cause immense political damage—for the divergencies between the opinion of the generals and that of the Führer are common talk—but may also constitute a danger for the morale of the troops. But I have no doubt that the Führer will be able to boost the morale of the people in an unexpected way when the right moment comes."

Autumn Manoeuvres 1938

On July 12th, 1938, the Supreme Command of the Army had issued its schedule for the regular army manoeuvres to be held during that autumn. It will be recalled that October 1st, 1938, had been mentioned as the date by which all preparations required under the current Directive "Green" had to be completed; and that Hitler had objected to the army manoeuvres being carried out too late in the autumn. The intention was, as we see, to use the military manoeuvres as a cover under which army and air force units were to be so placed that with a minimum of diversion they could go over to real warfare and strike at the heart of Czechoslovakia almost at a moment's notice. The smoke-screen was to be complete. The manoeuvres schedule, which is initialled by Zeitzler, states expressly that " foreign military delegations as well as foreign military attachés will be invited to attend the autumn exercises."

Meanwhile a difference had arisen between the Army and the Air Force over the fixing of D-Day—the Germans called it X-Day. On August 24th, 1938, Jodl sent a memorandum to Hitler in which he stated that in order to make the most of the element of surprise the Air Force wished the order to march to be given sufficiently late on X-minus-One to prevent mobilisation from becoming known to Czechoslovakia on that day. " The Army's efforts," says the memorandum, " are tending in the opposite direction. It intends to let the Supreme Command initiate all advance measures between X-minus-Three and X-minus-One which will contribute to the smooth and rapid working of the mobilisation. With this in mind the Army Supreme Command also demands that the X-Order be given not later than 1400 hours on X-minus-One."

Jodl then discusses the implications of the "incident" which is to set the whole operation in motion. It will be remembered that this was discussed between Hitler and Keitel when it was suggested that the assassination of the German Ambassador in Prague might suit such a purpose. How is this "incident" to be timed ?

" Operation 'Green' will be set in motion by means of an 'incident' in Czechoslovakia which will give Germany provocation for military intervention," writes Jodl. " The fixing of the exact time for this incident is of the utmost importance. It must come at a time when weather conditions are favourable for our superior air forces to go into action and at an hour which will enable authentic news of it to reach us in the afternoon of X-minus-One. It can then be spontaneously answered by releasing the X-Order at 1400 hours on X-minus-One. On X-minus-Two, Navy, Army and Air Force will merely receive an advance warning. If the Führer intends to follow this plan of action, all further discussion is superfluous. For in that case no advance measures may be taken before X-minus-One for which there is not an innocent explanation as we shall otherwise appear to have manufactured the incident. Orders for absolutely essential advance measures must be given in good time and camouflaged with the help of the numerous manoeuvres and exercises. Also, the question raised by the Foreign Office as to whether all Germans should be called back in time from prospective enemy territories must in no way lead to the conspicuous departure from Czechoslovakia of any German subjects before the incident. Even a warning of the diplomatic representatives in Prague is impossible before the first air attack, although the consequences could be very grave in the event of their becoming victims of such an attack, e.g., death of representatives of friendly or confirmed neutral powers. If, for technical reasons, the evening hours should be considered desirable for the incident, the following day cannot be X-Day but it must then be the day after that. In any case we must act on the principle that nothing must be done before the incident which might point to mobilisation, and that the swiftest possible action must be taken after the incident."

One observes that even for master conspirators it is not always easy to determine the best way to start a war unless one is prepared, at the same time, to kill a large number of one's own people.

Finishing Touches

September, the critical month, arrives, and the finishing touches are put to the plan. On September 3rd, 1938, Hitler has a conference at the Berghof with Brauchitsch and Keitel. Brauchitsch is to command the campaign against Czechoslovakia. He reports on the exact time when the troops earmarked for " Green " are to be transferred to " exercise areas." The field units are to be transferred on September 28th. They will then be ready for action. When X-Day becomes known, they will " carry out exercises in the opposite direction." Hitler objects to having the field units a two-day march away. He orders camouflage exercises to be carried out " everywhere." He is dissatisfied with the employment of troops for " Green." The prospects for the 2nd Army are smallest since it faces the strongest Czech fortifications, and this is, therefore, a waste of troops. A thrust in the 10th Army area, however, is promising. " The Czechs will stop opposite the 2nd Army and keep an assault army ready east of Prague. A thrust against it into the heart of Czechoslovakia is to be made. A thrust in the 14th Army area will fail because of transport difficulties. Therefore assemble all motorised and armoured divisions with the 10th Army and employ them in the thrust. Once we are through there, the Southern front which is built up opposite our 12th Army in three defence lines, will collapse. An army in the heart of Bohemia will bring about the decision. For the 2nd Army it would possibly be a repetition of Verdun. An attack there would mean bleeding to death for a task which cannot be accomplished." Brauchitsch objects " because of the state of the motorised divisions, supply and untrained leaders." But Hitler answers that the operation as he (Brauchitsch) has planned it, is exactly what the Czechs are expecting. " Opposite the 10th Army the enemy is not always in concrete emplacements. There is a possibility here of drawing in the Henlein people. The line here is very far back. There must be co-operation between 10th and 12th Armies. We must add motorised units to the army. How else can we gather experience ? Decisive is the co-ordination of equal speeds." Hitler then gives orders for the development of the Western fortifications and demands an improvement of the advance positions around Aachen and Saarbrücken. He orders the construction of 300 to 400 battery positions to take a total of 1,600 artillery pieces. One cannot help feeling that he knows what he is talking about.

On September 9th, 1938, Hitler calls Keitel and Brauchitsch to another conference, this time at Nuremberg. General Halder is also there, as well as a number of other officers. The meeting lasts from 10 p.m. until 3-30 a.m. The record of this discussion, for all its highly technical detail, is one of the most fascinating documents in our possession.

Gen. Halder explains the operational plan. The Czechoslovak army is to be prevented from retreating from the Bohemia-Moravia area. It is to be beaten. A rapid decision is to be brought about. " This mission can be accomplished by a pincer attack in the direction of Olmütz and Brno, to be carried out by the 2nd and 14th Armies. There is a difficult transport situation in Austria. For this reason the main effort lies in the area of the 2nd Army. The Czechoslovak frontier can only be lightly held, and a withdrawal of the Czech forces is certain. Several defensive lines which are favoured by the terrain will delay the second thrust and allow time to be gained for a Czech retreat and to retain a rear position. This is to be avoided. The Bohemian-Moravian heights which will confront the attacker in the last phase, will favour the probable Czech course of action. The pincer attack makes a "rear attack" from behind these heights possible. This operation will definitely succeed. Enemy reserves are in the first instance mainly local. There are further reserves near and south of Prague. The enemy will have no time to form further reserves. The enemy does not possess closed armoured forces. They are distributed and consist of light units."

Regarding the 2nd Army, the " weaknesses opposite its sector are recognized. The installations are only partly completed.

Most of them lack armed cupolas. There are great gaps. Olmütz will be reached on the second day. The so-called light motorised forces on the right flank are no danger. They consist partly of mounted units and will be engaged by the adjoining army. Were the attack, against expectations, to fail, then under no circumstances 'bleed to death' before the position. The strategic concentration is to be flexible. Rear sections will be brought up to the points where success has been achieved. The Czechs are fearing the Glatz mountain area. In this area only demonstrations are to be staged. There will be a tie-up of Czech forces. To provide cover eastwards, tanks will be valuable.

" The 12th and 14th Armies will work together. Their columns must necessarily support one another during the thrust and cause the front to collapse. Bohemia is only weakly occupied at the frontier—one division per every 120 kilometres. The operation is therefore promising. After the thrust in a northerly direction 12th Army faces east and races for Brno. The enemy will not be able to employ reserves according to plan. The 10th Army faces the Pilsen bolt which is strongly fortified. Roads are bad. Tanks must break through here and establish bridgeheads for the forces following up. Forces of the next wave will be brought up by lorry units. After the 3rd and 4th mobilization day six further divisions will be brought up to the second and third line and can be employed where success is in the balance."

That is Halder's plan. As at the previous meeting, Hitler takes a poor view of it and says so. He launches out into a strategic and tactical dissertation which is of absorbing interest. Even the condensed transcript of the minutes indicates that here he felt right " in his element " ; an armchair strategist, it is true, but one of unmistakable calibre. One understands that the generals of the older school must have hated him while the younger officers were fascinated by his undoubted military gifts.

" We should not plan the action," says Hitler, " on the operations as we desire them, but take into consideration the probable course of action pursued by the enemy. With regard to this course of action two factors are decisive: (1) At the time of our rearmament between 1934 and 1938 our opponent must have endeavoured to safeguard himself against a tearing of his East-West communications, in this case presumably between Troppau and Nikolsburg. Against us this would imply the building of fortifications on the Upper Silesian frontier. In the South an agreement with Austria would have achieved a defence north of the Danube, or an advance to the Danube to protect the southern flank. (2) This latter move is no longer possible (since the seizure of Austria). Therefore, as a result of the situation created in March 1938, it is all the more probable that they have streng-thened their fortifications opposite our 2nd Army. The enemy must hold there—otherwise there is no sense in holding the remaining front. Hence here the best regiments and forti-fications are to be expected. Holding the front facing the 2nd Army will decide the ' to be or not to be ' of Czecho-slovakia.

" There is no doubt that the planned pincer movement is the most desirable solution and should be carried out. But its success is nevertheless too uncertain for it to be depended upon, especially as a rapid success is necessary from a political point of view. The first eight days are politically decisive ; within that week a far-reaching territorial gain must be achieved. Our artillery (210 cm. howitzers) is not adequate against fortifications. Where an attack is expected the element of surprise is ruled out. Besides, one knows from experience that it is hard to abandon an action which has achieved only part-success. More and more units are thrown into breaches, and the bleeding-to-death, which one wanted to avoid, sets in. Tanks are used up and are not available for the subsequent territory-gaining operation. The result is that motorised divisions have to advance without armour.

" Also the objectives of the motorised units are not too far off and can be gained without fighting, so that they could be equally well gained by infantry troops. The motorised divisions will not be able to influence a decision to any extent. It is the task of the motorised forces to bridge areas free of the enemy. Where an attack opens up a large, free space the commitment of motorised forces is justified. They may be compared with the use of army cavalry at the beginning of the 1914 war. It is fatal for tanks to have to stop and wait for infantry. This contradicts all laws of logic. In the 14th Army sector fortifications can only have been begun since March. Hence the thrust towards Brno will be easier. The 2nd Panzer Division can therefore be left there. However, this division should operate with the 29th motorised division. Therefore the 29th must not arrive on the evening of the second day. The 2nd Panzer must constitute the advance column of the 29th Division (motorised). Are the roads suitable for the 29th ? The 13th Division, which has no prospects of success as a motorised division with the 12th Army, is to be transferred to the

Reichenau Army together with the 2nd Motorised Division. Thus two chances for victory will be created. If the pincer movement has no success, the 10th Army will open the way for the 12th Army, carrying strong forces into the heart of the country. If both operations are successful, this means the end of Czechoslovakia. In place of the two motorised divisions it is preferable to mobilize two further divisions which are to be brought up on lorries and buses. It may become necessary for the 10th Army to turn north-east towards Prague."

That, as far as one can see from the minutes, seems to have fixed the generals.

The generals, at this time, are still worried. Jodl notes in his Diary on September 8th, 1938, that he had a conversation with Gen. Stülpnagel (who was later to become military governor of Paris) in which the latter asked for a written assurance that the Army High Command will be informed five days in advance if the plan is to be carried out. "I agree," writes Jodl, " and add that the overall meteorological situation can be estimated to some extent only for two days in advance, and that therefore the plans may be changed up to that moment, i.e. X-minus-Two. Gen. Stülpnagel mentions that for the first time he wonders whether the previous basis of the plan is not being abandoned. It pre-supposed that the Western Powers would not interfere decisively. It gradually seems as if the Führer would stick to his decision even though he may no longer be of this opinion. It must be added that Hungary is at least moody and that Italy is reserved.

" I must admit," continues Jodl, " that I am worrying too, when comparing the change of opinion about political and military potentialities, as reflected in the Directives of June 24th, November 5th, and December 7th, 1937, and May 30th, 1938, with the last statements. In spite of that one must be aware of the fact that the other nations will do everything they can to apply pressure on us. We must pass this test of nerves, but because only very few people know the art of withstanding this pressure successfully, the only possible solution is to inform only a very small circle of officers of news that causes us anxiety, and not to have it circulate through the ante-rooms as heretofore."

Towards Mobilization

Events now move at a steady pace towards the fateful day.

On September 10th, 1938, Hitler signs a decree whereby the entire Reich Labour Service organization comes under the command of the Supreme Command of the Army with effect from September 15th. On September 15th, Keitel, Chief of the Supreme Command of the Armed Forces, issues the relevant instructions which reveal that, with one stroke, the entire labour force hitherto engaged on constructing the Western fortifications has become " militarily mobilized " and that, among others, all light road construction battalions are now suddenly " training units of the Army." Their members " are regarded as having been drafted into the Armed Forces for manoeuvre purposes and are soldiers." On September 11th, 1938, Jodl records that he had a conference with Secretary of State Jahnke of the Propaganda Ministry " on imminent common tasks." What was considered particularly important was the " joint preparation for the refutation of our own violations of international law, and the exploitation of its violations by the enemy." This ingenious document was actually worked out down to the smallest detail, and extracts of it were made available at Nuremberg. It was actually issued on October 1st, 1938, and the extracts alone, which contain only a handful of samples, comprise sixteen large pages.

Every conceivable eventuality is considered under five different headings, first, the nature of the incident, second, a practical example, third, the orthodox attitude of international law towards it, fourth, its justification by the laws of warfare, fifth, the explanation to be given by the Propaganda Minister. Thus in the category " bombing of extra-territorial buildings and areas," the example given is " the destruction of the British Embassy in an air raid on Prague." The position under international law is then quoted as " assuming that no orders for the bombing of extra-territorial buildings and areas will be given by us under any circumstances, the action in question would have been carried out by mistake." Justification by the laws of warfare of the same incident would be that " an accident of this kind can best be explained publicly by the fact that the British Embassy is in the immediate vicinity of military installations, the bombing of which was an indispensable military necessity. If, therefore, the British Embassy was hit by mistake, it is to be described as a regrettable accident." But this does not mean that the Propaganda Minister is compelled to put out this version. The column for his remarks is left blank.

One wonders what his " explanation " would be. The list goes into scores of cases, from the illegal employment of prisoners of war on munitions work, the use of churches as billets and stables, the destruction of the Hradshin in Prague to the bombing of Red Cross hospitals, and the compulsory evacuation of the civil population. Everything is provided for, and an answer ready.

On September 15th, 1938, Jodl notes in his Diary that at a conference with the Chief of the Army High Command and the Chiefs of the General Staffs of Army and Air Force, " the question was discussed what could be done if the Führer insists on an advancement of the date, owing to the rapid development of the situation." On September 16th, Keitel returns from Berchtesgaden and " graphically describes the results of the conference between Chamberlain and the Führer." An order is issued by Keitel on the same day to the railways to have empty rolling stock kept in readiness clandestinely for the strategic concentrations of the Army, so that it can be transported beginning on September 28th. Still on the same day, Jodl himself signs an order, enumerating a total of 302 battalions of the Reich Labour Service which are immediately to receive military training. On September 17th, he notes in his Diary that " contrary to the previous intention to transfer all Sudeten Germans with previous military training to the Replacement Army, the Führer issues orders to unite them into a Sudeten German Free Corps. The Supreme Command of the Armed Forces places Lt. Col. Koechling at the disposal of Konrad Henlein as an adviser." The same day, according to a message received by Schmundt, a conference lasting in all seven minutes took place between Hitler and Col. Koechling who " received far-reaching plenary powers from the Führer. The Sudeten German Free Corps remains responsible to Konrad Henlein alone. Purpose: protection of the Sudeten Germans, and maintenance of disturbances and clashes. The Free Corps will be established in Germany. Armament only with Austrian weapons. Activities of the Free Corps to begin as soon as possible."

The following day, September 18th, 1938, a schedule showing the disposition and movement orders for the various armies assigned for the campaign against Czechoslovakia is circulated. It shows that the Army Group Command is under Gen. Adams, with Gen. Wietersheim as Chief of Staff. The Second Army based on Cosel is commanded by Gen. v. Rundstedt, the Eighth

Army based on Freiburg by Gen. v. Bock, the Tenth Army based on Schwandorf by Gen. v. Reichenau, the Twelfth Army based on Passau by Gen. Ritter v. Leeb (with Gen. v. Manstein as Chief of Staff), and the Fourteenth Army, based on Vienna, by Gen. List—all of whom were later to achieve considerable notoriety either in France, the Balkans, or on the Russian Front.

On September 20th, Jodl notes that " Britain and France have handed over their demands in Prague, the contents of which are still unknown." He adds : " The activities of the Free Corps begin to assume such an extent that they may bring about, and already have brought about consequences harmful to the plans of the Army, in that they have caused the transfer of rather strong units of the Czech Army to the proximity of the border. By checking with Col. Koechling I attempt to lead these activities into normal channels. Toward the evening the Führer also takes a hand and gives permission to act only with groups up to 12 men each, after approval of the Corps HQ."

September 21st, 1938, is a critical day. A document circulated by the Supreme Command of the Armed Forces outlines, in 25 points, the military measures to be considered " if the Czechoslovak Government accepts the terms, i.e. cession of the Sudeten German territory, and a plebiscite in Czech-German areas." The measures contemplated for this event include the withdrawal by the Czechs, from this territory, of troops, police and gendarmerie and other military units ; immediate surrender of arms in these territories ; immediate surrender of all fortifications in the areas with all arms and equipment ; the withdrawal of all military power behind a security line, which will include the fortifications ; the right of the German Armed Forces to use all public transport and communications, especially railways, for military purposes ; the right to fly over the above territories ; demobilization of the entire Czech armed forces in the remaining area of the country, and discharge of all reserves ; immediate discharge of all Sudeten Germans in the armed forces from the whole of Czechoslovakia to be sent home into Sudeten Germany ; closing down of the entire armament industry until after the end of all negotiations ; prohibition of any new fortifications opposite the security line ; destruction of all existing fortifications situated beyond the future German borders ; demand of further cession of territory on military grounds, namely, the Bratislava bridgehead, the area northwest of Pilsen, the

F

Eger sector west of the Elbe to Laun ; security line must be 25 kilometres from the territory being ceded to Germany, or the territory being put to the vote ; cessation immediately of all military intelligence work against Germany ; immediate pardon and release of all Sudeten Germans, and Germans convicted of espionage ; transfer of all Czech air force personnel to their peace time garrisons, and prohibition of all military flying operations ; prohibition of destruction or sabotage of any military installations in the territories ceded ; the closing down and handing over to the German armed forces of all radio transmitters of a military, official, or private character in the areas to be ceded ; the handing over of all railway networks including rolling stock, undamaged ; the handing over of all public utilities (power stations, gas works, etc.) undamaged, etc., etc.

On the same 21st September, Jodl notes in his Diary at 1130 hours : " Telephone call from the adjutant of the Führer : ' The Führer has received news five minutes ago that Prague is said to have accepted unconditionally '." And at 1245 hours : " Department heads are informed and directive is issued to continue preparations for ' Green ', but nevertheless to get ready with everything necessary for a peaceful penetration."

The following day, September 22nd, Jodl notes, at 1920 hours, a telephone call from Godesberg by Gen. v. Stülpnagel on behalf of Keitel. " The Date (X-Day) cannot yet be ascertained ; continue preparations according to plan. If ' Case Green ' occurs, it will not be before September 30th. If it occurs sooner it will probably be improvised."

On September 25th, two SS battalions of the Death's Head formation are moved, by order of Hitler, into the " Ascher Zipfel " to the rear of Henlein's Free Corps.

On September 26th, Jodl records that the " Chief of the Supreme Command (Keitel) has stopped the intended approach march of the advance units to the Czech border, because it is not yet necessary, and because the Führer does not intend to march in before September 30th in any case. Order to approach towards the Czech frontier need be given on September 27th only. In the evening of September 26th, fixed radio stations at Breslau, Dresden and Vienna are placed at the disposal of the Propaganda Ministry for interference with possible Czech propaganda transmissions. Question by department ' Foreign Countries ' (Abteilung Ausland) whether Czechs are to be allowed to leave and cross through Germany. Decision from Chief of Armed Forces Supreme Command : yes. 1515 hours : Chief of Supreme Command informs Gen. Stumpf (of the Air Force) about the result of the Godesberg conversations and about the Führer's opinion. In no case will X-Day be before September 30th. It is important that we do not permit ourselves to be drawn into military engagements because of false reports, before Prague has replied. A question from Stumpf about Y-Hour results in the reply, that on account of the weather situation, a simultaneous intervention of the Air Force and Army cannot be expected. The Army needs the dawn, the Air Force can only start later on account of frequent fogs. The Führer has to make a decision for the commanders-in-chief who is to have priority. The opinion of Stumpf is also that the attack of the Army has to proceed. The Führer has not as yet made a decision about commitment against Prague."

Towards Munich

It is September 27th, 1938. There are two more days until the Munich Conference. There is no doubt whatsoever that Hitler has everything ready to strike at Czechoslovakia, and to strike in such a manner that the entire country will fall into his hands at one sweeping blow. Should Czechoslovakia, however, give in and consent to negotiations, he has his demands ready. The 25 points, drawn up on September 21st, are so complete that they will leave the rump of Czechoslovakia wholly at Hitler's mercy. At Munich, we know, Czechoslovakia was made to accept them. They had by then been in Hitler's pocket, ready to be pulled out, for a full week. But he did not rely on them. In fact, he relied on nothing except his army and air force. He was fully determined to go to war.

On September 27th, 1938, at 1320 hours, Jodl notes in his Diary that "the Führer consents to the first wave of attack being advanced to a line whence they can arrive in the assembly area by September 30th." The actual order which is in our possession states that these assault units comprise approximately 21 reinforced regiments, or 7 divisions. On the same day, at 1920 hours, Keitel issues this order :

" The Führer has approved the mobilization without warning of the five regular west divisions (Numbers 26, 34, 36, 32, and 35). The Führer and Supreme Commander of the Armed Forces has expressly reserved the right to issue the order for employment in the fortification zone, and the evacuation of this zone by workers of the Todt Organization. It is left to the Supreme Command of the Army to assemble as far as possible, first of all, the sections ready to march and subsequently, the remaining sections of the divisions in marshalling areas behind the western fortifications."

One wonders whether the French General Staff was aware how thinly and flimsily manned the Siegfried Line was at the time when at Munich, M. Daladier and Mr. Chamberlain bought what they believed to be the security of the West at the price of a Czech Army " up to date in armament and equipment " ? Would the Siegfried Line have held even those three weeks which Gen. Wietersheim gave it ? One cannot cease to wonder.

The vital question of " Co-ordinated Time of Attack by Army and Air Forces on X-Day " is still not solved. On September 27th, Jodl calls a conference to settle the matter once and for all. " The Army wishes to attack at dawn, i.e. about 0615 hours, and it also wishes to conduct some limited operations during the preceding night, which, however, would not alarm the entire Czech front. The time of attack for the Air Force depends on weather conditions. During the last few days, for instance, the weather would have delayed the start until, between 0800 and 1100 hours, owing to low ceiling in Bavaria." In the end they decide that synchronization is not possible, and that " the attack by the Army, independent of the attack by the Air Force, will take place at the time desired (0615 hours), and that the Air Force will attack at a time most suitable to them." It is not as easy as all that, even for Hitler, to arrange for a proper " blitzkrieg."

Still on the same day, September 27th, Keitel issues this " Most Secret " order : " As a result of the political situation, the Führer has ordered mobilization measures for the Armed Forces, without the political situation being aggravated by issuing the mobilization (X) order or corresponding code-words. Within the scope of these mobilization measures, it is necessary for the Armed Forces authorities to issue requests to the various Party authorities and their organizations which are connected with the previous issuing of the Mobilization Order, the advance measures or special code-names. The special situation makes it necessary that these requests be met immediately even if the code-word has not been previously issued, and without being referred to higher authorities. The Supreme Command requests that subordinate offices be given immediate instructions to this effect, so that the mobilization of the Armed Forces can be carried out according to plan." In other words, the political situation is so delicate and in the balance, that even the issuing of the agreed code-words for mobilization might upset it. But since mobilization cannot be postponed any longer, it is ordered, so to speak, underhand without the agreed code-word being issued at all.

On September 28th, 1938, Jodl notes in his Diary : " Stumpf reports about a conference with Goering, where the latter states that a Great War can hardly be avoided any longer. It may last seven years, and we shall win it."

The same day, Keitel and Jodl issue a whole sheaf of orders. Spheres of responsibility on the German-Czechoslovak frontier are defined for the frontier guards, police units, customs officials and party organizations. The Henlein Free Corps are to receive their instructions direct from Hitler, and will be subordinate to the Supreme Command of the Army from the moment the Army crosses the frontier. Four battalions of SS (Death's Head units) are to come under the authority of the Commander-in-Chief of the Army immediately, and are to be employed in the West, along the Upper Rhine. They are the second and third battalions of the Second SS Regiment Brandenburg, stationed at Brieg in Upper Silesia, and the first and second battalions of the Third SS Regiment Thuringia, stationed at Radebeul and Koetzschenbroda near Dresden. The two SS battalions operating in the Asch Promontory, are the first and second battalions of the SS Regiment Upper Bavaria, and they will come under Army command immediately the army crosses the Czech border. In the West two special units are established on the French-German border ; they are the " Special Group Siegfried Kz9145 " and " Special Group Siegfried Kz9148," and their task, among others, is the preparation of organisation for the reception of refugees.

At 1700 hours on September 28th, Jodl notes in his Diary : " Tension relaxes. The Führer has decided on a conference with Chamberlain, the Duce, and Daladier in Munich."

And the following day September 29th, 1938, he notes : " The pact of Munich is signed. Czechoslovakia as a power is finished. Four zones as set forth, will be occupied between October 2nd and 7th. The remaining part of mainly German character, will be occupied by October 10th. The genius of the Führer, and his determination not to shun even a world war, have again won the victory without the use of force. There remains the hope that the incredulous, the weak, and the doubtful, have by now been converted and remain converted."

The Planners Look Ahead

On September 30th, 1938, Keitel, on behalf of Hitler, issues " Directive No. 1 " relative to the " Occupation of territory separated from Czechoslovakia." The first article of the directive states the various zones of ceded territory, and the time and manner in which they are to be occupied. The second article declares :

" The present degree of mobilized preparedness is to be maintained completely, for the present also in the West. Orders for the rescinding of measures taken are held over. The entry is to be planned in such a way that it can easily be converted into operation ' Green '."

A subsequent order, issued on the same day, on the same subject, opens with this paragraph :

" By order of the Supreme Commander of the Armed Forces, the occupation of the Sudeten German areas by the Armed Forces will be executed in a manner which will allow a change-over to military operations at any time. For the advance of the troops to coincide with the withdrawal of the Czechs, particularly in the fortified zones, and on account of the possibility of local resistance, it is necessary for the march-in to be arranged in a way suited to the conduct of military operations."

Hitler is taking no chances, neither in Czechoslovakia, nor in the West. What is more, it almost looks as if he were anxious to discover a hitch, in the form of local resistance or some kind of " provocation " which would enable him, right now, to tear up the Munich Agreement—which gave him only part of what he wanted—and occupy the whole of Czechoslovakia in one blow, after all. But nothing happens. The occupation proceeds.

Directive No. 1 of September 30th, 1938, states that " the conduct of the field units must be based on the realization that they are occupying a territory whose population, after being harassed for years, looks upon the German Armed Forces as liberators." It also states that " armed resistance in the area cleared for occupation must be broken. Czech soldiers and other armed personnel found within the sector must be disarmed and taken prisoner. The boundary of the sector against the Czechs is not to be crossed under any circumstances. Hostile action against the Czechs on or beyond this boundary is to be avoided." A number of administrative instructions are issued. The rate of exchange is issued at 100 Czech crowns for 10 Reichsmark. The German Penal Code is introduced in the occupied areas. Representatives of the Berlin Propaganda Ministry are dispatched into the ceded areas. Requisitioning is prohibited, and mobilization measures may not be taken among civilian personnel.

On October 1st, 1938, Keitel requests permission from Hitler, after Zone V has been occupied, to dissolve the military formations of the Labour Service in the West and to take the five serving divisions out of the Siegfried Line and back to their home stations. Hitler has Schmundt telephone from the Opera House in Saarbrücken that he agrees.

On October 10th, 1938 Keitel sends a further telegram to Hitler suggesting that after the occupation of Zone V the following measures be taken : suspend operation ' Green ' but maintain a sufficient state of preparedness on the part of the Army and Air Force to make intervention possible if necessary ; all units not needed, to be withdrawn from the occupied area and reduced to peacetime status, as the population of the occupied area is heavily burdened by the concentration of troops ; dissolve the lorry-borne regiments as a matter of urgency, in the interests of economy ; in the west, gradual reversal of all mobilization measures without prejudice to the work in the lines ; intention of the Commander-in-Chief of the Army (Brauchitsch) to relinquish his executive powers on October 15th, 1938. Hitler agrees with all proposals except the withdrawal of units not needed in the occupied area. He orders Keitel to meet him at Essen on October 13th, when they will make a decision. Brauchitsch, on October 11th, 1938, sends a message to Hitler suggesting that he be relieved as from October 15th, and that " the administration of the area be taken over on that date by Reich Commissar Henlein, providing that further military operations are no longer necessary.". The change-over is actually made on October 21st, 1938, and on October 18th, Brauchitsch gets a letter of thanks from Hitler. On October 17th, it is decided that by October 20th, about half of the army units still remaining in Sudeten German territory, comprising 14 divisions and 3 SS Regiments, should be moved out, to enable the discharge of the older age groups and the reassignment of recruits. Large parts of the Air Force are also moved out of the area on that date, and as from October 21st, the Reich Labour Service ceases to be under the command of the Supreme Command of the Armed Forces.

But Hitler, while agreeing to all these measures, keeps his eyes fastened on the rest of Czechoslovakia, that part which eluded his grip at the Munich Conference. On October 11th, 1938, a bare twelve days after the conference, he sends a new questionnaire to Keitel. This time he wants to know: " (1) What reinforcements are necessary in the present situation to break all Czech resistance in Bohemia and Moravia? (2) How much time is required for the regrouping or moving up of new forces? (3) How much time will be required for the same purpose if it is executed after the intended demobilization and return measures? (4) How much time would be required to achieve the state of readiness of October 1st, 1938?" Here are Keitel's answers. Question 1 : Army Groups 4 and 5 require no reinforcements ; Army Group 1 needs one division ready to march and one mobile division ; Army Group 3 needs one mobile division, and Army Group for Special Duties needs one armoured brigade and two mobile divisions. Question 2 ; Regrouping would need two days, moving up of new forces from the Reich 4 to 5 days. Question 3 : time required in the southeast about 10 to 11 days, in the east 9 to 10 days. Question 4 : time required for the army would be 6 days. If reserves are called up by radio, 3 days at least. A further question elicits the answer that on October 10th, 1938, there were altogether 24 divisions in the ceded areas.

What was to be the next step?

Goering takes a hand

It is useful, at this stage, to take a brief look at Germany's internal situation. Among the Nuremberg Documents are the minutes of a conference which took place on October 14th, 1938—a fortnight after the Munich Agreement—between Goering and his economic planning staff. They show the extraordinary economic situation in which Germany then found herself, and the long black shadow this situation was casting ahead.

Goering opened the meeting by declaring that he intended to give instructions for the work during the next few months. Everybody knew from the press what the world situation looked like, and therefore the Führer had issued an order to him to carry out a gigantic programme, compared to which previous achievements were insignificant. There were difficulties in the way which he would overcome with the utmost energy and ruthlessness.

" The amount of foreign exchange, " Goering declared, " has completely dwindled on account of the preparation for the Czech enterprise, and this makes it necessary that it should be strongly increased immediately. Furthermore, foreign credits have been greatly overdrawn, and thus strongest export activity—stronger than up to now—moves into the foreground. For the next few weeks an increased export is a first priority in order to improve the foreign exchange situation. The Reich Economy Ministry must draw up a plan for the raising of export activity by pushing aside current difficulties which prevent export.

" These gains made through export are to be used for increased armament. Armament must not be curtailed by export activity. I have received the order from the Führer to increase the armament to an abnormal extent, the Air Force having first priority. Within the shortest time the Air Force is to be increased five-fold, the Navy must also be armed more rapidly, and the Army must obtain large amounts of offensive weapons at a faster rate, particularly heavy artillery and heavy tanks. Along with this, fuel, powder, and explosives have also been moved into the foreground of attention. This should be coupled with accelerated construction of highways, canals, and particularly railways.

" Substitutes produced under the Four Year Plan are to be brought rapidly into circulation. The Reich Economy Ministry and other agencies should make suggestions by the beginning of November for rapidly increasing introduction of substitutes. The import of materials for which we possess substitutes has to be drastically curtailed.

" How can these requirements be fulfilled ? " Goering asks. And he answers :

" I am faced with unheard-of difficulties. The treasury is empty, the industrial capacity is crammed with orders for many years. In spite of these difficulties, I am going to change the situation under all circumstances. Memoranda are no help, I desire only positive proposals. If necessary, I am going to convert the economy with brutal methods in order to achieve this aim. The time has come for private enterprise to show whether it has a right to continued existence. If it fails I am going over to state enterprise without any regard. I am going to make barbaric use of the plenipotentiary powers given to me by the Führer. All the wishes and plans of the state, party, and other agencies who are not entirely in this line, have to be rejected without pity. Also the ideological problems cannot be solved now, there will be time for them later. I urgently caution against making promises to the workers which I cannot keep. The wishes of the Labour Front recede entirely into the background. The industry has to be fully converted. An immediate investigation of all productive plants is to be initiated in order to determine whether they can be converted for armament and export, or whether they are to be closed down. The problem of the machine tool industry has first consideration in this respect. There is no place for printing and laundry machines, and other machines of that kind, they all have to produce machine tools. In the field of machine tools the priorities of the orders are to be investigated, and wherever possible, an increase in productive capacity must be aimed at. It follows without saying that work has to be carried out in three shifts.

" It remains now to decide who is going to carry out this task—the state or self-administrative industry. I warn all agencies, particularly the Labour Front, price controllers and others, not to interfere with these proposals in any way. I am going to proceed ruthlessly against every interference on the part of the Labour Front. The Labour Front will cease to receive raw materials and workers for its tasks. Similarly, all other party requirements have to be set aside without consideration. Foreign workers may continue to be employed except in particularly secret sections of enterprises. At the present time plants must not be burdened with unnecessary demands, such as sports fields, casinos or similar desires of the Labour Front. Measures proposed by the Labour Front have to be submitted to me for approval.

" Raw materials and power must be subjected to the strictest management. Similarly the distribution of workers has to be organized in an entirely different way than has been done until now. Retraining does not function ; all agencies have failed. I shall organize the employment of youth in industry on a very large scale. Large state training centres are to be created, and plants will be compelled to employ a certain number of apprentices. Retraining of hundreds of thousands of people will have to take place. Much more work will have to be performed by women than until now. Above all, young women have to be employed to a larger extent. Work periods of eight hours do not exist any more ; wherever necessary overtime is to be worked, double and triple shifts are a matter of course. Where the workers protest, as in Austria, for example, I shall proceed with forced labour ; I shall create camps for forced labour. The Labour Front should not carry false social ideas among the workers. It is a fact that the previous generation has driven the cart into the mud through mutiny of the workers, and by being guilty of not having these workers shot on the spot. Therefore, we have to put the matter in order again.

" Much is to be done at once in the field of transport. The Transport Ministry is to submit a request for construction of rolling stock and other requirements. In agriculture it is of importance to employ foreign workers. Similarly, the problem of agricultural machines needs urgent attention. Of particular importance is the building of store-houses. The Sudetenland has to be exploited with all means. I count upon the complete industrial assimilation of Slovakia. Bohemia, Moravia and Slovakia will become German dominions. Everything possible must be taken out. The Oder-Danube Canal is to be speeded up. Search for oil and ore are to be conducted in Slovakia."

This said, the discussion turned abruptly to the Jewish question. Goering declared, according to the minutes, that the Jewish problem had to be tackled now with all methods because the Jews had to get out of the economy. However, the wild bustle of commissars as it had developed in Austria, had to be prevented under all circumstances. These wild actions had to cease. The settling of the Jewish problem should not be regarded as a system for providing for inefficient party members. At this point Councillor Fischböck, one of the officials attending the meeting, revealed that in the beginning there were 25,000 commissars in Austria alone. Today there were still 3,500 who were useless almost without exception. In Austria the Party was of the opinion that " aryanization " was a duty of the Party, and that it was connected with the compensation of old Party members. In Austria there was still a total of 2 milliards of Jewish property. Large enterprises were being bought up by the Control Bank, but it was difficult to oust the Jews from small industrial enterprises. Goering intervened to take a strong stand against the opinion that " aryanization " was the duty of the party. It was the duty of the state alone. However, he would not release foreign exchange to ship away the Jews. In an emergency situation ghettos should be created in large cities. Councillor Schmeer thereupon cautioned against more lenient methods in the fight against the Jews. Jewish labour units should be created. If that were done, people would emigrate of their own accord. But Councillor Neumann, another worthy, warned and expressed the opinion that " one should use more precaution in this matter, particularly in Austria." Whereupon Goering closed the meeting.

Liquidation of the Remainder

Exactly a week after this meeting which was to put German war production into top gear in order to achieve the " abnormal extent " demanded by Hitler, the Führer issued a new interim directive. It is dated October 21st, 1938, and opens with this paragraph :

" The future tasks of the Armed Forces and the preparations for the conduct of war resulting from these tasks will be laid down by me in a later Directive. Until this Directive comes into force, the Armed Forces must be prepared at all times for the following eventualities :

(1) The securing of the frontiers of Germany, and the protection against surprise air attacks ;

(2) The liquidation of the remainder of Czechoslovakia ;

(3) The occupation of the Memelland."

Under Article Two the Directive then orders :

" It must be possible to smash at any time the remainder of Czechoslovakia if her policy should become hostile towards Germany. The preparations to be made by the Armed Forces for this contingency will be considerably smaller in extent than those for ' Green '; they must, however, guarantee a continuous and considerably higher state of preparedness since planned mobilization measures have been dispensed with. The organization, order of battle, and state of readiness of the units earmarked for that purpose are in peace-time to be so arranged for a surprise assault that Czechoslovakia herself will be deprived of all possibility of organized resistance. The object is the swift occupation of Bohemia and Moravia and the cutting off of Slovakia. The preparations should be such that at the same time ' Grenzsicherung West ' (Measures of Frontier Protection in the West) can be carried out. The detailed mission of Army and Air Force is as follows :

" Army : The units stationed in the vicinity of Bohemia-Moravia and several motorized divisions are to be earmarked for a surprise type of attack. Their number will be determined by the forces remaining in Czechoslovakia. A quick and decisive success must be assured. The assembly and preparations for the attack must be worked out. Forces not needed will be kept in readiness in such a manner that they may be either committed in securing the frontiers or to follow up the attack.

" Air Force : The quick advance of the German Army is to be assured by an early elimination of the Czech Air Force. For this purpose the commitment in a surprise attack from peace-time bases has to be prepared. Whether for this purpose still stronger forces may be required can be determined only from the development of the military situation in Czechoslovakia. At the same time a simultaneous assembly of the remainder of the offensive forces against the West must be prepared."

A good deal could be said by way of comment on these documents. One might point out in detail the ever-recurring inconsistencies between Hitler's public statements and his real intentions as revealed in his secret orders ; one could show in greater detail than has been done hitherto, how German machinations systematically brought about within Bohemia, Moravia and Slovakia that state of insecurity and final helplessness which was to serve Hitler as the pretext for intervening once more and seizing finally what he was prevented from taking at Munich. But, as has been said before, it is not the purpose of this study to prove that Hitler lied, cheated and deceived. That proof has been given. We are here concerned merely with the plan and its execution as seen from inside the German Supreme Command, not with its motives and morals. We are trying to discover, not by speculation but by piecing together official German state papers, how each phase of the overall plan develops from the preceding phase, how they are dove tailed into each other, and how they lead on to the next stage. We know the original motive for it all ; indeed, we have it from Hitler's own mouth. We know where it all lead in the end. All we wish to do here is to retrace the road of the planners in as many of its turnings and windings as we can discover, and to see how they got there. As we approach the final stage, the documents speak increasingly loudly for themselves, and it becomes increasingly superfluous to add any comment to them.

Danzig Moves Up

Four weeks after the issue of the interim directive on Bohemia and Moravia, a new name appears in the secret papers of the German Supreme Command. It is Danzig. The pattern is being followed scrupulously. No time is lost by the planners. Austria was still being " digested " when the first moves were made towards the invasion of Czechoslovakia. The ink on the Munich Agreement is hardly dry when the first instructions are issued for the seizure of Bohemia and Moravia. The remainder of Czechoslovakia has not yet been overrun, but Hitler already works on his next objective.

On November 24th, 1938, Hitler issues a " First Supplement to Instructions dated October 21st, 1938," which we have just quoted. It bears Keitel's signature and reads as follows :

" The Führer has ordered :

Apart from the three contingencies mentioned in the instructions of October 21st, 1938, preparations are also to be made to enable the Free State of Danzig to be occupied by German troops by surprise.

The preparations will be made on the following basis :

Condition is a quasi-revolutionary occupation of Danzig, exploiting a politically favourable situation, not a war against Poland.

Occupation by the army has to take place from East Prussia. The troops to be employed for this purpose must not simultaneously be earmarked for the occupation of Memelland, so that both operations can, if necessary, take place simultaneously. The Navy will support the Army's operation by attack from the sea according to detailed orders from the C-in-C. Navy. The forces participating are to be instructed to cooperate with the Army. The details of the support to be given by the Navy are to be agreed between the branches of the Armed Forces concerned.

How far Air Force units can collaborate in the occupation is to be investigated by the Reich Marshal of the Air Force and the C-in-C. Air Force, and to be agreed in direct cooperation with the other two branches of the Armed Forces.

The plans of the branches of the Armed Forces (Supreme Commands of Army, Navy and Air Force) are to be submitted by January 10th, 1939."

Five days before this date, on January 5th, 1939, Hitler was having a conversation with Beck, the Polish Foreign Minister, at Berchtesgaden. According to the minutes which are in our possession, Hitler, after discussing briefly Polish-Russian relations and stating that he himself was " interested in the Ukraine from the economic viewpoint but had no interest in it politically," went on to discuss Danzig. He emphasised that " as it was a German city, sooner or later it must return to the Reich. In his opinion it would be possible, by way of mutual agreement, to find some way out and achieve a form of guarantee for the legitimate interests of both Poland and Germany. If an agreement was reached on this question, all difficulties between the two States could quite definitely be settled and cleared out of the way." Beck pointed out that Danzig was " a very difficult problem " and " Polish opinion was particularly sensitive in this respect." Hitler declared that " the Minister could be quite at ease, there would be no *faits accomplis* in Danzig and nothing would be done to render difficult the situation of the Polish Government."

It seems true, judging from the Directive of November 24th, 1938, that Hitler at this stage did not seek war with Poland over Danzig, and was even anxious that the seizure of Danzig should not result in a conflict with Poland. The reason for this was not that he believed in an understanding with Poland, as he told Beck. It was, as we shall see later, that he was at this stage in two minds which to tackle first—Poland or the West. That he would tackle Poland eventually, he was certain. But he did not wish the Danzig question to develop in such a manner that it might force his hand in this larger question. For the rest, the *fait accompli* which he had assured Beck Poland need not fear, was at that time being busily prepared by the three branches of the Armed Forces.

Nothing more is heard of Danzig for the time being. The problem of Bohemia and Moravia remains to be solved.

The Big Blow on Saturday

On December 17th, 1938, Keitel, Chief of the Supreme Command of the Armed Forces, passes on the following letter of instructions from Hitler to the Supreme Commands of the three Services :

" Reference ' Liquidation of the Rest of Czechoslovakia '
the Führer has given the following additional order :

The preparations for this eventuality are to continue on the assumption that no resistance worth mentioning is to be expected.

To the outside world too it must clearly appear that it is merely an action of pacification and not a warlike undertaking.

The action must therefore be carried out by the peace-time Armed Forces only, without reinforcements from mobilization. The necessary readiness for action, especially the ensuring that essential supplies are brought up, must be effected by adjustment within the units.

Similarly the units of the Army detailed for the march-in must, as a general rule, leave their stations only during the night prior to the crossing of the frontier, and will not previously form up systematically at the frontier. The transport necessary for previous organization should be limited to the minimum and will be camouflaged as much as possible. Necessary movements, if any, of single units, and particularly motorized forces, to the training areas situated near the frontier, must have the approval of the Führer. The Air Force should take action in accordance with similar general directives.

For the same reasons the exercise of executive power by the Supreme Command of the Army is valid only for the newly occupied territory and only for a short period."

We do not possess the actual orders which set the German Army rolling into Bohemia and Moravia and occupying Prague on the morning of March 16th, 1939. But we possess a few documents which, without shedding much new light on it, illustrate this phase from one or two new angles.

Thus on March 13th, 1939, three days before the invasion, Ribbentrop sent the following telegram in secret code to the German Embassy in Prague :

" In case you should get any written communication from President Hacha, please do not make any written or verbal comments or take any other action on them but pass them on here by cypher telegram. Moreover, I must ask you and the other members of the Embassy to make a point of not being available if the Czech Government wants to communicate with you during the next few days."

On the same day, March 13th, 1939, Horthy, the Regent of Hungary, sent this telegram to Hitler :

" Your Excellency—my sincere thanks. I can hardly tell you
how happy I am because this Head Water Region—I dislike
using big words—is of vital importance to the life of Hungary.
In spite of the fact that our recruits have only been serving for
five weeks, we are going into this affair with eager enthusiasm.
The dispositions have already been made. On Thursday, the
16th of this month, a frontier incident will take place which
will be followed by the big blow on Saturday. I shall never
forget this proof of friendship, and your Excellency may rely
on my unshakable gratitude at all times. Your devoted friend.
Horthy."

Still on that same day, March 13th, 1939, Hitler had the
Slovak Prime Minister Tiso called to Berlin and talked to him
for 35 minutes. The record of his harangue is available,
and its purpose is obviously to press the Slovak Government
to dissolve its connection with Prague and declare its independence. Most of what Hitler said that evening was blatant
propaganda, easily recognizable as such, and of no relevance to
the subject of this inquiry. But it does contain a number of
astonishing remarks.

The Czechs, Hitler told Tiso, were violating the Munich
Agreement and were behaving in a provocative manner intolerable to Germany. At Munich, Germany had solved the Czech
question according to her *Weltanschauung* (meaning presumably
that she was interested only in the German minority and " did
not want any Czechs.") but if " this solution leads to no results,
we have decided absolutely to pursue it to its conclusion, without
consideration for this ideological principle." The attitude of
Slovakia was also a disappointment to him. " In the past year,"
the record states, " the Führer had to face the difficult decision
whether or not to permit Hungary to occupy Slovakia. He
had been under a wrong impression as he had of course believed
that Slovakia wished to be annexed to Hungary. This error
was caused by the fact that Slovakia was further away from
Germany and by the importance of the more serious problems
which then overshadowed this question. It was only in the crisis
that the Führer was dissuaded from this opinion. It was then
that he first heard and noted that Slovakia wished to conduct
her own affairs.

" Now he had permitted Minister Tiso to come here in order
to make his position clear in a very short time. Germany had
no interests east of the Carpathian mountains. It was indifferent
G

to him what happened there. The question was whether Slovakia wished to conduct her own affairs or not. He did not wish for anything from Slovakia. But he wanted to secure final confirmation as to what Slovakia really wanted. He did not wish that reproaches should come from Hungary that he was preserving something which did not wish to be preserved at all. He took a liberal view of unrest and demonstrations in general, but in this connection, unrest was only an outward indication of internal instability. He would not tolerate it and he had for that reason permitted Tiso to come in order to hear his decision. It was not a question of days but of hours. He had stated at the time that if Slovakia wished to make herself independent, he would support this endeavor and even guarantee it. He would stand by his word as long as Slovakia made it clear that she desired independence. If she hesitated or did not wish to dissolve her connection with Prague, he would leave the destiny of Slovakia to the mercy of events for which he was no longer responsible."

Hitler then asked Ribbentrop whether he had anything to add, and Ribbentrop repeated that a decision must be made within hours and not days. " He showed the Führer a message he had just received which reported Hungarian troop movements on the Slovak frontiers. The Führer read this report, mentioned it to Tiso and expressed the hope that Slovakia would soon make her decision."

Thus was Slovakia got out of the way.

Two days later, on March 15th, 1939, Hitler called President Hacha to Berlin. The detailed record of this historic interview in which Hitler bullied and bludgeoned Hacha into signing away what remained of Czechoslovakia's independence and accepting the status of Protectorate, is in our possession, but except for Hitler's customary ranting which here goes to extraordinary lengths, it contains hardly any facts or aspects that are not, in their essence, known already. The interview is of the same character and spirit as that with Schuschnigg a year earlier. As Hitler accused Schuschnigg of having broken the Berchtesgaden Agreement, so he now accused Hacha of having violated the Munich Agreement with the result that he (Hitler) no longer had any confidence in the ability of the Czech Government to maintain orderly conditions.

" Thus it was that the die was cast last Sunday (March 12th)," the minutes record Hitler as stating. " We were now confronted with this fact. He had given the order to the German troops to march into Czechoslovakia and to incorporate Czechoslovakia into the German Reich. At 6 o'clock in the morning the German army would invade Czechoslovakia from all sides, and the German air force would occupy the Czech airfields. There existed two possibilities. The first was that the invasion would lead to a battle. In this case resistance would be broken by all means with physical force. The other possibility was for the invasion of the German forces to take place in a bearable form. In that case it would be easy for the Führer to give Czechoslovakia and the new organization of Czech life a generous measure of autonomy and a certain national liberty. That was the state of affairs, and the reason why he had asked Hacha to come. This invitation was the last good deed which he (Hitler) could offer to the Czech people. The visit of Hacha could perhaps prevent the extreme. The hours went past. At 6 o'clock the troops would march in. The military action was not a small one but planned with all generosity,"

The outcome of the meeting is known.

Case White

" The bloodless solution of the Czech conflict in the autumn of 1938 and spring of 1939 and the annexation of Slovakia, rounded off the territory of Greater Germany in such a way, that it now became possible to consider the Polish problem on the basis of more or less favourable strategic premises."

Thus General Jodl in his Munich speech on November 7th, 1943.

On March 25th, 1939, a week after the occupation of Prague, the Supreme Commander of the Army had an interview with Hitler, at the conclusion of which he made, among others, the following notes on what Hitler had told him :

" L. (Lipski, the Polish Ambassador to Berlin) will return from Warsaw on Sunday, March 26th. He was charged to inquire whether Poland would be prepared to come to terms with Germany with regard to Danzig. The Führer left Berlin during the night of March 25th as he does not wish to be here when L. returns. Ribbentrop shall negotiate first. The Führer does not wish, though, to solve the Danzig problem by the use of force. He would not like to drive Poland into the arms of Britain by doing so. A military occupation of Danzig would have to be taken into consideration only if L. gives a hint that the Polish Government could not take the responsibility toward their own people of ceding Danzig voluntarily and the solution would be made easier for them by a *fait accompli*.

" For the time being the Führer does not intend to solve the Polish question. However, it should now be worked upon. A solution in the near future would have to be based on especially favourable conditions. In that case Poland shall be knocked down so completely that she need not be taken into account as a political factor for the next decades. The Führer has in mind, for such a solution, a border line advance from the Eastern border of East Prussia to the Eastern tip of Upper Silesia. Evacuation and resettlement are questions that remain open. The Führer does not want to go into the Ukraine. Possibly one could establish a Ukrainian State. But these questions also remain open."

A glance at the map will show what the advanced German frontier in the East, with which Hitler is toying at this time, implies. It is almost exactly the line along which Poland was partitioned between Germany and the Soviet Union in August, 1939.

The code name for the invasion of Poland was " Case White."

The first Directive for this campaign appears to have been issued on April 3rd, 1939. A further set of instructions, dealing with " Case White " and signed by Hitler was issued on April 11th, 1939. More instructions, signed by Hitler and Keitel, appear on May 10th and 12th, 1939. A further operational order, signed by Keitel, is issued on June 22nd, and another on June 24th, 1939. The final Directive, with Hitler's signature and containing date and time of the attack, is issued on August 31st, 1939. Complete texts of these documents were, unfortunately, not made available at Nuremburg, but merely extensive extracts. Although in this way much instructive detail is missing, the broad outlines of the strategic planning and timing and possibly rather more than that, remain visible. Reference will be made to them in the following pages as they appear in their chronological sequence.

The instructions issued over Keitel's signature on April 3rd, 1939, bear the routine heading " Directive for the Armed Forces 1939-40." They state :

" The Directive for the Uniform Preparation of War by the Armed Forces for 1939-40 is being re-issued. Part I (Frontier Defence) and Part III (Danzig) will be issued in the middle

of April. Their basic principles remain unchanged. Part II
(" Case White ") is attached herewith. The signature of the
Führer will be appended later. The Führer has added the follow-
ing Directives to ' Case White ' :

> (1) Preparations must be made in such a way that the
> operation can be carried out at any time from September
> 1st, 1939, onward.
>
> (2) The High Command of the Armed Forces has been
> directed to draw up a precise time-table for ' Case
> White ' and to arrange the synchronized timing between
> the three branches of the Armed Forces.
>
> (3) The plans of the branches of the Armed Forces and the
> details for the time-table must be submitted to the
> Supreme Command of the Armed Forces by May 1st,
> 1939."

A tentative date for the attack on Poland was thus set as far
back as April 3rd, 1939, and it proved to be the final one—
September 1st, 1939. Complete plans including a detailed
time-table were to be ready a full four months before the attack,
and Hitler gave his General Staff less than one month to prepare
them.

The second Directive, equally " Top Secret " and signed
by Hitler is dated April 11th, 1939. It refers again to the " Directive for the Uniform Preparation of War by the Armed Forces
1939-40," and announces that Hitler will lay down in a later
directive the "future tasks of the Armed Forces and the preparations to be made in accordance with these for the conduct of
the war." Until that Directive comes into force " the Armed
Forces must be prepared for the following eventualities : (1) Safe-
guarding of the frontiers of the German Reich and protection
against surprise air attacks (Annexe I) ; (2) "Case White "
(Annexe II) ; and (3) the annexation of Danzig (Annexe III).
Annexe IV contains regulations for the exercise of military
authority in East Prussia in the event of a warlike development.
The annexes contain much that is instructive.

Annexe I contains instructions of a general nature to the
three Services for the defence of the Reich frontiers and
air and sea defences. Preparations for this must be made in such
a way that an effective defence is possible at any time without
a general or partial mobilization. The code word is " Frontier
Defence " (Grenzsicherung). Under the sub-heading of "Legal
Basis " it is here stated : " It should be anticipated that a State

of Defence or State of War as defined in the Reich Defence Law of September 4th, 1938 will not be declared. All measures and requests necessary for carrying out a mobilization are to be based on the laws valid in peacetime."

Annexe II contains the directives for " Case White." The first article, headed " Political Hypotheses and Aims," states that quarrels with Poland should be avoided. Should Poland, however, change her present policy which is based on the same principle and adopt a threatening attitude towards Germany, a " final settlement " will be necessary notwithstanding the pact with Poland. The Free State of Danzig will be incorporated into Germany at the outbreak of the conflict at the latest. " Our policy aims at confining the war to Poland, and this is considered possible in view of the internal crisis in France and British restraint as a result of this. Should Russia intervene, this would imply Poland's destruction by Bolshevism. German military exigencies will determine the attitude of the Baltic States. Hungary is not a certain ally. Italy's attitude is determined by the Berlin-Rome Axis."

Hitler has not abandoned his old idea that the best moment for him to strike is when France is in internal difficulties. He believes that such a period of acute crisis in French affairs has now come, and that Britain, taking this into account, will be unwilling to commit herself.

Article Two, headed " Military Conclusions," is unhappily not included in the extracts. The strategic design at this stage remains therefore somewhat obscure. The remaining paragraphs set out the tasks and operational objectives of the three Services. "A camouflaged or open (general) mobilization will not be ordered before X-Day-minus-One, at the last possible moment." The Army may, on its Southern flank, enter Slovak territory. In the North, a junction between Pomerania and East Prussia must be quickly established. " The preparations for the opening of operations are to be made in such a way that—without waiting for the planned assembly of mobilized units—positions can be taken up immediately by the first available troops."

Annexe II is supplemented by further " Special Orders for ' Case White'." Here again it is stated that a state of Defence or War will not be declared. The special orders refer to mobilization—a clandestine mobilization will not include the civil sphere and the armaments industry whereas a public one will— the area of operations and executive power, the organization of frontier guards, Goering's special powers, clearing the frontier areas, receiving refugees, evacuation measures, division of responsibilities, communications, etc. As regards feeding the troops, the instructions say that they may take food from the occupied area on orders from the Army High Command, but the German minority should be spared because of its distressed condition. Requisitioning may be carried out " in accordance with the Hague Land War Convention." Supplies from people of German race must however be paid for in German currency.

A later Annexe V, dated May 12th, 1939, and signed by Hitler, defines the operational areas for the Army under reference to a map which is attached, and states with regard to these areas : " If our troops advance beyond the Reich frontier or the further frontier of the Slovak protected zone, the operational area will be extended accordingly in the direction of the advance."

Annexe III deals with the seizure of Danzig, saying that " a lightning annexation of the Free State of Danzig may be carried out independently of ' Case White ', to exploit a favourable political situation, and stipulates the tasks of the three Services in preparing and carrying out this operation." It adds : " The annexation should be considered as an act of restoring a purely German area to German sovereignty after a long separation. In this case, too, a State of Defence or War will not be declared. Mobilisation is not intended as the coup will be carried out by only a part of the peace-time army."

Goering Explains the Situation

On April 15th, 1939, as the Directives for " Case White " were going out and preparations were beginning in full earnest against Poland, Goering had a meeting with Mussolini, at which Ciano was also present. The minutes of what Goering told the Italians are available and they give a good impression of how Hitler and Goering appreciated the international situation as it stood at that period.

Referring to the recent incorporation of Bohemia and Moravia, Goering pointed out that " the heavy armament of Czechoslovakia showed how dangerous that country could have been, even after Munich, in the event of a serious conflict. Because of Germany's action the position of both axis countries had improved, among other reasons owing to the economic possibilities which resulted from the transfer to Germany of the great production capacity of Czechoslovakia. That contributes towards a considerable strengthening of the axis against the Western powers. Furthermore, Germany now need not keep in readiness a single division for protection against that country in case of a larger conflict. This, too, is an advantage from which in the last analysis both axis countries will benefit."

Turning to Poland, Goering observes : " The action taken by Germany in Czechoslovakia is to be viewed as an advantage for the axis in case Poland should finally join the enemies of the axis powers. Germany could then attack Poland from two flanks and would be within only 25 minutes flying distance from the new Polish industrial centres which had been moved further into the interior of the country, nearer to the other Polish industrial districts, because of their proximity to the border. Now by the turn of events they were located again in the proximity of the border."

Finally, the record states, " the Fieldmarshal happened to talk about the date at which Germany would be prepared best for a greater test of strength. In this connection he pointed out that Germany at the moment was comparatively weak at sea, because both new battleships which had been launched recently would be ready for commissioning only next year, and two additional battleships would be launched only next year. In the Air Force also, regrouping and adaptation to a new type of bomber, the 'JU 88,' the production of which had yet to begin, was taking place. This new German bomber had such a range that it would be possible not only to attack Britain herself, but to push beyond in a western direction and bomb ships which reach Britain from the Atlantic. Of course, Germany was ready for action, if suddenly a conflict should arise. But if one was considering at what period of time the armament situation was most favourable, both the above-mentioned facts—insufficient armament at sea and conversion of the Air Force to a new type of bomber—should not be disregarded. Besides, in the autumn already a monthly production of 280 aircraft of the 'JU 88' type and at the end of the year, of 350 machines could be counted upon. On the basis of these calculations he came to the conclusion that in nine months or one year the situation for the axis, from a military point of view, would be more favourable. On the other hand, it was true that the rearmament in Britain and France had not made very much progress. In many cases the factories for the production of war material were only in the state of construction. Britain

would most likely not be able to show any results worth mentioning before 1942 for her newly begun high pressure rearmament
in the air.

"Furthermore, the Führer considered it almost out of the
question that Britain and France would not stand together.
According to the German point of view, the two countries
would in any conflict eventually support each other to the utmost.
Only if Britain should carry out a complete reversal of her
policy and the costs and risks of her present political line become
too high, would she perhaps confine her efforts to the preservation
of the Empire and give the authoritarian countries a free hand
for securing their vital necessities. At the present time Britain
had a weak government which had yielded to the pressure of
the Left. Britain had deviated from her old line of policy which
was to offer assistance only on the basis of her own judgement
of the situation, in each individual case ; she had turned away
from her traditional policy and was now committing herself in
advance to render support, and that under conditions which could
be determined by the other partner. It was another question,
of course, how Britain could fulfil her guarantee obligation.
How was she going to help Poland or Rumánia, for instance ?
She had no means of sending troops, and could actually fulfil
her obligations only by igniting a general war.

"All in all, however, it had to be stressed that the situation
of the axis was very strong and that it could defeat all possible
opponents in a general conflict."

At the First Suitable Opportunity

Preparations for " Case White " continued.

On May 10th, 1939, Keitel issued a further Directive, dealing
with the exercise of military powers in the operational areas
of the Army, and Hitler, on the same day, supplemented his
earlier instructions by an Annexe VI, covering "instructions for
the economic war and the protection of our own economy."
The Commanders-in-chief of the three Services are requested
to report to the Supreme Command of the Armed Forces on
the measures taken in consequence of these instructions by
August 1st, 1939.

The annexe itself states that Navy and Air Force are directed
to make preparations for the immediate opening of economic
warfare, principally against Britain, and as a second priority,
against France, in the event of " Frontier Defence " being ordered.

The measures to be taken by Army, Navy, and Air Force are described in detail and based on the assumption that the operations will be offensive in character. Regarding " Case White " this same document sets out as the main objective the capture, in undamaged condition, of Polish economic installations. A speedy occupation of the industrial areas of Polish Upper Silesia and Teschen is considered important. Poland must be cut off from imports by sea, and this must be borne in mind when dealing with ships sailing under neutral flags and perhaps carrying goods for Poland to neutral ports.

On May 3rd, 1939, Hitler held one of his periodical briefing conferences with his commanders-in-chief. This time, Goering, Raeder, Keitel, Brauchitsch, Milch, Halder, Bodenschatz, Jeschonnek, Warlimont and several others were present. Col. Schmundt was in attendance and the minutes of the meeting, kept by him, are in our possession. It is a document of considerable significance, and frequent reference is made to it elsewhere in these studies, owing to the wide range of subjects Hitler covered in his speech.

Hitler began by analysing the present situation. It must be considered, he said, from two points of view : (a) the actual development of events between 1933 and 1939 ; (b) the permanent and unchanging situation in which Germany is placed. He comes to these conclusions :

" In the period 1933-1939 progress was made in all fields. Our military situation improved enormously. Our position with regard to the rest of the world has remained the same. Germany has dropped from the circle of Great Powers. The balance of power has been effected without the participation of Germany. This equilibrium is disturbed when Germany's demands for the necessities of life make themselves felt and Germany re-emerges as a Great Power. All demands are regarded as ' encroachments.' The British are more afraid of dangers in the economic sphere than of the simple threat of force. A mass of 80 million people has solved its ideological problems. In the same way economic problems must be solved. No German can evade the creation of the necessary economic conditions for this. The solution of the problems demands courage. The principle whereby one evades solving the problem by adapting oneself to circumstances, is inadmissible. Circumstances must rather be adapted to aims. This is impossible without the invasion of foreign states or attacks on foreign property."

We may think back, for a moment, to a similar secret briefing speech made by Hitler on November 5th, 1937, contained in the " Hossbach Minutes." His ideas, his planning have remained absolutely consistent. He then said that " never has space been found without an owner. The attacker always comes up against the proprietor. The question for Germany is where the greatest possible conquest can be made at the lowest cost." In the intervening years he has come up against the proprietors of Austrian and Czechoslovak space and knocked them out of the way. Now for Poland. Is it here that " the greatest possible conquest can be made at the lowest cost ? " One thing is certain : he is determined not to cut his coat according to his cloth. That is the one solution which is " inadmissible." He will get the extra cloth, and if it happens to be " foreign property," so much the worse for the owner. There are many astonishing and remarkable things in Hitler's secret speeches. This ranks, without doubt, among the most noteworthy.

" Living space," Hitler continues, " in proportion to the magnitude of the state, is the basis of all power. One may refuse for a time to face the problem, but finally it is solved one way or the other. The choice lies between advancement and decline. In 15 or 20 years' time we shall be compelled to find a solution. No German statesman can evade the question longer than that." But the present time, he argues, is particularly propitious. " We are at present in a state of patriotic fervour which is shared by two other nations, Italy and Japan. The period which lies behind us has indeed been put to good use. All our measures have been taken in the correct sequence and in harmony with our aims. After six years, the situation today is as follows :

" The national-political unity of the Germans has been achieved, apart from minor exceptions. Further successes cannot be attained without the shedding of blood. The demarcation of frontiers is of military importance. Poland is no ' supplementary enemy.' Poland will always be on the side of our adversaries. In spite of the treaties of friendship, Poland has always had the secret intention of exploiting every opportunity to do us harm.

" Danzig is not the subject of the dispute at all. It is a question of expanding our living space to the East, of securing our food supplies, and of settling the Baltic problem. Food supplies can be expected only from thinly populated areas. Over and above the natural fertility, thoroughgoing German exploitation will enormously increase the surplus. There is no other possibility. Colonies are no solution. Germany should beware of gifts of colonial territory. They don't solve the food problem since they can easily be blockaded. The answer, therefore, lies in Poland.

"The Polish problem is inseparable from conflict with the West," Hitler points out. "If fate brings us into conflict with the West, the possession of extensive areas in the East will be an advantage. We shall be even less able to rely upon record harvests in time of war than in time of peace. The population of non-German areas will perform no military service and will be available as a source of labour. Poland's internal power of resistance to bolshevism is doubtful. Thus Poland is of doubtful value as a barrier against Russia. It is questionable whether military success in the West can be achieved by a quick decision ; questionable, too, is the attitude of Poland. The Polish Government will not resist pressure from Russia. Poland sees danger in a German victory in the West, and will attempt to rob us of our victory. There is therefore no question of sparing Poland, and we are left with the decision : to attack Poland at the first suitable opportunity."

It will be seen presently, from a later document, that for some time Hitler was not certain whether, after the liquidation of Austria and Czechoslovakia, he should make war first on the West or on Poland. That eventually he was going to invade both was always a certainty. Living space in the South-east and East alone was not enough. It had to be acquired in all directions. But it was a question of sequence and timing. In his speech of May 23rd, 1939, he had made his decision if, indeed, he had not made it earlier. His reasoning, translated into customary language, is simple : if and when we fight the West, extra food-producing areas in the East will increase our otherwise doubtful staying power. A military success in the West, against Britain and France, will not be achieved overnight but may necessitate a long campaign. During this campaign Poland will not look on idle. She will stab us in the back. We must therefore, in order to fight the West with a good chance of winning, wipe out Poland first.

But will it be possible to deal with Poland without getting embroiled in a simultaneous war with the West ? And if this is not possible, how can the West be kept at arm's length while we are dealing with Poland ? It is the old problem which now, at last, has beome acute.

For, continues Hitler, " we cannot expect a repetition of the Czech affair. This time there will be war. Our task is to isolate Poland. The success of this isolation will be decisive. Therefore I must reserve the right to give the final order for the attack. There must be no simultaneous conflict with the Western Powers. If it is not certain that the German-Polish conflict will not lead to war in the West, the fight must primarily be against Britain and France. Fundamentally therefore : the conflict with Poland, beginning with an attack on Poland, will only be successful if the Western Powers keep out of it. If this is impossible, it will be better to attack in the West and to settle Poland at the same time."

It was precisely this situation which Hitler endeavoured so desperately, until the last moment, to create and which in the end he failed to bring about. When he saw that he had failed, it was too late to concentrate primarily on the West and deal with Poland at the same time. The dynamics of events had themselves reversed the course.

However, he considers the proposition in some detail.

" If there were an alliance of France, Britain and Russia against Germany, Italy and Japan," he speculates, " I should be constrained to attack Britain and France with a few annihilating blows." He doubts the possibility of a peaceful settlement with Britain. " We must prepare ourselves for the conflict. Britain sees in our development the foundation for a hegemony which would weaken her. Britain is therefore our enemy, and the conflict with Britain will be a life-and-death struggle. What will this struggle be like ? Britain cannot subjugate Germany with a few powerful blows. It is imperative for Britain that the war should be brought as near to the Ruhr basin as possible. French blood will not be spared in attempts to break through the West Wall. The possession of the Ruhr basin will determine the duration of our resistance. The Dutch and Belgian air bases must be occupied by armed force. Declarations of neutrality must be ignored. If Britain and France intend the war between Germany and Poland to lead to a conflict between Germany and themselves, they will support Holland and Belgium in their neutrality and make them build fortifications in order finally to force them into cooperation. Albeit under protest, Holland and Belgium will yield to pressure. Therefore, if Britain

intends to intervene in the Polish war, we must occupy Holland
with lightning speed. We must aim at securing a new defence
line on Dutch soil up to the Zuider Zee.

" The idea that we can get off cheaply is dangerous. There is
no such possiblity. We must burn our boats. It is no longer a
question of justice or injustice, but of life or death for 80 million
human beings. Every country's armed forces or government
must aim at a short war. The Government, however, must also
be prepared for a war of 10 or 15 years' duration. History shows
that people always believed wars would be short. In 1914 the
opinion still prevailed that it was impossible to finance a long
war. Even today this idea persists in many minds. But on the
contrary, every state will hold out as long as possible, unless
it immediately suffers some grave weakening, as for instance
the loss of the Ruhr basin. Britain has similar weaknesses.
Britain knows that to lose a war will mean the end of her world
power."

The remainder of Hitler's address deals with ways and means
of defeating Britain. These are discussed in detail elsewhere in
these studies. (Chaper III, Operation Sea-Lion.)

Economic Mobilization

" The period that lies behind us has indeed been put to good
use."

What are the facts behind this statement ? How does Germany's
material preparedness compare with the aims set by Hitler ?
What did Goering achieve since he made his " barbaric "
speech ? Are the sights set more or less correctly ? On May
24th, 1939, the day after Hitler's secret briefing address, Maj.
Gen. Thomas, Chief of the War Economy Department of the
German Supreme Command—a man to whose punctilious
habit of making extensive notes and writing detailed memoranda
we owe a great deal of invaluable information—gave an address
at the Berlin Foreign Office on the activities of his department.
Extracts from this speech are available.

Gen. Thomas began by reminding his audience that under
the Versailles Treaty the German Army had been limited to
seven divisions, that an air force was prohibited, and the Navy
forbidden to build ships of over 10,000 tons or submarines. " The
production of arms, ammunition and military equipment was
limited to a few authorised plants. Until the end of 1933,
in spite of secret, camouflaged attempts, no essential change

occurred in the situation, so that we can state that the present rearmament represents the work of four years."

The 100,000 men army of seven infantry and three cavalry divisions of 1933 compared in May, 1939, Gen. Thomas explained, with a peace-time army of 18 corps headquarters, 39 infantry divisions, among them four fully motorised and three mountain divisions, five Panzer divisions, four light divisions and 22 machine-gun battalions. In addition there were at the frontier a large number of permanent border protection units. Since large-scale procurement of new arms for the 100,000 men army was out of the question, but the development of new types was busily carried on in secret, " our present army could be equipped in all fields with the most modern weapons and it certainly leads the world in its infantry armament, and in the large number of its types of guns. Completely new and developed only in the last 5 years are the five Panzer divisions, the modern battle cavalry and the light divisions."

Conditions in the field of material, Gen. Thomas continued, were the same. The entire equipment of the armoured divisions and the light divisions was newly created. In addition an enormous number of special motor vehicles, sometimes of the most difficult construction, had been developed. The artillery had been partly motorised and provided with the most modern sound and light measuring equipment. The great increase in the number of technical troops was making special demands on the armament industry. To this manifold rearmament had to be added the construction of frontier fortifications which were at first begun in the East and which were started in the West as soon as the situation permitted.

The German peace-time army before the last war, Gen. Thomas said, had been increased from 43 divisions to 50 divisions in the period from 1898 to 1914, i.e. in 16 years. "Our rearmament from seven infantry divisions to 51 divisions represents the work of four years." The Navy in 1933 had in addition to a few obsolete pre-war ships of the line, one armoured ship of 10,000 tons, 6 light cruisers and 12 torpedo-boats. "Since 1933 we have put into service 2 battleships of 26,000 tons each, 2 armoured ships of 10,000 tons each, 17 destroyers and 47 submarines, a total tonnage of 125,000. Also launched were: 2 battleships of 35,000 tons, 4 heavy cruisers of 10,000 tons, 1 aircraft carrier, 5 destroyers and 7 submarines totalling 106,000 tons. The launching of additional ships is impending."

The Air Force, too, had risen again, and now had a strength of 260,000 men. " Today already the Air Force possesses 21 squadrons consisting of 240 echelons. Its increase is in process. The anti-aircraft arm with its four types is certainly the most modern in the world and already comprises almost 300 anti-aircraft batteries. Anti-aircraft guns of still larger calibres are being introduced."

German armament industry had been developed to the same extent, Gen. Thomas claimed. The few factories permitted by the Versailles Treaty had developed into the mightiest armament industry existing in the world. "It has attained performances which in part equal German war-time performances, and in part even surpass them. Germany's crude steel production is today the largest in the world after America's, the aluminium production exceeds that of America and of the other countries in the world very considerably. Our output of rifles, machine-guns and artillery is at present larger than that of any other country. Our powder and explosive production in the coming year will again reach the volume of the Hindenburg programme (of the last war)."

Gen. Thomas finally explained the organization behind this prodigious production. A personnel organization " in the form of a military economic organization " had been built up. The World War had made Germany sufficiently aware of the lack of an economic mobilization organization. Consequently already a few years after the World War certain soldiers had begun to set up an organization which was to handle economic preparations for war. From this nucleus had grown the present " great military defence economy organization which has its centre in the economic division with the Supreme Command of the Armed Forces and the branch agencies which have been set up in the defence industry inspectorates under the jurisdiction of each corps headquarters." This organization was devoting itself chiefly to the handling of the armament industry proper and in particular had carried out the mobilizational preparation of these plants. The preparation of the mobilization of the rest of industry was originally in the charge of the Ministry of Economics, but this had now been unified and " all economic preparations for war are now being made in accordance with uniform directives which are worked out jointly by the economic division of the Army and the Commissioner General of the Armed Forces."

" In conclusion we can state that the total German rearmament in the field of personnel as well as material represents an accomplishment of the German people probably unique in the world. The great financial and labour efforts of German industry and of the German people have no doubt yielded the desired result and we can perceive today that German armament in its breadth and its state of preparedness has a considerable start over the armament of all other countries."

The Time-table is Ready

On June 22nd, 1939, Keitel issues a document headed "Preparations for ' Case White'" which states that " the Supreme Command of the Armed Forces has submitted to the Führer and Supreme Commander a ' preliminary time-table for ' Case White'" based on the particulars so far available from the Navy, Army and Air Force. Details concerning the days preceding the attack and the start of the attack were not included in this time-table. Keitel goes on to say that Hitler is in the main in agreement with the intentions of the three services, but has a number of suggestions to make. In particular Hitler orders that " so as not to disquiet the population by calling up reserves on a larger scale than usual for the manœuvres scheduled for 1939, as is intended, civilian establishments, employers or other private persons making inquiries should be told that men are being called up for the autumn manœuvres and for the exercise units which it is intended to form for these manœuvres." Hitler also orders that " for reasons of security the clearing of hospitals in the frontier area which the Army High Command proposes to carry out from the middle of July, must not be carried out."

On June 24th, 1939, Keitel, as Chief of the Supreme Command, in a memorandum on " Case White" instructs the Army High Command " to prepare all measures necessary for the capture, in undamaged condition, of the bridges over the Lower Vistula. On the completion of preparations, the Army High Command will report to the Supreme Command." Besides, Army and Navy High Commands are " again to examine whether the element of surprise in sudden attacks against the bridge at Dirschau will be impaired by preceding actions of the Navy in the Danzig Bay. In view of the importance of the bridge it should be stated if the consent of the Army High Command to the intended measures of the Navy (mining before X-day) is upheld."

H

The bridge at Dirschau was indeed important. It was intended to be one of the main jumping-off points from Danzig territory into the Corridor.

The Last Two Weeks

The diplomatic history immediately preceding the German attack on Poland and the outbreak of war is known through the British and French official publications, and the Nuremberg Documents have little or nothing new to contribute to it. Some new light is thrown on the role played by Italy in these last weeks, and in particular on Mussolini's abortive attempt to postpone the war by calling an international conference. The most instructive document in this connection is the record of two conversations which Ciano, the Italian Foreign Minister, had with Hitler at Berchtesgaden on August 12th and 13th, 1939, and this is discussed in Chapter II, " Otto to Alaric " which deals with German-Italian relations generally. But the document contains a number of other remarks and observations of Hitler's, chiefly with reference to the Western Powers and of a more general nature, and these contribute a certain amount of further information of the state of German planning at this stage—a fortnight before the actual outbreak of war.

Hitler, with the aid of maps, showed Ciano the present position of Germany from a military point of view. He particularly emphasized the German fortifications in the West. There were the points at which in earlier times the French, for geographical and strategic reasons, had always attempted a break-through. These points had now been protected with special care so that a break-through was impossible at any of them. The western fortifications had been carried along the Luxembourg and Belgian frontiers to the borders of Holland, so that a violation of the Belgian frontier would no longer bring any advantages to France but would involve the serious risk that Belgium, in order to defend her neutrality and under pressure from the Flemish element in her population, would place herself on the German side. The one remaining possibility of attack was, theoretically, across the Netherlands, but according to the view of the Führer, the Dutch would defend their neutrality with energy because they knew that if they took part in a general war, they would lose to Japan their almost undefended East-Asiatic colonies. Furthermore, in view of the countless rivers and canals, and of the possibility of flooding wide areas of the lowlands, the

Netherlands offered very unsuitable territory as a starting-off point for a great army. Germany would obviously invade the Netherlands in the event of a violation of Dutch neutrality and, owing to the very short distance of the German frontier from the Meuse, could reach this river within a few hours. Finally the Rhine, which in Holland was 1-1½ miles wide, offered a natural protection against attacks from this direction.

The point to note here is that Hitler asserts he would "obviously invade Holland in the event of a violation of Dutch neutrality," whereas in his secret briefing speech of May 23rd, 1939, he stated bluntly that he would "occupy Holland with lightning speed" immediately upon the outbreak of war, and that "declarations of neutrality must be ignored." It is unlikely that he changed his mind and softened in his attitude towards the Low Countries. It is more likely that he feared to shock the wavering Italians unduly if he revealed to them the full ruthlessness of his plans.

"The third possibility of an attack on Germany," the record continues, "consisted in a blockade by the British Navy. In this connection it should be remembered that the great range of the latest German bombers brought the whole of Britain within their sphere of action and would allow them to attack the blockading ships from the air. There were no other possibilities of attacking Germany. The Scandinavian countries would doubtless remain neutral, and they were certain that neither side would attack them because the occupation of countries as large as Norway and Sweden was not a practical proposition. Similarly Switzerland would certainly oppose to the utmost any attempt on her neutrality."

Hitler here looks at Scandinavia from the point of view of German defence and not attack. He is certain that neither Sweden nor Norway will attack Germany or lend themselves as bases for an attack on Germany. But his reference to these two countries may mean more than just that. The remark that these countries are too large to make their occupation a practical proposition is open to interpretation. It may mean that Hitler thinks the Scandinavian countries believe that their occupation is not practical and that therefore it will not be attempted ; it may also mean that he himself subscribes to this view and does not consider, at this stage, such an occupation a practical proposition. The point is interesting in view of the later invasion of Norway. We shall presently deal with a number of documents which would seem to indicate that this was actually Hitler's view and that he had to be won over to the opposite stand-point.

" In the East," the record continues, " Germany had also erected strong defences. The Führer showed Count Ciano the various defence systems of East Prussia. On the other frontiers strong fortifications were being constructed, and along the Polish frontier opposite Berlin they were being built up into an impregnable system of staggered lines. The capital was, however, only 150 kilometres from the Polish frontier and therefore exposed to air attacks especially because, owing to its great size, it could be bombed from a very great height without attacking particular targets with a certainty that bombs would fall somewhere within the city area."

Turning to the military position of the Western Powers, Hitler again pointed out the vulnerability of Britain from the air. " British aircraft production had made progress, but protective measures against raids were still very much in arrear. It was known that Britain had decided only in the previous autumn upon the definite type of anti-aircraft gun they were going to use. Germany's experience of her own seven years of rearmament assured her that large-scale production was possible only some long time after the selection of the prototype, so that no real anti-aircraft protection could exist in Britain for another year or two. Furthermore London and all the large British cities and centres of industry suffered from the same disadvantages as Berlin in relation to air attack. Bombing can be carried out from a great height and out of range of British anti-aircraft guns with complete certainty that the results would always be successful."

At sea, Hitler went on, Britain had for the moment no immediate reinforcements in prospect. Some time would elapse before any of the ships now under construction could be taken into service. As far as the land army was concerned, after the introduction of conscription 60,000 men had been called to the colours. If Britain kept the necessary troops in her own country she could send to France at best two infantry divisions and one armoured division. For the rest she could supply a few bomber squadrons but hardly any fighters since, at the outbreak of war, the German Air Force would at once attack Britain and British fighters would be urgently needed for the defence of their own country. With regard to the position of France,

Hitler said that " in the event of a general war, after the destruction of Poland—which would not take long—Germany would be in a position to assemble hundreds of divisions along the West Wall and France would then be compelled to concentrate all her available forces from the colonies, from the Italian frontier and elsewhere, on her own Maginot Line for the life-and-death struggle which would then ensue."

The Polish Army, Hitler explained, was most uneven in quality. There were a few parade divisions, and for the rest large numbers of troops of less value. Poland was very weak in anti-tank and anti-aircraft defence and at the moment neither France nor Britain could help her in this respect. If however, Poland were given assistance by the Western Powers over a long period, she could obtain these weapons and German superiority would thereby be diminished. " In contrast to the fanatics of Warsaw and Cracow, the population showed very sharp differences ; furthermore, it was necessary to consider the position of the Polish State. Out of 34,000,000 inhabitants, $1\frac{1}{2}$ million were German, about 4 million were Jews and 9 million Ukrainians, so that the number of genuine Poles was far less than the total population and their striking power was not to be valued highly. In these circumstances Poland could be struck to the ground by Germany in the shortest time.

" Since the Poles, through their whole attitude, had made it clear that, in any case, in the event of a general conflict they would stand on the side of the enemies of Germany and Italy, a quick liquidation at the present moment could only be of advantage for the unavoidable conflict with the Western Democracies. If a hostile Poland were to remain on Germany's eastern frontier, not only would the eleven East Prussian divisions be tied down, but also further contingents would be kept in Pomerania and Silesia. This would not be necessary in the event of a previous liquidation."

The conversation then turned to the Balkans, and finally Ciano explained Italy's position. This part of the conversation is examined in Chapter II, " Otto to Alaric." The following day the conversations were continued and Hitler made some additional observations on the Polish situation.

The danger of delaying action too long into the autumn, he explained, was that Poland would be able to carry out what Hitler described as " her relatively limited aims." Danzig could be made to submit by slow pressure and the treaty position was extremely favourable to Poland. Danzig could be blockaded and slowly ruined or even starved out from the second half of September and particularly from the beginning of October.

The Poles " could easily occupy the place." This occupation would be followed by the re-conquest of the Corridor and Danzig, on the part of Germany, but any further military operations would be impossible at the present time of year. Danzig therefore would fall into ruin, and the heavily motorised German forces which were necessary for deep penetration into Poland could not be used. In a severe winter, it would be possible to undertake certain military operations, but weather conditions would make the emergency landing fields and the usual aerodromes unusable. If Germany used these aerodromes the flying distances would be much lengthened, more petrol would be consumed and a considerable small weight of bombs could be carried.

" It was therefore necessary," the record quotes Hitler as stating, " that within the shortest time Poland should clearly state her intentions and no further provocation should be endured by Germany. If these provocations were allowed to pass, the affair would be prolonged until October when tanks and aircraft could not be used. The Polish General Staff knew these climatic conditions and their effect upon the German forces, and therefore Poland was playing for time. The Führer had therefore come to two definite conclusions : (a) in the event of any further provocation, he would immediately attack ; (b) if Poland did not clearly and plainly state her political intentions, she must be forced to do so. It should not be forgotten that the war of nerves which the Poles had started by means of continuous provocations had now lasted for three months. Any sign of giving in would, in view of the Slav mentality, bring a violent reaction of over-confidence on the part of the Poles. Surrender would not in any way strengthen the German position, but would be regarded by every other country as a sign of weakness."

It is not difficult to discern what here is pure propaganda, served up for the benefit of the Italian visitor, and what are Hitler's genuine calculations. What is not always quite clear is to what extent Hitler actually, at one time or another, believed in the genuineness of his own pretexts and excuses. He possessed an extraordinary gift of imputing to others the sinister motives he himself was harbouring, and having effected this mental transfer, of convincing himself—or at least so it sometimes seems— that this was now the true and real position and to act upon it.

Goering and Ribbentrop always knew when they were telling a lie. With Hitler one is not always so certain. For all his ice-cold calculations and hard, brutal planning in which, as has been seen, he knew precisely what he was doing and recognized only facts, he had a sure instinct where and when it was of advantage so to befog and befuddle himself that he was capable of really believing anything he himself uttered. It is a rare quality which few men possess, and it is therefore seldom recognised for what it is, when it appears. It seems too absurd to be real. Hitler's absurdity was his reality, and conversely his reality was his absurdity. It was so staggering that it almost carried him to his goal.

Canaris has his Doubts

On August 17th, 1939, Admiral Canaris, Chief of the German Counter-Intelligence, had a conversation with Keitel, Chief of the Supreme Command of the Armed Forces. It revolved round the question of whether the Western Powers, especially Britain, would intervene. We possess Canaris' notes on this conversation and their authenticity has been confirmed by Keitel.

The Chief of the Supreme Command was confident that Britain would not intervene. Canaris notes : " I tried to contradict his views and say that the British would certainly at once institute a blockade and would destroy our merchant shipping. Keitel believed this to be of no great importance as we would receive oil from Rumania. I answered that this was not the decisive factor and that we could not resist a blockade for a long time. Britain would fight us with all her means if we should use force against the Poles and if there were to be bloodshed. I told him that the British would have acted in precisely the same manner had any bloodshed occurred when we marched into Czechoslovakia. I tried to explain to Keitel the consequences of economic warfare for Germany and tell him that we have only very few means to counteract it. Just a short while ago I had heard that we could send only 10 submarines into the Atlantic Ocean. Keitel thought that it would be easy to force Rumania to surrender her oil after the conquest of Poland. I called his attention to the actions of the British in the Balkans and tried to explain to him that the British would certainly have everything prepared in the Balkans for such an eventuality. Bulgaria would not be useful to us as an ally as she would be attacked at once by Rumania and Turkey."

Strike or be Destroyed

It will be remembered that Hitler's instructions regarding " Case White " called for all preparations to be completed by September 1st, 1939. Although this was not then the fixed date for the beginning of the invasion of Poland, it was a tentative date and the aim towards which the efforts of the Armed Forces were directed.

On August 22nd, 1939, a week before this dead-line was reached, Hitler once more called all his Commanders-in-Chief to his house at Berchtesgaden for a secret briefing conference. The minutes of his address were among the files of the Supreme Command of the Armed Forces captured at Flensburg, and are available.

Hitler told his officers that he had called them together in order to give them a picture of the political situation, so that they might have an insight into the individual elements on which he had based his decision to act, and in order to strengthen their confidence. He then said :

" It was clear to me that a conflict with Poland had to come sooner or later. I had already made this decision in spring, but I thought that I would first turn against the West in a few years' time, and only afterwards against the East. But the sequence cannot be determined in advance. One cannot close one's eyes to a threatening situation. I wanted to establish an acceptable relationship with Poland in order to fight first against the West. But this plan, which suited me, could not be executed since essential points have changed. It became clear to me that Poland would attack us in case of a conflict with the West. Poland wants access to the sea. The further development became obvious after the occupation of the Memel region, and it became clear to me that in certain circumstances a conflict with Poland could arise at an inopportune moment."

This is a summary of his earlier views, and it will be seen that it is reasonably consistent. It will be remembered that in his speech of November 5th, 1937, recorded in the " Hossbach Minutes," he considered the idea of striking at some time between 1943 and 1945. In the light of what he now says when he refers to " in a few years' time," it was apparently then his plan to strike against the West. The "establishment of acceptable relations with Poland " is seen as a move to keep Poland quiet until the war with the West was over. This plan " suited " Hitler. Eventually it had to be reversed because " essential points had changed." This is presumably a reference to the contact established between the British and Polish Governments in the spring of 1939 which led to the British guarantee for Poland and eventually to the Anglo-Polish Alliance. Hitler perceived rightly that this new bond was now restricting his freedom of action. He was certain that in the event of his attacking in the West first, Poland would join in and "stab him in the back." He said as much in his speech of May 23rd, 1939. It can be said that he was by now quite clear in his own mind about what was likely, even certain to happen, whatever move he made. There was no more room for doubt, and he did not pretend there was, at any rate not in his inner circle of military advisers and commanders. What he said to the world is a very different matter and does not concern us here.

Continuing his exposé, Hitler stressed a number of personal factors. First of all there was his own person. " Essentially everything depends on me, on my existence, because of my political activity. Furthermore on the fact that probably no one will ever again have the confidence of the whole German people as I have it. There will probably never again be a man in the future with more authority than I command. My existence is therefore a factor of great value. But I can be eliminated at any time by a criminal or an idiot." Next there was Mussolini. " His existence is also decisive. If something happens to him, Italy's loyalty to the alliance will no longer be certain. The basic attitude of the Italian court is against the Duce. Above all, the court sees in the expansion of the Empire a burden. The Duce is the man with the strongest nerves in Italy." Finally there was Franco. Spain was not yet under firm totalitarian rule, but Franco's personality would guarantee benevolent neutrality if no more. On the enemy side, as far as decisive personalities were concerned, there was " a negative picture. There is no outstanding personality in Britain or France.

" For us it is easy to make a decision. We have nothing to lose. We can only gain. Our economic situation is such, because of our restrictions, that we cannot hold out for more than a few years. Goering can confirm this. We have no other choice. We must act. Our opponents risk much and can gain only little. Britain's stake in a war is unimaginably great. Our enemies have men who are below average. There are no personalities, no masters, no men of action."

Besides these personal aspects, the political situation was

also favourable for Germany. In the Mediterranean there was rivalry between Italy, Britain and France. In the Near and Middle East there was tension which had roused and alarmed the Mohammedan world. The British Empire did not emerge strengthened from the last war. From a maritime point of view it achieved nothing. There was conflict between Britain and Ireland. The South African Union acquired greater independence. Concessions had to be made in India. Britain was in great danger. An unhealthy state prevailed in her industries. A British statesman could look into the future only with concern. France's position had also deteriorated, particularly in the Mediterranean. In the Balkans further favourable factors could be discerned. Since (the Italian seizure of) Albania there was an equilibrium of power in the Balkans. Yugoslavia carried the germ of collapse because of her internal situation. Rumania was not growing any stronger. She was liable to be attacked and vulnerable, being threatened by Hungary and Bulgaria. Turkey, finally, since Kemal's death had been ruled by small minds and weak, unsteady men.

"All these favourable circumstances will no longer prevail in two or three years from now. No one knows how long I shall live. Therefore it is better to have the conflict now."

The creation of Greater Germany, Hitler went on, was a great achievement politically, but militarily it was questionable since it was achieved through a bluff on the part of the political leaders. "It is now necessary to test the military. If at all possible, this should be done not in the course of a general settlement but by solving individual tasks." In other words : we have not really as yet tested the efficiency and striking power of our armed forces. We cannot be sure how good they are. Therefore it is advisable not to shoulder them with too big a task to which they might prove unequal. Let us work in instalments and see what we can achieve.

" Our relations with Poland have become unbearable. My Polish policy hitherto was in contrast to the ideas of the people. My proposals to Poland relating to Danzig and the Corridor were upset by Britain's intervention. Poland changed her tone towards us. The initiative cannot be allowed to pass to the others. This moment is more favourable than in two or three years' time. An attempt on my life or that of Mussolini can change the situation to our disadvantage. One cannot eternally stand opposite one another with cocked rifles. A suggested compromise would have demanded that we change our convictions and make agreeable gestures. They talked to us again in the language of Versailles. There was danger of losing prestige. Now the probability is still great that the West will not intervene. We must accept this risk with reckless resolution. A politician must accept a risk just as much as a military leader. We are facing the alternative to strike or be destroyed with certainty sooner or later. I have always accepted a great risk in the conviction that it may succeed. Now we are again faced with a great risk. We need iron nerves and iron resolution."

Hitler then gave a number of special reasons which strengthened his conviction that this was the best time to strike. Britain and France were both under obligations but neither was in a position to honour them. There was no actual rearmament in Britain, but merely propaganda. " It has done much damage that many hesitant Germans said and wrote to English people after the solution of the Czech question :' The Führer carried his point because you lost your nerve, because you capitulated too soon.' This explains the present propaganda war. The British speak of a war of nerves. It is one element of this war of nerves to boost the increase in armament. But how does British re-armament stand in actual fact ? " The construction programme of the Navy for 1938 had not yet been filled. Only the reserve fleet had been mobilized. A considerable strengthening of the British Navy was not to be expected before 1941 or 1942. Little had been done on land. Britain would be able to send a maximum of three divisions to the continent. A little had been done for the Air Force but it was only a beginning. Anti-aircraft defence was in its initial stages. At the moment Britain had only 150 anti-aircraft guns. Fire directors were lacking. Britain was still vulnerable from the air. This could change in two or three years. At the moment the British Air Force had only 130,000 men, France 72,000 and Poland 15,000. Britain did not want the conflict to break out for another two or three years.

It was characteristic of Britain, Hitler said, that when Poland wanted a loan from her for rearmament she only gave Poland a credit in order to make sure that Poland would buy in Britain although Britain was unable to deliver. This meant that Britain did not really want to support Poland. She was unwilling to risk 8 million sterling in Poland although she willingly put half a milliard into China. Britain's position in the world was very precarious. She was unwilling to accept any risks. France, owing to the decline in her birth rate, lacked men. Little had been done for her re-armament. Her artillery was antiquated. She did not want to enter on this adventure.

Summing up, Hitler estimated that there were only two possibilities for the West to fight Germany. " First, the blockade. This will not be effective because of our self-sufficiency and because we have sources of aid in the East. Second, attack from the West from the Maginot Line. I consider this impossible. A third possibility is the violation of Dutch, Belgian and Swiss neutrality. I have no doubts that all these states as well as Scandinavia will defend their neutrality with all available means. Britain and France will not violate the neutrality of these countries. In actual fact, Britain cannot help Poland. There remains an attack on Italy. A military attack is out of the question. No one is counting on a long war. If Gen. von Brauchitsch had told me that I should need four years to conquer Poland I should have replied : In that case it cannot be done. It is nonsense to say that Britain wants to wage a long war."

And he concludes by announcing : " We shall hold our position in the West until we have conquered Poland. Our enemies are little men. I saw them at Munich."

This speech was made on August 22nd, 1939. The following day the conclusion of the Non-Aggression Pact between Germany and the Soviet Union was announced. Anticipating it, Hitler said :

" Now Poland is in the position in which I wanted her. The publication of the Non-Aggression Pact with Russia will hit like a bombshell. The consequences cannot be overlooked. The effect on Poland will be tremendous." He adds : "We need not be afraid of a blockade. The East will supply us with grain, cattle, coal, lead and zinc. It is a big aim which demands great efforts. I am only afraid that at the last moment some dirty pig will make a proposal for mediation. The political aim is set farther. A beginning has been made for the destruction of Britain's hegemony. I have made the political preparations. The way is now open for the soldier."

Start on Saturday Morning

Hitler made a second speech on August 22nd, 1939. We possess the record of it but it does not tell us before what audience this address was made. From its general character one may conclude that it was made to a group of high officers for the purpose of buttressing their morale and fighting spirit. The record is not the usual full one but consists merely of notes of the main points made by Hitler.

With regard to Britain and France, Hitler said in this second speech, things might also turn out differently. "One cannot predict the course of events with certainty. I anticipate rather a kind of trade barrier than a blockade, and along with it a severance of diplomatic relations. On our side we require the most iron determination. We must retreat before nothing. Everybody must be quite clear in their minds that we are determined from the beginning to fight the Western Powers. It is going to be a struggle for life and death. A long period of peace would not do us any good. Therefore it is necessary to be prepared for anything. We must show manly bearing. It is not machines that fight each other but men. We have the better quality of men. Mental factors are decisive. The opposite camp has weaker people. In 1918 the nation collapsed because the mental prerequisites proved inadequate.

" The destruction of Poland stands in the foreground. The aim is the elimination of her fighting forces, not the arrival at a certain line. Even if war should break out in the West, the destruction of Poland will remain the primary objective. A rapid decision must be obtained on account of the season.

" I shall give a propagandist cause for starting the war," said Hitler. " Never mind whether it be plausible or not. The victor will not be asked, later on, whether we told the truth or not. In starting and waging a war, it is not Right that matters but Victory. Have no pity. Adopt a brutal attitude. Eighty million people shall get what is their right. Their existence has to be secured. Right is on the side of the strongest. Act with the greatest severity. Our first aim is to advance to the Vistula and Narew. Our technical superiority will break the nerves of the Poles. Every newly created Polish force shall again be broken at once. There will be a constant war of attrition. There will be a new German frontier according to healthy principles, possibly with a protectorate as a buffer. But military operations will not be influenced by these reflections. Complete destruction of Poland is the military aim. To be fast is the main thing. Pursue until complete elimination.

" The start will be ordered probably for Saturday morning."

There has been some uncertainty as to whether Hitler always intended to launch his campaign on September 1st, 1939, or whether at some interim stage an earlier date had been envisaged. He told Ciano during their conversation on August 12th, 1939, that "the end of August" was the latest date on which to start the campaign. The only marching order for "Case White" actually in our possession is, in fact, dated August 31st, and it gives the date of the attack as September 1st, 1939, at 04.45 hours. The Saturday morning, on the other hand, which Hitler mentions was August 26th, 1939. Was the attack scheduled for this day and then postponed? The Nuremberg Documents leave no doubt that it was.

On August 23rd, 1939, Jodl notes in his diary:

" 11.00 hours-13.30 hours : Discussions with Chief of Armed Forces Supreme Command. X-Day has been announced for August 26th. Y-Time has been announced for 04.30 hours." August 23rd, 1939, was the day after the Hitler speech just quoted. It was the day on which the treaty between Germany and the Soviet Union was signed and became effective. It was, incidentally, also the day on which Jodl was appointed Chief of the Armed Forces Executive Office (Wehrmacht-Führungsstab).

When was this decision cancelled and the new date fixed? We have no precise answer to that. Goering says it was on August 24th, while Ribbentrop maintains that it was on August 25th, 1939. Goering's statement occurs in a testimony taken during an interrogation at Nuremberg on August 29th, 1945. He declared that " on the day when Britain gave her official guarantee to Poland the Führer called me on the telephone and told me that he had stopped the planned invasion of Poland. I asked him whether this was merely temporary or for good. He said : ' No, I shall have to see whether we can eliminate British intervention'." Goering added that orders for the beginning of the campaign were issued by the Supreme Command of the Armed Forces, of which Keitel was chief, on behalf of Hitler and "that the time had to be chosen in such a way that the Supreme Command could always cancel the campaign twenty-four hours before the proposed date."

Ribbentrop, in a similar testimony, also taken at Nuremberg on August 29th, 1945, confirmed this and actually claimed to have been the originator of this postponement. In a somewhat confused and garbled statement he said : "The Führer had already decided to go ahead when the British guarantee signature came. When I heard about this British guarantee—I learned from the press it had been signed in London—I went at once to the Führer and hearing that military steps had been taken against Poland, asked him to cancel them and stop the advance. The Führer immediately agreed to do this. He gave orders to his military adjutant, who was Schmundt, who passed the orders on to the military people to stop the advance into Poland." Asked by the interrogator when this took place, Ribbentrop answered : " I think it was on August 25th, 1939. Then the negotiations with Henderson started in Berlin, and only after this last attempt with Britain did not come off, the Führer made again an offer of friendship and of close collaboration with Britain. When this didn't come off, the Führer decided to treat directly with the Poles. And when the Polish intermediary didn't come, the Führer acted and took military steps."

One wonders whether Ribbentrop knew what he was saying. He obviously did not know that Goering was being interviewed at the same time on the same subject. Ribbentrop's interrogation lasted from 14.00 to 16.30 hours, Goering's from 14.30 to 16.40 hours. Thus Ribbentrop once more repeated the time-worn propaganda phrases of the " offer of friendship and close colla- boration with Britain " when a few cells down the corridor Goering bluntly stated, to another interrogator, that Hitler wanted to see whether he could " eliminate British intervention." And that was really all that was behind the postponement of the attack. There was never at any time even the slightest prospect of getting the war against Poland stopped altogether. Nor was there ever, at any time, the slightest prospect of avoiding war between Britain and Germany. Hitler was determined to have both. That he got them both at the same time, was his mis- fortune. But, as he himself said, " one cannot predict the course of events with certainty."

Directive Number One

The final order to attack Poland bears the heading " Directive No. 1 for the Conduct of the War." It is dated Berlin, August 31st, 1939, and is signed by Hitler. It reads as follows :

" Now that all the political possibilities of disposing by peaceful means of a situation on the Eastern frontier which is intolerable for Germany are exhausted, I have determined on a solution by force.

" The attack on Poland is to be carried out in accordance with the preparations made for ' Case White,' with the alterations which result, where the Army is concerned, from the fact that it has in the meantime almost completed its dispositions.

" Allotment of tasks and the operational target remain unchanged.

" Date of attack—September 1st, 1939.

" Time of attack—04.45 hours.

" This time also applies to the operations at Gdynia, Bay of Danzig and the Dirschau Bridge.

" In the West it is important that the responsibility for the opening of hostilities should rest unequivocally with Britain and France. At first purely local action should be taken against insignificant frontier violations. The neutrality assured by us to Holland, Belgium, Luxembourg and Switzerland should be scrupulously observed. The German land frontier in the West is not to be crossed at any point without my express consent. The same applies to warlike actions at sea or any which may be so interpreted. Defensive measures on the part of the Air Force should at first be confined exclusively to the warding off of enemy air attacks on the frontiers of the Reich. In doing so the frontiers of the neutral states should be respected as long as possible when dealing with single aircraft and smaller units. Defensive operations over neutral territory should only be permitted if French and British attacking squadrons are operating over neutral territory against German territory in considerable forces and air defence in the West is thus no longer assured. It is of special importance that the Supreme Command of the Armed Forces should be informed with the least possible delay of any violation of the neutrality of these states on the part of our opponents in the West.

" If Britain and France open hostilities against Germany, the task of those sections of the Armed Forces which are operating in the West is to maintain, while conserving their strength as far as possible, those conditions necessary for the successful conclusion of the operations against Poland. Within the scope of this duty, damage should be done to enemy forces and their economic sources of supply. In any event I reserve for myself the order to commence attack operations.

" The Army is holding the West Wall and is making preparations to prevent it being turned. The Western Powers would be violating Belgian or Dutch territory in doing so. If French forces move into Luxemburg, the frontier bridges may be blown up.

"In its warfare on merchant shipping the Navy is concentrating on Britain. In order to intensify the effect of this, a declaration of danger zones is to be expected. The Supreme Command of the Navy announces in which areas and within what limits danger zones are considered expedient. The wording of the public declaration should be prepared in conjunction with the Foreign Office and should be submitted to me for approval through the Supreme Command of the Armed Forces. The Baltic should be secured against penetration by the enemy. The Commander-in-Chief of the Navy decides whether the approaches to the Baltic should be mined for this purpose.

" The primary task of the Air Force is to prevent the French and British Air Forces from operating against the German Army and German 'living space.' In waging war against Britain, preparations should be made for the use of the Air Force in causing damage to sea transport, the armament industry and troops transports to France. Full use should be made of favourable opportunities to make an effective attack on massed British naval units, especially on battleships and aircraft carriers. The decision regarding attacks on London rests with me.

" Attacks on the British Isles should be prepared, bearing in mind that whatever happens, inadequate success with part forces is to be avoided."

Jodl on the Phoney War

In his secret speech of November 7th, 1943, Gen. Jodl, reviewing the period immediately following the outbreak of war, stated :

" This brings me to the actual outbreak of the present war, and the question which next arises is whether the moment for the struggle with the Poland—in itself unavoidable—was favourably selected or not. The answer to this is all the less in doubt since the opponent, after all not inconsiderable in himself, collapsed with unexpected rapidity, and the Western Powers who were his friends, while declaring war on us and forming a second front, for the rest made no use of the possibilities open to them of snatching the initiative from our hands. Regarding the course taken by the Polish campaign, nothing further need be said than that it proved, in a measure which made the whole world sit up and take notice, a point which up till then had not been certain by any means, namely the high state of efficiency of the young Armed Forces of Greater Germany.

I

" The main effect of this success was however that we now had no opponent in the East and that in view of the agreements with Russia, the front problem might be regarded as solved for the time being. As a result of all this the point of gravity in the conduct of the war naturally shifted to the West where the most urgent task was clearly defined as the protection of the Ruhr basin from invasion, through Holland, by the British and French. Even before the Polish campaign had been concluded, the Führer had already decided upon an attack against this enemy, the aim of which could only be the complete subjection of the opponent. The fact that this decision was not carried out as originally planned, namely in the late autumn of 1939, was mainly due to weather conditions but in part it was also influenced by our situation with regard to armaments.

" In the meantime however we were confronted by yet another problem which had to be settled promptly ; the occupation of Norway and Denmark. The point here lay in opening up a theatre of war which, while it lay outside the zone of immediate danger, yet possessed twofold importance from the point of view of our general conduct of the war. In the first place there was danger that Britain would seize Scandinavia and thereby, apart from effecting a strategic encirclement from the North, stop our imports of iron and nickel which were of such importance to us for war purposes. Secondly, it was the realization of our own naval necessities which made it imperative for us to secure for ourselves free access to the Atlantic through a number of air and naval support points or bases. Here, too, therefore defensive and offensive requirements combined to form an indissoluble whole.

" The course and conclusion of this campaign are known. In the main it was completed in such good time that it was possible to start upon the campaign in the West with the setting in of the most favourable season of the year, in May 1940."

These passages are instructive. They show that the attack in the West, opening with the invasion of the Low Countries, was originally planned for the autumn of 1939 and had to be postponed for weather reasons and, as Jodl claims, because of munitions shortages. The invasion of Norway and Denmark was planned simultaneously and in the event received priority. The Nuremberg Documents bear this out in some detail.

Rosenberg Sells Norway

It will be remembered that in his remarks to Ciano on August 12th, 1939, Hitler made a reference to Scandinavia which seemed to indicate—although it is admittedly open to interpretation— that he did not think an occupation of either Norway or Sweden a "practical proposition." Other documents relating to Scandinavia seem to bear this out. The view that the invasion of Scandinavia was Hitler's "pet operation," that he conceived the idea and was particularly insistent on its execution, a view held rather widely during the war, is not supported by these documents. The truth, as far as one can discern it from the incomplete evidence available, is that the invasion of Norway was primarily the idea of Vidkun Quisling.

We shall see that Quisling sold the idea to Rosenberg and Rosenberg tried very hard to sell it to Hitler. But the Führer refused to buy it. Rosenberg thereupon did the next best thing and sold it to Raeder, the Commander-in-Chief of the Navy, and Raeder in the end succeeded in selling it to Hitler. Rosenberg and Raeder were the two main advocates of this plan. Hitler was won over to it only after considerable difficulties.

Rosenberg was exceedingly proud of the part he played in preparing the invasion of Norway and most anxious that his share in it should be recognized, and he be given full credit for it. Thus, on June 17th, 1940, he submitted to Hitler via Hess a long document entitled "The Political Preparations of the Norway Action" in which he sets out in great detail the activities of his office (the "Office of Foreign Relations of the National Socialist Party") in connection with the invasion of Norway. The text of this memorandum is in our possession. It is a long and, at least in parts, tedious document evidently designed to boost Rosenberg, and it can only be summarized here.

Rosenberg states that his office had been in contact with Quisling for years. In 1939 Quisling sent Rosenberg "an estimate of the situation and his opinion about the possible intentions of Britain with regard to Scandinavia in the event of a conflict between Britain and Germany." Rosenberg received Quisling in Berlin shortly afterwards, and Quisling pointed out to him the importance of Norway and the "advantages gained by the power in control of the Norwegian coast in case of an Anglo-German conflict." Anglo-Saxon propaganda was successful in Norway, but since he (Quisling) was convinced that this time the neutrals would be involved in a war, he requested support for his party and press. Rosenberg thereupon put Quisling in touch with a number of German officials and had a memorandum sent to Hilter on the subject at the end of June, 1939.

Arrangements were made, upon Quisling's request, for 25 of Quisling's party members to receive special training in Germany, but the question of financial subsidies to Quisling made no progress. Goering had taken charge of these money matters, but the outbreak of the Polish war delayed things and Rosenberg remarks that a further reminder which he gave Goering "in the course of a talk about the importance of Norway in connection with the matters set forth originally by Quisling had no practical results." Meantime Quisling continued to inform Rosenberg's office through his deputies in Germany on developments in Scandinavia. Anglo-Saxon propaganda was gaining further ground and Germany had acquired the odour of being a secret ally of Soviet Russia and the real culprit in Finland's misfortunes. Under the cloak of helping Finland, Britain was planning to seize Norway and possibly also Sweden in order to effectively close the blockade and gain further air bases against Germany.

In the early part of December, 1939, Quisling again came to Berlin and pressed Rosenberg to do something, "to tie Norway's fate to that of Greater Germany." Quisling's deputy in Germany, Hagelin, at that time arranged for an interview between Quisling and Raeder which duly took place. Rosenberg, on his part, in one of his reports to Hitler "again mentioned Norway, pointing out her importance in the case of Britain deciding to occupy that country with the tacit consent of its government." Finally Raeder prevailed upon Hitler to receive him in order to hear from him what Quisling had had to say. Raeder persuaded Hitler to see Quisling personally and two interviews took place, on December 16th and 18th.

" During these interviews the Führer emphasized repeatedly that the most preferable attitude of Norway as well as the rest of Scandinavia would be one of complete neutrality. He had no intention to enlarge the theatres of war and draw other nations into the conflict. If, however, the enemy were preparing an enlargement of the zones of war with the aim of further strangling and threatening Germany, he would, of course be compelled to arm against such steps." Hitler then promised Quisling financial support for his movement and for the purpose of combating increasing enemy propaganda. "The military side of the question was now transferred to a special military staff which assigned special missions to Quisling and heard his opinions." The political treatment was to be in the hands of Rosenberg, expenses were to be carried by the Foreign Office and the Foreign Minister was to be kept informed at all times. Scheidt, an official in Rosenberg's office, was appointed liaison officer with Quisling and for this purpose was attached to Commander Schreiber, the German naval attaché in Oslo. In January, 1940 it was decided to give Quisling an initial subsidy of 20,000 Reichsmark.

Rosenberg's account of the sequence of events appears to be reasonably correct as far it goes. We shall presently return to it. Meanwhile it is of interest to note that at least with Raeder and Doenitz, his own and Quisling's ideas fell on fruitful ground. We possess two documents which show that even during the Polish campaign both naval men were thinking in the same direction.

In a Naval War Diary which was kept by Raeder's Chief of Staff, and of which extensive extracts are available, it is noted on October 3rd, 1939 :

" The Chief of the Naval War Staff (Raeder) considers it necessary that the Führer be informed as soon as possible of the opinions of the Naval War Staff on the possibilities of extending the operational base to the North. It must be ascertained whether it is possible to gain bases in Norway under the combined pressure of Russia and Germany, with the aim of improving our strategic and operational position. The following questions must be given consideration : (a) what places in Norway can be considered as bases ? (b) can bases be gained by military force against Norway's will, if it is impossible to carry this out without fighting ? (c) what are the possibilities of defence after the occupation ? (d) will the harbours have to be developed completely as bases or have they already advantages suitable for supply position ? The Flag Officer U-boats (Doenitz) already considers such harbours extremely useful as equipment and supply bases for Atlantic U-boats to call at temporarily. (e) What decisive advantages would exist for the conduct of the war at sea in gaining bases in Northern Denmark, e.g., Skagen ? "

On October 9th, 1939, Doenitz (Flag-Officer, U-boats) sent a most secret memorandum to Raeder on the subject " Base in

Norway." He points out that any such base must answer three requirements. It must be situated outside the Shetlands-Norway Straits ; it must be ice-free ; and it must have rail communications. Only two harbours, Doenitz indicates, answer these requirements—Trondheim and Narvik. For Trondheim he quotes a number of advantages. It is situated within the fjord and therefore unaffected by artillery action from the sea. It has deep-water channels which are difficult for the enemy to mine. It has several entry and exit routes and, in view of its southern position, short lines of communication with Germany, better climatic conditions and a shorter route to the Atlantic. There are bases which are suitable for U-boats and industrial installations which would facilitate repairs and supply. Against these advantages Trondheim has the disadvantage of lying at a short distance from the bases of the British Air Force and is therefore liable to be attacked. Narvik, Doenitz points out, has roughly the same advantages as Trondheim and lies at a greater distance from British bases but its disadvantages are considerable. Lines of communication with Germany are long, climatic conditions unfavourable, the route to the Atlantic long. It has communication only with the Baltic since the Gulf of Bothnia is not ice-free, it has no basins and very few industrial installations. Doenitz therefore concludes that Trondheim is the more suitable place and proposes that a base be established there which would include the possibility of supplying fuel, compressed air, oxygen and provisions ; repair opportunities for overhaul work after engagements at sea ; good arrangements for billeting U-boat crews, as well as anti-aircraft protection. He finally recommends the use of Narvik as an alternative fuel supply point.

Case Yellow

While these plans went forward, preparations for the invasion of the Low Countries were being pushed ahead vigorously. It will be recalled from Jodl's speech that it was originally planned to launch this campaign immediately following the Polish war, in the autumn of 1939. On October 9th, 1939, the day Doenitz submitted his proposals for a German submarine base at Trondheim, Hitler issued his first Directive for the campaign against Holland and Belgium.

The code-word for this campaign was "Case Yellow." The Directive bears the number 6 and is signed by Hitler. It reads as follows :

"(1) If it becomes evident in the near future that Britain, and France acting under her leadership, are not disposed to put an end to the war, I am determined to take action, and offensive action, without letting much time elapse.

(2) A long waiting period results not only in the ending, to the advantage of the Western Powers, of Belgian and perhaps also Dutch neutrality but it also strengthens the military power of our enemies to an increasing degree, causes confidence of the neutrals in German final victory to wane and does not help to bring Italy to our aid as a brother-in-arms.

(3) I therefore issue the following orders for the further conduct of military operations :

(a) Preparations should be made for offensive action on the northern flank of the western front, crossing the area of Luxembourg, Belgium and Holland. This attack must be carried out as soon and as forcefully as possible.

(b) The object of this attack is to defeat as strong sections of the French Fighting Army as possible, and her ally and partner in the fighting, and at the same time to acquire as great an area of Holland, Belgium and Northern France as possible, to be used as a base which offers good prospects for the conduct of air and naval war against Britain and to provide ample coverage for the vital Ruhr area.

(c) The time of the attack is dependent on the operational readiness of the armoured and motorised units, which should be expedited with the utmost effort, and on the state of the weather at the time and the weather forecast.

(4) The Air Force will prevent the combined French and British Air Forces from interfering with the Army and, where necessary, give direct support to its operations. In this connection it will be very important to prevent the combined French and British Air Forces from gaining a foothold, and also British troops from landing, in Holland. The cutting of the supply routes of the British troops once they have landed will be the task of the Air Force since U-boats will soon have to cease operating in the Channel on account of great losses.

(5) The conduct of the war at sea must concentrate entirely on being able to give direct or indirect support to the Army and Air Force operations throughout this attack.

(6) In addition to these preparations for the start of the offensive in the West according to plan, the Army and Air Force

must be ready at any time and in increasing strength, to be able to make an immediate stand against a combined French and British entry into Belgium, and this in as advanced a position as possible on Belgian territory, while at the same time they must be able to occupy Holland as extensively as possible while pushing towards the West Coast.

(7) The disguising of preparations must take the line that nothing more than precautionary measures against the threatening concentration of French and British forces on the Franco-Luxembourg and Belgian frontiers are being taken.

(8) I request the Commanders-in-Chief, acting on this order, to submit reports on their intentions to me individually as soon as possible and to keep me informed through the Supreme Command of the Armed Forces of the state of their preparations."

Although we know that Hitler was anxious to start this campaign as soon as possible and that he was certainly reckoning on carrying it out in the late autumn of 1939, we have no precise information regarding the date for which the invasion was first scheduled. But we possess a chronological file of brief orders issued by Keitel between November 7th, 1939, and May 9th, 1940, informing the three Services in each case that the date for the attack has again been postponed and advising them when the next decision regarding X-Day will be made. The first of these orders is dated November 7th, 1939, and states :

" On November 7th, 1939, the Führer and Supreme Commander of the Armed Forces, after hearing reports on the meteorological and railway transport situation, has ordered :

A-Day is postponed for the time being by three days. The next decision will be made at 1800 hours on November 9th, 1939."

This order presupposes that A-Day had previously been fixed, presumably for November 7th or 8th. The postponement of three days would take us to November 9th or 10th. On November 10th, however, Keitel issued a new order to the effect that Hitler on November 9th had decided that " the earliest date for A-Day is November 19th," but a decision on this would be made on November 13th. On November 13th, however, Keitel announces that " A-Day will definitely not be before Wednesday, November 22nd," but the next decision would be made on November 16th. On that day a further order states that A-Day was "definitely not before Sunday, November 26th," and the next decision would be made on November 20th.

On November 20th there is another postponement. This time the attack is not due before December 3rd, and the next decision will be made on November 27th, 1939.

On November 20th, 1939, however, Hitler through Keitel issues a new Directive on " Case Yellow." It is " Directive No. 8 " and states :

" (1) The state of alert must be maintained for the time being so that the deployment which has been initiated may be continued at any time. Only in this way is it possible to take immediate advantage of a favourable weather situation.

"The Armed Forces will make preparations so that the attack can still be stopped, even if the order for stopping it should arrive at the higher command only at A-Day-minus-One at 23.00 hours. The code-word—

> 'Rhine' - carry out the attack
>
> *or* 'Elbe' - stop the attack

will be transmitted to the higher commands not later than at the above-mentioned time. The Supreme Command of the Army and the Supreme Command of the Air Force are requested to report immediately after the designation of attack day to the Supreme Command of the Armed Forces, Department Air Force, the hour at which the beginning of the attack is planned by mutual agreement.

" (2) Contrary to previously issued instructions, all action intended against Holland may be carried out without a special order when the general attack opens. The attitude of the Dutch armed forces cannot be anticipated ahead of time. Wherever there is no resistance, the entry should have the character of a peaceful occupation.

" (3) The operations on land are to be conducted on the basis of the deployment order of October 29th, 1939. The following will apply :

(a) All arrangements are to be made, in order to shift quickly the main effort of the operations from Army Group B to Army Group A, in case faster and greater successes should develop at Army Group A than Army Group B, as one might well assume from the present distribution of enemy forces.

(b) In the first instance the Dutch area including the West Frisian Islands situated just off the coast, for the present excluding Texel, is to be occupied up to the Grebbe-Maas line.

" (4) Blockade measures against the Belgian and, contrary to earlier orders, also against the Dutch harbours and navigable waters are authorised for the Navy, namely for submarines during the night before the attack and for surface fighting craft and aircraft from the time of the attack by the Army. The span of time between the beginning of the blockade operations and the time of the attack on land must however be kept as short as possible for the deployment of the submarines. Battle actions against Dutch naval forces are authorised only if they take a hostile attitude. The Navy will take over the artillery defence of the coast against attacks from the sea in the coastal territories which are to be occupied. Preparations for this are to be made.

" (5) The missions of the Air Force remain unchanged. They are supplemented by special orders which the Führer has given orally about airborne landings and support of the Army in the seizure of the bridges west of Maastricht. The 7th Airborne Division will be committed for the airborne operation only after possession of the bridges across the Albert Canal has been secured. The quickest transmission of this message is to be assured between the Supreme Command of the Army and the Supreme Command of the Air Force. Localities, especially large open cities and industries are not to be attacked without compelling military reasons either in the Dutch or in the Belgian or Luxembourg areas.

" (6) Shutting of the borders : until the beginning of the attack traffic and news services across the border are to be maintained in their present volume across the Dutch, Belgian and Luxembourg borders, in order to assure the element of surprise. Until the beginning of the attack, civil authorities are not to participate in the preparations for the closing of the borders. With the beginning of the attack the Reich frontier against Holland, Belgium and Luxembourg is to be blocked for all non-military traffic and news services across the border. The Supreme Commander of the Army will issue the relevant orders to the military and civil offices concerned. With the beginning of the attack the supreme Reich authorities concerned will be informed by the Supreme Command of the Armed Forces that the measures for the closing of the frontiers have been ordered direct by the Supreme Commander of the Army, and that this also applies to the Dutch frontier not in the area of operations. Along the other Reich frontiers opposite neutral countries there will be, in the first instance, no restrictions in traffic and news services across the border after the beginning of the attack."

The deployment order of October 29th, 1939, mentioned in this Directive is unfortunately not in our possession, and it is therefore not possible to study in greater detail the military preparations made. But it is clear from this Directive that plans for the invasion of Holland were changed between this and the previous Directive which would appear to have been No. 7, since Hitler's Directive of October 9th, 1939, bore the number 6. Evidently special measures had been envisaged with regard to Holland ; there was to have been a special order authorising the attack on Dutch territory, and blockade measures against Dutch harbours were not, it seems, originally envisaged. All this is changed in Directive No. 8 which prescribes an identical treatment for all three countries. It will be noted that in this order the bombing of large open cities is not authorised " without compelling military reasons." Here again, second thoughts must have prevailed which led, in the event, to the destruction of Rotterdam and other cities from the air.

The defence of the Ruhr basin and the danger of losing it through an Anglo-French offensive conducted across Dutch and Belgian territory seems to have greatly preoccupied the German military leaders. We possess a secret circular signed by Keitel which, referring to the Directive just quoted, places special emphasis on this. It says that this aspect was specially discussed with Hitler and the result was as follows :

" The protection of the Ruhr area, by moving Aircraft Reporting Service and the Air Defence as far forward as possible in the area of Holland, is of no inconsiderable significance to the whole conduct of the war. The more Dutch territory we occupy the more effective can the defence of the Ruhr be made. This viewpoint must determine the choice of objectives by the Army even if the Army and Navy are not directly interested in such a territorial gain. It must be the object of the Army's preparations, therefore, to occupy, on receipt of a special order, the territory of Holland, in the first instance, as far as the Grebbe-Maas line. It will depend on the political and military attitude of the Dutch as well as on the effectiveness of their flooding whether the objective must and can be still further extended. Preparations are likewise to be made to take possession, with the support of the Navy, of the West Frisian Islands, at first with the exception of Texel, as soon as the Northern coast of Groningen is in our hands. These are of great importance as bases for the Aircraft Reporting Service, and Britain must be deprived of the possibilities of seizing them for similar purposes."

This, then, was the situation on November 20th, 1939. Three days later, on November 23rd, 1939, Hitler once again called together all his Commanders-in-Chief to give them a secret briefing speech. The text of this speech was captured with the archives of the German Supreme Command at Flensburg.

The Old Story

This speech is an exceedingly long, rambling and disorganized dissertation, and the hard facts it contains are not always easy to discover among the jumble and tangle of historical reminiscences and political and "philosophical" reflexions. Even when closeted with his closest military associates Hitler cannot refrain from recalling, in a long and tedious introduction, his own past achievements from 1919 onwards which reads little differently from his public speeches.

He admits that there were many doubters when he marched into the Rhineland, reintroduced conscription, and ordered the general rearmament. Even the seizure of Austria was considered a hazardous step. But "it brought about a considerable reinforcement of the Reich. The next step was Bohemia, Moravia and Poland. It was not possible to accomplish this step in one campaign. First of all, the western fortifications had to be completed. It was not possible to reach the goal in one effort. It was clear to me from the first moment that I could not be satisfied with the Sudeten-German territory. That was only a partial solution. The decision to march into Bohemia was made. Then followed the establishment of the Protectorate, and with that the basis for the action against Poland was laid. But I was not quite clear at that time whether I should start first against the East and then in the West or vice versa. Under pressure the decision came to fight Poland first. One might accuse me of wanting to fight and fight again. In struggle I see the fate of all beings. Nobody can avoid a struggle if he doesn't want to lose. The growing number of our people requires a larger living space. My goal was to create a logical relation between the number of people and the space for them to live in." It is the familiar story known from earlier briefing speeches. To cut one's coat according to one's cloth is a "cowardly" solution and is rejected. "It is the one eternal problem," says

Hitler, " how to set the number of Germans in a proper relationship to the available space. No calculating cleverness is of any
help. The problem can only be solved by the sword."

Hitler goes on to state that 1914, with its war on several fronts,
" did not bring the solution of these problems. Today the second
act of this drama is being written. For the first time in 67 years
it must be made clear that we do not have to wage a two-front
war. What had been desired since 1870 and had been considered
as impossible of achievement, has come to pass. For the first
time in history we have to fight on only one front. The other
front is at present free. But no one can know how long that will
remain so. I have doubted for a long time whether I should
first strike in the East and then in the West. Basically I did not
organize the armed forces in order not to strike. The decision
to strike was always in me. Sooner or later I wished to solve the
problem. Under pressure it was decided that the East was to
be attacked first. If the Polish war was won so quickly it was due
to the superiority of our armed forces. We had an unexpectedly
small expenditure in men and material. Now the Eastern front
is held by only a few divisions. It is a situation which we viewed
previously as unachievable. Now the situation is such that the
opponent in the West lies behind his fortifications. There is no
possibility of coming to grips with him. The decisive question is :
how long can we endure this situation ? "

Hitler then reviews the position of Russia (discussed in detail
in Chapter V, Case Barbarossa) and comes to the conclusion
that the pact with the Soviet Union must be regarded as securing
Germany's rear, for "we can oppose Russia only when we are
free in the West." No time must, however, be lost since the
situation might change. The death of either Stalin or Mussolini
might " present us with a new situation." Scandinavia " is
hostile to us because of Marxist influences but is neutral now."
This is the only reference to Scandinavia in the whole speech.
It is noteworthy that Hitler ascribes Scandinavia's hostility
toward Germany to Marxist influences whereas in his dealings
with Quisling and his preparations for the invasion of Norway
this hostility is traced back to Anglo-American propaganda.
But at the time of this speech the contacts with Quisling through
Raeder had not been made, and the decisive interview had not
yet taken place. America, Hitler considers, " is not yet dangerous
to us because of her neutrality laws. The strengthening of our
opponents by America is still not important. The position of

Japan is still uncertain. It is not certain whether she will join us against Britain." And he decides that " everything is determined by the fact that the present moment is favourable whereas in six months it might no longer be so."

Again he tells his military leaders " in all modesty " that he considers himself " irreplaceable," and continues : "Neither a military nor a civilian person could replace me. Assassination attempts on me may be repeated. I am convinced of the powers of my intellect and decision. Wars are always ended only by the destruction of the opponent. Whoever believes differently is irresponsible. Time is working for our adversary. At present we have a relationship of forces which can never be more propitious but can only deteriorate for us. The enemy will not make peace when the relationship of forces is unfavourable for us. There can be no compromise. We must show sternness against ourselves. I shall strike and not capitulate. The fate of the Reich depends only on me. I shall deal accordingly."

It is in passages such as this that the personality of Hitler emerges in its full and fearful proportions.

He reviews once more the state of armament of his enemies, particularly the British Navy and British anti-aircraft defences and comes to the conclusion that Germany possesses superiority in material all along the line. But certain flaws in army personnel must have come to light during the Polish campaign. For Hitler goes on to say :

" I am most deeply pained when I hear the opinion that the German Army is not individually as valuable as it should be. The infantry in Poland did not accomplish what one should have expected from it. Discipline was lax. But I believe that the soldiers must be judged in their relative value in comparison with the opponent. There is no doubt that our armed forces are the best. Every German infantryman is better than the French. He is inspired not by exhilaration of patriotism but by tough determination. I am told that the troops will only advance if the officers lead the way. In 1914 that was also the case. I am told that we were better trained then. In reality we were only better trained on the barrack square but not for war. I must pay the present leadership the compliment that it is better than it was in 1914. Remember the collapse while storming Liège. There was nothing like this in the campaign in Poland. Five million Germans have been called to the colours. Of what importance if a few of them collapse ? We need daring in the

Army, Navy and Air Force. I cannot bear it when it is said that the Army is not in good shape. Everything lies in the hands of the military leaders. I can do anything with the German soldier if he is well led."

The Ruhr—An Achilles Heel

At last Hitler comes round to discussing the campaign now in preparation. He declares :

" We have an Achilles Heel—the Ruhr. The progress of the war depends on the possession of the Ruhr. If Britain and France push through Belgium and Holland into the Ruhr, we shall be in the greatest danger. That could lead to a paralysis of the German power of resistance. Every hope of compromise is childish. It is victory or defeat. It is not a question of the fate of National Socialist Germany but who is to dominate Europe in the future. Certainly Britain and France will go over to the offensive against Germany when they are completely armed. Britain and France have means of pressure to induce Belgium and Holland to ask for British and French assistance. In Belgium and Holland sympathies are all with Britain and France. If the French Army marches into Belgium in order to attack us, it will be too late for us. We must anticipate them. It is a difficult decision for me. None has ever achieved what I have achieved. My life is of no importance in all this. I have led the German people to a great height, even if the world does hate us now. I am setting this work on a gamble. I have to choose between victory and destruction. I choose victory. My decision is unalterable. I shall attack France and Britain at the most favourable moment. The breach of the neutrality of Belgium and Holland is meaningless. No one will question it when we have won. We shall not bring about the breach of neutrality as idiotically as it was done in 1914. If we do not break the neutrality of these countries, Britain and France will. Without attack the war cannot be ended victoriously. The question whether the attack will be successful no one can answer. Everything depends on the favourable moment. The military conditions are favourable. A prerequisite, however, is that the leadership gives an example of fanatical unity from above. There will be no failure if the leaders always have the courage the rifleman must have. Our chances are different today from what they were during the offensive of 1918. Numerically we can commit more than 100 divisions. The material situation is good. What is not ready today must be ready tomorrow. As long as I live I shall think only of the victory of my people. I shall shrink from nothing and shall destroy everyone who is opposed to me. I have decided to live my life so that I can stand unashamed if I have to die. I want to destroy the enemy. Behind me stands the German people whose morale can only grow worse. Only he who struggles with destiny can have a good intuition. During the last few years I have experienced many examples of intuition. Even in the present development I see a prophecy. I shall stand or fall in this struggle. I shall never survive the defeat of my people."

This is probably Hitler's most remarkable and revealing speech. It shows him at his best and at his worst—depending on which way one looks at him. It certainly shows the whole man in terrifying, over-life-size proportions. Once again one shudders to think what he would have done had he won the war.

More Postponements of " Case Yellow "

After Hitler's secret briefing speech to his Commanders-in-Chief on November 23rd, 1939, with its repeated emphasis on the necessity of losing no more precious time, it must have seemed as if the invasion of the Low Countries would now be undertaken in earnest almost any moment. Yet there was a series of further postponements.

On November 27th Keitel had to announce that the earliest date for A-Day (the day of attack) would be December 9th, but a new decision would be made on December 4th, 1939.

On November 28th, 1939, he issued a "most secret " memorandum dealing with the employment of the 7th Airborne Division to which reference has already been made. It states that "should the quick break-through of the Sixth Army, north of Liège, fail owing to the demolition of the bridges over the Maas and the Albert Canal, the intended employment of the 7th Airborne Division will be cancelled. Special orders for this event will be issued." The Führer, the memorandum states, was of the opinion that the 7th Airborne Divison " must on the first day of the attack be employed on another task and requests that the following possibilities be examined : (a) the occupation of Walcheren Island and thereby Flushing harbour or some other Southern Dutch island especially valuable for our air and naval warfare ; (b) taking one or more Maas crossings between Namur and Dinant with the object of keeping them open until the arrival of the mobile troops employed in the Fourth Army sector ; (c) securing of the territory north of Carignan and north-east of Sedan so that the mobile troops employed in the sector of Army Group A may be able to escape from the wooded heights south-west and south-east of Bouillon." Hitler requests the Supreme Commander of the Army, the Naval War Staff and the Commander-in-Chief of the Air Force to explore these possibilities "as quickly as possible." Once again he is seen to devote personal attention to the most detailed tactical questions.

But more postponements are to come. On November 29th, 1939, the time-table for "Case Yellow" is issued, but on December 4th, Keitel sends word to the three Service Chiefs that the earliest date is now December 11th. This is postponed further until December 17th, and on December 12th Keitel orders that "Christmas leave may be arranged by the three Services," since the earliest date for the attack is now January 1st, 1940. On December 27th, 1939, the weather forecast imposes a further postponement by "at least a fortnight," and on January 9th, 1940, it is announced that the next decision will not be made before January 10th, 1940.

On January 10th, 1940, a decision is made. An order issued by Keitel the following day (January 11th) states :

"On January 10th, 1940, the Führer and Supreme Commander of the Armed Forces, after receiving reports from the Commanders-in-Chief of the Navy and Air Force, and from the Chief of the General Staff of the Army, has ordered the following :

(1) A-Day and X-Hour :

A-Day is Wednesday, January 17th, 1940.

X-Hour is 15 minutes before sunrise at Aix-la-Chapelle - 08.16 hours.

The code-names " Rhine " or " Elbe " will be issued before 23.00 hours on A-Minus-One, provided the weather forecast permits.

" (2) Employment of the 7th Airborne Division.

The operation is to be carried out according to the instructions so far given, with the following modifications : for the 7th Airborne Division, besides the 'North' and 'South' drives a third drive (code-name 'Einsatz-Festung') is to be prepared for obtaining possession of the heart of the Dutch fortress. The Supreme Command of the Army makes preparations to enable it to break quickly into the Dutch fortress beyond the goal hitherto designated, i.e. the Maas-Grebbe line, should 'Einsatz-Festung' be the order given to the 7th Airborne Division.

K

The decision on the 'Einsatz-Festung' will be made at the latest on the morning of A-Day-minus-One. The 'North' and 'South' drives can only be considered if by A-Day a sufficient depth of snow improves jumping and landing conditions near Ghent and along the Maas which at the moment are fraught with difficulties.

"(3) Air Force attack on the enemy Air Force.

If the weather is suitable, the Air Force will on January 14th, 1940, attack with all available forces the majority of the occupied enemy air-fields in north-eastern and eastern France by surprise, with the principal aim of destroying the fighter and reconnaissance aircraft stationed there. For this attack the Air Force is at liberty to fly across Luxembourg and, as far as necessary, also across Belgian and Dutch territory."

But A-Day was not to be on January 17th, 1940. On January 13th, 1940 it was postponed until January 20th and thereafter nothing more was heard of it until May 7th, 1940. For in the meantime something untoward had happened.

On January 10th, 1940, a Staff Major of the 7th Airborne Division which had its headquarters in Berlin, made a forced landing on Belgian territory. The Major had been attached to Unit 220 of Troop Transport by Air and had been flying to Cologne to discuss the operational plan at 22nd Infantry Division Headquarters. He was arrested and interned, and in his aircraft there was found a sheaf of secret papers, containing instructions to the Commander of the Second Air Fleet which was stationed in the West. Allied Intelligence has since ascertained that the 22nd Division was specially trained for landing from the air in enemy territory. The secret papers which are in our possession contained not only detailed intelligence about British and French dispositions in France but what is more, very precise instructions where and how the 22nd Division was to drop and operate. It is highly probable that once he was reasonably certain that this officer and his papers had fallen into Belgian hands, Hitler saw his entire venture in jeopardy and felt obliged to think again. It must have been clear that with these precise and detailed operational plans in the hands of the enemy, the entire campaign had to be replanned and remapped. This alone, if nothing else—and we may assume that the weather continued to play its delaying part—would be sufficient to account for the long postponement which followed.

Operation " Weser Exercise "

Planning for the invasion of Norway had meanwhile been going ahead steadily. Preliminary work, it seems, had been cloaked with the code-word " Study N." On January 27th, 1940, Keitel issued an order which shows that things were beginning to take shape. It reads as follows :

" The Führer and Supreme Commander of the Armed Forces desires that ' Study N ' should be worked on, from now on, under my direct and personal guidance, and in closest conjunction with the general war policy. For these reasons the Führer has commissioned me to take over the direction of further preparations."

" A working staff has been formed for this purpose at the Supreme Command of the Armed Forces Headquarters and this represents at the same time the nucleus of a future Operational Staff."

Keitel then requests the Supreme Commands of the three Services to nominate one officer each for this staff and announces that " all further plans will be made under the code-name ' Weser Exercise '."

Political preparations, at this time, show some odd divergencies. Returning once more to Rosenberg's long report of June 17th, 1940, we find that while Quisling and Hagelin continued to send increasingly alarming information about the " active intervention of the Western Powers in Norway with the consent of the Norwegian Government," these reports were not confirmed by the German Legation in Oslo. " The Legation," Rosenberg says, " believed in the neutral intentions of the Norwegian Government and was further convinced that the Government would take up arms in defence of its neutrality policy. The Foreign Office (in Berlin) held the same opinion." Thus Rosenberg was hard put to it to prove that Ribbentrop's advice was worthless and that the information received by him from Quisling represented the true facts. Quisling's and Hagelin's reports grow more and more colourful, particularly after the *Altmark* incident, which Hagelin assured Rosenberg was a " pre-arranged affair " between the British and Norwegian Governments. But again " in complete contrast to these opinions the German Legation in Oslo, even after the *Altmark* incident, relied fully upon the good-will of the Norwegians. The Ambassador cited the signing of the German-Norwegian trade agreement as weighing heavily in favour of his point of view." However, Rosenberg succeeded in arranging for Quisling a further subsidy of £10,000 in British currency per month for three months commencing on March 15th, 1939. The remainder of this lengthy and cumbrous report is a highly-coloured narrative of British machinations in Norway, Norwegian connivance and urgent warnings from Quisling to take action before it was too late. It is designed to prove throughout that Rosenberg and Quisling were right in their forecasts, and Ribbentrop's Foreign Office wrong, and that events confirmed this. It contributes no further information on the actual planning of the invasion.

Dual Planning

" Case Yellow " and " Weser Exercise " were now being planned simultaneously, and it was a question which of the two was to be carried out first. We shall see that a decision on this vital question was not made until early in March, 1940.

Some insight into the later stages of this planning can be obtained from entries in Gen. Jodl's War Diary. They do not give us a complete sequence but the general development becomes visible.

On February 5th, 1940, Jodl notes that the special staff "Weser Exercise" met for the first time, was welcomed by Keitel (under whose orders it was going to work) and given its instructions.

The following day, February 6th, 1940, Jodl makes a remarkable entry. " New idea : carry out ' H ' (Holland) and ' Weser Exercise ' only, and guarantee Belgium's neutrality for the duration of the war." Nothing further is heard of this variant.

On February 21st, 1940, Hitler has a talk with Gen. v. Falkenhorst and charges him with the preparations for " Weser Exercise." Jodl notes that " Falkenhorst accepts gladly, and instructions are issued to the three branches of the Armed Forces." Gen. Fromm makes a proposal that the following units should be employed in Norway : 7th Airborne Division, 22nd Division, one regiment of the First Mountain Division, two divisions of the 7th Wave and a motorised brigade. It will be observed that the 7th Airborne Division and the 22nd Division were units earmarked for the invasion of Holland and Belgium and much discussed in this connection. Apparently a redistribution of forces is planned.

On February 26th, 1940, " the Führer raises the question whether it is better to undertake ' Weser Exercise ' before or after ' Case Yellow.' The Chief of the Home Defence (Gen.

Warlimont) is charged with examining this problem. The Führer decides that the Navy will have to wait with mine-laying from the air until the employment of a large force of aircraft is possible." On February 28th, 1940, Jodl proposes first to Keitel and later to Hitler himself that " Case Yellow " and " Weser Exercise " must be prepared " in such a way that they will be independent of one another as regards both time and forces employed. The Führer agrees completely if this is in any way possible." That afternoon the " Staff Falkenhorst" reports on preparations so far and Jodl explains to them the new basis for their preparations. According to his notes, Jodl suggested the following forces to be employed :

N (Norway) : 4 Parachute Companies
2 Mountain Divisions
22nd Infantry Division or 16th Infantry
2 Divisions of the 7th Wave. [Regiment
D (Denmark) : 1 Corps Headquarters
1 Police Division
1 Division of the 3rd Wave
1 Lines of Communication Division.

Jodl adds that " it is still under consideration whether the reinforced Rifle Brigade 11 should go to Group D (task force for Denmark) and then to N (Norway) or straight to N (Norway)."

On February 29th, 1940, Falkenhorst reports to Hitler who agrees with the proposals and shows himself very satisfied. " Führer wishes also to have a strong task force in Copenhagen and a plan, elaborated in detail, showing how individual coastal batteries are to be captured by shock troops."

On March 1st, 1940, the Directive for "Weser Exercise" is issued. It is signed by Hitler. It runs as follows :

"(1) The development of the situation in Scandinavia requires the making of all preparations for the occupation of Denmark and Norway by a part of the German Armed Forces (' Case Weser Exercise '). This operation should prevent a British encroachment on Scandinavia and the Baltic, further it should guarantee our ore base in Sweden and give our Navy and Air Force a wider start line against Britain. The parts which the Navy and Air Force will have to play, within the limits of their capabilities, are to protect the operation against the interference of British naval and air striking forces.

" In view of our military and political power in comparison with that of the Scandinavian States, the force to be employed in 'Case Weser Exercise' will be kept as small as possible. The numerical weakness will be balanced by daring actions and surprise execution. On principle we shall do our utmost to make the operation appear as a peaceful occupation, the object of which is the military protection of the neutrality of the Scandinavian States. Corresponding demands will be transmitted to the governments concerned at the beginning of the occupation. If necessary, demonstrations by the Navy and Air Force will provide the required emphasis. If in spite of this resistance should be encountered, all military means will be used to crush it.

" (2) I place in charge of the preparations and the conduct of the operation against Denmark and Norway the Commanding General of the XXI Army Corps, Gen. v. Falkenhorst (Commander of 'Group XXI'). In questions of the conduct of operations the above-named is directly under my orders. The staff is to be completed from all three branches of the Armed Forces. The force which will be selected for the purpose of 'Case Weser Exercise' will be under separate command. They will not be allocated to other operational theatres. The part of the Air Force detailed for the purposes of 'Weser Exercise' will be tactically under the orders of Group XXI. After the completion of their task they revert to the command of the Commander-in-chief of the Air Force. The employment of forces which are under direct Naval and Air Force command will take place in agreement with the Commander of Group XXI. The administration and supply of the forces posted to Group XXI will be ensured by the branches of the Armed Forces themselves according to the demands of the Commander.

" (3) The crossing of the Danish border and the landings in Norway must take place simultaneously. I emphasize that the operations must be prepared as quickly as possible. In case the enemy seizes the initiative against Norway, we must be able to apply immediately our own counter-measures. It is most important that the Scandinavian States as well as the Western opponents should be taken by surprise by our measures. All preparations, particularly those of transport, drafting and embarkation of the troops, must be made with this factor in mind. In case the preparations for embarkation can no longer be kept secret, the leaders and the troops will be deceived with fictitious objectives. The troops may be acquainted with the actual objectives only after putting to sea.

" (4) Occupation of Denmark ('Weser Exercise South ').

The task of Group XXI : occupation by surprise of Jutland and of Fünen immediately after the occupation of Seeland. In addition, having secured the most important places, the Group will break through as quickly as possible from Fünen to Skagen and to the east coast. In Seeland bases will be captured early on. The Navy will provide forces for the securing of the connection Nyborg-Korsör and for swift capture of the Little Belt Bridge as well as for landing of troops, should the necessity arise. The Navy will also prepare the defence of the coast. The Air Force will provide squadrons of which the primary object will be demonstration and dropping of leaflets. Full use of the existing Danish ground defences and air defences must be secured.

" (5) Occupation of Norway (' Weser Exercise North '.)

The task of Group XXI : capture by surprise of the most important places on the coast by sea and airborne operations. The Navy will take over the preparation and execution of the transport by sea of the landing troops as well as the transport of the forces which will have to be brought to Oslo at a later stage of the operation. The Navy will escort supplies and reserves on the way over by sea. Preparations must be made for speedy completion of coastal defence in Norway. The Air Force, after the occupation has been completed, will ensure air defence and will make use of Norwegian bases for air warfare against Britain.

" (6) Group XXI will make regular reports to the Supreme Command of the Armed Forces concerning the state of preparations and will submit a chronological summary of the progress of preparations. The shortest necessary space of time between the issue of the order for ' Weser Exercise ' and its execution must be reported.

Code-names are : ' Weser Day ' - the day of operation.
' Weser Hour ' - ' H ' hour."

The Directive shows that this is a complicated Combined Operation with a not fully unified command. Falkenhorst, in fact, has only conditional command of the naval forces which are to support his land forces, and units of the Air Force are only temporarily under his orders. Jodl notes in his Diary on March 3rd, 1940, that the " Commander-in-Chief of the Air Force opposes any subordination of units of the Air Force to 21st Army Corps." On the same day he notes : " Führer expressed himself very sharply on the necessity for a swift entry into Norway with strong forces. No delay by any branch of the Armed Forces. Very rapid acceleration of the attack necessary." And he adds the crucial sentence :

"Führer decides to carry out 'Weser Exercise' before 'Case Yellow' with a few days' interval."

On March 5th, 1940, there is "a big conference with the three Commanders-in-Chief about 'Weser Exercise.' Field-marshal (Goering) in a rage because not consulted until now. Won't listen to anyone and wants to show that all preparations so far made are worthless." Nevertheless, the results of the conference are recorded as (a) stronger forces to Narvik ; (b) Navy to leave ships in the ports (*Hipper* or *Lützow* in Trondheim) ; (c) Christiansand can be left out at first ; (d) 6 divisions envisaged for Norway ; (e) a foothold to be gained immediately in Copenhagen."

On March 7th, 1940, Jodl notes that Falkenhorst has a conference with the Commander-in-Chief of the Air Force, and the differences between him and Goering are apparently ironed out. "The preparations are now taking firm shape. The Führer signs a Directive containing all changes subsequent to the conference of March 5th, 1940. Nothing is to be changed any more now." This revised directive of March 7th is not in our possession.

On March 13th, 1940, Jodl's Diary contains this entry : "Führer does not yet give order for 'Weser Exercise.' He is still looking for an excuse." On March 14th, 1940, it is the same. "Führer has not yet decided what reason to give for 'Weser Exercise.' British keep vigil in the North Sea with 15 or 16 submarines ; it is not clear whether their reason is to protect their own operations or prevent operations from the German side." The Commander-in-Chief of the Navy (Raeder) suggests that it is "open to question whether it would not be better to undertake 'Case Yellow' before 'Weser Exercise.' There is the danger that in that case the British would immediately land at Narvik as we would have been the first to violate Norwegian neutrality."

A week later, on March 21st, 1940, misgivings are noted among 21st Army Group about the long interval between taking up readiness positions at 05-30 hours and the close of diplomatic negotiations. "Führer rejects any earlier negotiations as otherwise calls for help will go out to Britain and America. If resistance is put up, it must be ruthlessly broken. The political plenipotentiaries must emphasize the military measures taken and even exaggerate them."

Two entries in the War Diary kept by Raeder's Chief-of-Staff and containing naval orders in connection with " Weser Exercise " illustrate the kind of preparation the Navy was making.

On March 24th, 1940, it is noted :

" Orders for Reconnaissance Forces.

XI. Behaviour during entrance into the harbour.

All ships darkened, lights to be put on only by order of the Flag Officer Reconnaissance Forces. No personnel on deck except gun crews and other upper deck action stations. All army troops below deck. The disguise as British craft must be kept up as long as possible. All challenges in morse by Norwegian ships will be answered in English. In answer to questions a text with something like the following content will be chosen : ' Calling at Bergen for a short visit, no hostile intent.' Challenges are to be answered with the names of British warships :

Köln	- H.M.S. *Cairo*
Königsberg	- H.M.S. *Calcutta*
Bromsö	- H.M.S. *Faulkner*
Karl Peters	- H.M.S. *Halcyon*
Leopard	- British Destroyer
Wolf	- British Destroyer
E-boats	- British motor torpedo boats.

Arrangements are to be made enabling British war flags to be illuminated. Continual readiness for making smoke."

Also on March 24th, 1940, the following order is recorded :

" Prepared Signals Group III for possible traffic with passing ships and with land during entry into Bergen harbour.

The following is laid down as guiding principle should one of our own units find itself compelled to answer the challenge of passing craft.

(a) To challenge :	(In case of *Köln*) *H.M.S. Cairo.*
(b) To order to stop :	(1) Please repeat last signal.
	(2) Impossible to understand your signal.
(c) In case of a warning shot:	Stop firing. British ship. Good friend.
(d) In case of an enquiry as to destination and purpose :	Going Bergen. Chasing German steamers.

Enthusiasm for " Weser Exercise " seems none too great among the three services. Mishaps occur, too. On March 28th, 1940, Jodl notes in his Diary : " The Norwegians are interning U21, seemingly because of maladroit statements of the commander who did not claim engine trouble, but mistaken navigation. But it may also be that a mistake was made in translation. Individual naval officers seem to be lukewarm concerning ' Weser Exercise ' and need a stimulus. Also |Falkenhorst and the other two commanders are worrying about matters which are none of their business. In the evening, the Führer visits the map room and roundly declares that he won't stand for the Navy clearing out of Norwegian ports right away. Narvik, Trondheim and Oslo will have to remain occupied by naval forces. Bad impression on land forces."

On March 29th, 1940, " Führer talks to Raeder alone about the retention of the ships. Raeder rejects Narvik but wants to examine whether Trondheim cannot be set up as a base immediately."

On March 30th, 1940, Doenitz, Commander-in-Chief of U-boats, signs his own secret order with regard to the participation of U-boats in " Weser Exercise." It states that the code-word for the beginning of the invasion is " Hartmut " and that " the naval force will, as they enter the harbour, fly the British flag until the troops have landed, except presumably at Narvik." The order bears Doenitz's signature.

On April 2nd, 1940, at last, everything is ready. Jodl notes :

" At 15.30 hours Commanders-in-Chief of Navy and Air Force and Gen. v. Falkenhorst with the Führer. All confirm preparations completed. Führer orders ' Weser Exercise ' to be carried out on April 9th, 1940."

It was the final date.

Not One Day Longer

The second half of the double programme is carried out to the accompaniment of considerable excitement.

After a silence of many weeks on " Case Yellow ", a new order is at last issued on May 7th, 1940. This time it is signed by Jodl on behalf of Hitler. It states :

" A new A-Day will be ordered, according to the weather situation, at 12.00 hours on A-Day-minus-One only. A new X-hour will be given accordingly. Next decision at 12.00 hours on May 8th, 1940."

The former interval of five clear days has been cut down to 24 hours.

On May 8th, 1940, Jodl notes in his Diary :

" Alarming news from Holland. Cancelling of leave, evacuations, road-blocks, other mobilization measures. According to reports of the Intelligence Service, the British have asked for permission to march in, but the Dutch have refused. According to reports, the Dutch measures are partly directed against the coast and partly against us. It is not possible to obtain a clear picture, whether the Dutch are working hand in glove with the British, or whether they really want to defend their neutrality against the first attacker. Evaluation of the weather shows slow improvement of the general situation but development of fog in the next few days must be reckoned with.

" The Führer does not want to wait any longer. The Field-marshal (Goering) wants a postponement until May 10th, at least. The Chief of the Armed Forces Supreme Command (Keitel) presses for early action. The Führer is very agitated. In the end he consents to postponement until May 10th, which is against his intuition, as he says. But not one day longer."

The next day, May 9th, 1940, Jodl has this entry :

" Führer decides that he will definitely make a start on May 10th, 1940. Departure with Führer train at 17.00 hours from Finkenkrug. After a report from Jeschonnek that the weather will be favourable on May 10th, the code-word 'Danzig' is given at 21.00 hours."

The code-words for the starting and cancelling of the attack have been changed since the last directive. They used to be " Rhine " and " Elbe." They are now " Danzig " and " Augsburg."

On May 9th, 1940, Keitel issues the last of his many orders for " Case Yellow." It reads :

" The Führer and Supreme Commander has decided :

A-Day   May 10th, 1940.
X-hour   05.35 hours.

The code-words ' Danzig ' or ' Augsburg ' to reach branches of the Armed Forces by 21.30 hours on May 9th, 1940, at the latest."

The first stage of the Big Plan has been completed.

II

Otto to Alaric

German-Italian Relations 1937-43

On May 17th, 1935, Papen, the German Ambassador to Vienna, writes a long letter to Hitler in which he develops a complicated scheme how to undermine the Schuschnigg régime and force it into co-operation with the Reich. He suggests pitting Schuschnigg and his followers against Starhemberg who was then acting in very close concert with Mussolini, and compelling them to enter into a coalition with the illegal Austrian Nazi party, on the basis of which Germany would then offer a "settlement" to Austria, culminating in Germany's participation in the Danube Pact.

This plan is noteworthy for the view it takes of Mussolini's position. Hitler had met Mussolini a year earlier, at Venice, and the meeting had not been a success. At its conclusion the Italians had announced that the independence of Austria was secure ; a month later Dollfuss was murdered in Vienna and Mussolini sent his troops to the Brenner Pass ; his most important newspaper called Hitler's cabinet "a government of assassins and pederasts." The two men were far from being friends.

Thus Papen calculates carefully. His plan is designed to exploit both the German-Italian tension and the comparative unpopularity of Italy in the Danube countries. He foresees, in his letter, that "Schuschnigg may not be willing to follow such a pattern "—his own, Papen's plan—" but that he will in all probability immediately communicate our offer to our opponents." Who are these opponents? The next sentence makes it clear. "If Schuschnigg finally says No and makes our offer known to Rome—" "But," continues the Ambassador, "I consider it completely possible that in view of the widespread dislike in the Alpine countries of the pro-Italian course and in view of the sharp tensions within the Federal Government, Schuschnigg will grasp this last straw." There is, at this time, no love lost between the two dictatorships.

Two years later compulsory military service has been re-introduced in Germany, and the Rhineland has been occupied. On June 24th, 1937, Blomberg, then Reich Minister for War and Commander-in-Chief of the Armed Forces, issues a

" Directive for the Unified Preparation for War of the Armed Forces." In it the conquests of Czechoslovakia and/or Austria figure as primary objectives, and French intervention is foreseen. The Directive says : " Although we can in all probability, as matters stand at present, reckon with one or more allies in particular, individual circumstances, all elaborations and plans are to be based on the fundamental assumption that we stand alone for the time being." Who are the potential allies Blomberg envisages at this stage ? It is possible but not certain that Italy figures among them, for in a later paragraph the same Directive says that, in case of a war on two fronts with its focal point in the West, " at least benevolent neutrality is expected from Italy, Hungary, and Yugoslavia." It is of secondary importance what Germany and Italy are saying about each other at this stage ; their public utterances are made for propaganda and publicity purposes. What is important and significant is the parts they assign to each other in case of conflict with the rest of the world. Their true relationship is reflected in their secret memoranda, and here it appears that concerted action with Italy has, at this time, not even tentatively entered Hitler's calculations.

The Mediterranean Calculation

A few months later, Hitler's plans have matured considerably. On November 5th, 1937, he holds a secret briefing conference with his Service chiefs (the record of which has become known as the " Hossbach Minutes "), in which he discusses at length possible repercussions of the situation then existing in the Mediterranean, on his expansion plans in the direction of Czechoslovakia and Austria. He thinks it likely that the Spanish civil war, which he reckons will last another three years, will sooner or later involve Britain and France in a conflict with Italy, and this might give him the necessary freedom of action.

Britain, he explains, is greatly preoccupied because of " her opposition in the Mediterranean to Italy which—by virtue of her history, driven by necessity, and led by a genius—expands her power position and must consequently infringe British interests to an increasing extent. The outcome of the Abyssinian War is a loss of prestige for Britain which Italy is endeavouring to increase by stirring up discontent in the Mohammedan world."

This development suits him extremely well. But he sees further possibilities of Italy indirectly assisting his designs. Italian consolidation on the Balearic Islands, he believes, is bound to get Mussolini into trouble with both Britain and France, and he therefore determines to strengthen the Italians in their fight to hold on to the Balearics. (See Chapter IV, Felix and Isabella.) "The subjugation of Italy in such a war appears very unlikely. Additional raw materials could be brought to Italy via Germany. The Führer believes Italy's military strategy would be to remain on the defensive against France on the Western frontier and carry out operations against France from Libya against French North Africa. As a landing of French and British troops on the Italian coast can be discounted, and as a French offensive across the Alps into Upper Italy would be extremely difficult and would probably stagnate before the strong Italian fortifications, the Italian Navy would be able to interfere with French lines of communication and paralyze to a large extent the transport of fighting personnel from North Africa to France. Therefore, at her frontiers with Italy and Germany, France would have at her disposal solely her metropolitan fighting forces."

" If Germany profits from this war by disposing of the Czecho-slovak and Austrian questions, the probability may be assumed that Britain—being at war with Italy—would not decide to commence operations against Germany. Without British support warlike action by France against Germany is not to be anticipated.

" The date of our attack on Czechoslovakia and Austria must be made dependent on the course of the Italian-British-French war and would not be simultaneous with the conclusion of military agreements with Italy, but commence in full independence. By exploiting this uniquely favourable opportunity he (Hitler) wishes to begin the execution of operations against Czechoslovakia."

It should be noted, and has been explained elsewhere in these studies, that at this stage Hitler was planning the conquest of Czechoslovakia and Austria in a single, combined operation, with the proviso that if circumstances necessitated it, Czecho-slovakia—the more important prize—should have priority.

Among those present, Blomberg, the War Minister, Fritsch, the Commander-in-Chief of the Army, and Neurath, the Foreign Minister, voice their doubts. The generals state that " the war with Italy would not bind the French army to such an extent that it would not be in a position to commence operations on the Western frontier with superior forces." Fritsch estimates the French forces " which would presumably be employed on the Alpine frontier against Italy to be in the region of 20 divisions, with the result that strong French superiority would still remain on our Western frontier." Neurath remarks that " an Italian-British-French conflict is not as near as the Führer appears to assume." Hitler answers that " the date which appeared to him to be a possibility was summer 1938. Should the Mediterranean conflict lead to a general mobilization in Europe, we would have to commence operations against Czechoslovakia immediately. If, however, the powers who are not participating in the war should declare their disinterestedness, Germany would for the time being have to side with this attitude."

The pattern of things to come begins to show itself, although the calculation itself proves to be faulty. But Italy's role is already defined. She is a pawn in Hitler's game, and the prospect of a military agreement appears for the first time.

Case Otto

The Mediterranean War did not take place. Hitler's plans had to be revised. Without the Western Powers being engaged, at least partly, by Mussolini, the conquest of both Austria and Czechoslovakia in one single sweep must have seemed too big and hazardous an undertaking. The operation had to be carried out in stages, and if the first stage was to be Austria, Hitler could not count on Mussolini covering his flank and rear. Indeed, the memory of Mussolini's reaction at the Brenner Pass after the coup of 1934 seems to have been strong enough to prompt Hitler to exclude Italy completely from his calculations and present Mussolini with an accomplished fact. There is nothing to indicate that at any time during the preparatory stages of " Case Otto " (the invasion of Austria) Hitler took Mussolini into his confidence or at least dropped him a hint, but there is a good deal pointing at the opposite.

If Mussolini knew what was going on in Austria in the early days of March, 1938, he did not know it from Berlin. He received his information from Vienna where Schuschnigg kept in touch with him. But he decided not to intervene. The precise sequence of events is of interest at this point.

The plebiscite arranged by Schuschnigg for the following

Sunday was cancelled on March 11th, 1938, at 6 p.m. At 7.30 p.m. Schuschnigg resigned. At about 10 p.m. the German army crossed the frontier into Austria.

The previous day, March 10th, 1938, Gen. Jodl notes in his diary at 13.00 hours : " The Führer wants to transmit an ultimatum to the Austrian Cabinet. A personal letter is dispatched to Mussolini and the reasons are developed which force the Führer to take action." This letter was actually dispatched on the evening of March 10th, 1938, approximately 24 hours before German troops crossed the frontier. The bearer was Prince Philip of Hesse, son-in-law of King Victor Emmanuel. He telephoned Hitler immediately after he had seen Mussolini and delivered the letter, at 22.25 hours, on March 11th, 1938. That same night Jodl issued a special " Top Secret " Directive for " policy towards Czechoslovakian and Italian troops or militia units on Austrian soil " which says that Czech units encountered in Austria are to be regarded as hostile, while " the Italians are everywhere to be treated as friends especially as Mussolini has declared himself disinterested in the solution of the Austrian question." Since it was only from his telephone conversation with Philip of Hesse that Hitler learned that " Austria was immaterial to Mussolini," this Directive was clearly based on this late information, and it thus appears that Hitler and his army chiefs were still not absolutely certain about Mussolini's reaction to the Austrian coup at the time when the German troops had already crossed the frontier.

The German army clearly expected the Italians at least to repeat the 1934 performance, and to find Italian units on Austrian soil. It is probably true that Hitler would have regarded such Italian intervention, even if it took only the form of a " friendly participation " in the occupation of Austria and a securing of an Italian sphere of influence, as a very serious embarrassment. This fear, and his anxiety to avoid such a clash, would account for the rattled and somewhat hysterical tone of his letter and the fumbling manner in which he tries to explain his action to Mussolini. The text of the letter was published at the time by the German Government, and there is no need to reproduce it here. In contrast to the Hitler of later years, it betrays a remarkable lack of self-assurance and a good deal of nervousness. Although undoubtedly intended at the same time as a public proclamation to the rest of the world, it was in the first instance addressed to Mussolini whom it was meant to pacify. It speaks, therefore, for the lack of a community of outlook and absence of personal intimacy between the two men, that Hitler should have thought it necessary to regale Mussolini with a long and tortuous propaganda story which would have been quite superfluous if closer relations had existed between the two, and which Mussolini can hardly have swallowed. Hitler is at great pains to placate Mussolini whom he apparently believes to be very angry, and summons every argument that comes to his mind. He suggests to him that he would have acted in precisely the same manner, had he been in his place ; he reminds him that " in an hour critical for Italy "—during the sanctions period—" I have proved to you the firmness of my sympathy " ; he begs him to believe that this sympathy will not change in the future ; and finally assures Mussolini that the Brenner frontier is final, and that he has no designs on South Tyrol. It is the letter of a very worried man, full of pleas and promises and unsolicited assurances.

Mussolini's reaction was most gratifying. During the telephone conversation with Philip of Hesse, of which we possess the transcript, one can almost hear Hitler sigh with relief. Philip of Hesse reports that he has just come back from the Palazzo Venezia. " The Duce accepted the whole thing in a very friendly manner. He sends you his regards. He had already been informed from Austria. Schuschnigg gave him the news. He had then told Schuschnigg that it (the holding of the plebiscite) would be a complete impossibility, that it would be a bluff, that such a thing could not be done. He was told that unfortunately it was already arranged in this manner and could not be changed any more. Whereupon Mussolini said that Austria would be immaterial to him."

This is what Hitler had hoped to hear. He bursts forth : " Then, please, tell Mussolini that I shall never forget this." Hesse says he will tell him so. Hitler goes on : " Never, never, never, whatever happens, I am still ready to make a quite different agreement with him." Hesse answers that he has already told him that. But Hitler insists. " As soon as the Austrian affair has been settled, I shall be ready to go with him through thick and thin, and nothing matters." Hesse answers " yes, my Führer," and still Hitler carries on. " Listen, I shall make any agreement. I am no longer in fear of the terrible position which would have existed militarily in case we had got into a conflict. You may tell him that I do thank him ever so

L

much, never, never shall I forget that." Hesse answers that he
has understood. But Hitler is so carried away that he underlines
it once more. " I will never forget it, whatever happens. If he
should ever need any help or be in any danger, he can be
convinced that I shall stick to him whatever might happen,
even if the whole world were against him." At last Philip of
Hesse is able to bring the conversation back to the business
in hand. But it is obvious that Hitler has lost interest. He
answers "yes" to whatever his envoy says.

This telephone conversation requires no comment. It shows
the Hitler-Mussolini relationship, in a flash, as what it really
was at the time of the invasion of Austria. Hitler was terrified
at the idea that Mussolini might stab him in the back at a moment
when a European conflict, however localized, would have meant,
the undoing of his régime. When the danger is averted he thanks
him with sweat on his brow and promises him the moon and the
tars. In the upshot it was the military alliance between Germany
and Italy, the Pact of Steel, the " Axis." But it took another
year before it was concluded. Two days after this telephone
conversation, the same sigh of relief is heard over the Berlin-
London telphone wire. Goering is telling Ribbentrop what has
happened, and adds : " Besides, I must say, Mussolini behaved
wonderfully." And Ribbentrop answers from London : " Very
good, indeed. We always thought so ! " One has reason to
doubt that they did.

Mussolini's reply to Hitler's letter was contained in an official
communiqué issued on the morning of March 13th, 1938, after
a session of the Fascist Grand Council at which the letter had
been read. It seems that Mussolini must have been rather grateful
to Hitler for having furnished him, ready-made, with all the
propaganda slogans and phrases needed for the occasion.
Mussolini served them up as he had received them, placed the
entire blame on Schuschnigg and washed his hands of Austria.
After the exhaustions of the Abyssinian campaign and in view
of the strain imposed by the Spanish civil war, this was the only
thing he could do and could be expected to do. He was in no
mood to start a fresh quarrel with anyone, or even have a
" misunderstanding." He stood in dire need of all the help
and sympathy he could get. In the circumstances, although the
presence of the German army at the Brenner frontier was an
uncomfortable thought, nothing more welcome could have
happened than that Hitler should have felt his debtor. Two

months after the successful execution of " Case Otto," Hitler visited Italy, and a few days later, on May 14th, 1938, Mussolini made a speech in which he reverted once more to Austria and said :

" At 6 p.m., on March 11th, 1938, Italy once again found herself at a cross-roads which called for a decision."

What had happened at 6 p.m.? Two things—Schuschnigg had cancelled his plebiscite (of which Mussolini had disapproved), and the French Ambassador had inquired whether Italy was ready, in execution of the Stresa Pact, to take joint action with France and oppose Hitler's march into Austria with the force of arms, a *démarche* which Mussolini had rejected. The odd conclusion which one may draw from this is that Mussolini had already quite made up his mind what to do (or not to do) at a time when Hitler presumably was still cogitating how best to put the whole matter to him, and had most probably not even begun to write his letter. Mussolini concluded : " It was our sense of duty, of our honour and our loyal friendship towards Germany which prompted us to do what we did. Now these two worlds, the Germanic and the Roman, are in immediate contact. Their friendship is lasting."

The New Basis

The understanding over the Austrian question, imposed as it was by the force of circumstances, thus reveals itself as the basis from· which German-Italian relations develop from now on. It is not intended here to retrace this development in all its stages, since most of it is public knowledge, but merely to indicate the new points which emerge from the captured documents.

It is still a long way until the military alliance but considerably more trust begins to be shown by the Germans at this stage. Hitler is preparing the second half of what he had originally conceived as a double-barrelled operation against Austria and Czechoslovakia. This time the Italians are taken into his confidence, up to a point. Thus on July 18th, 1938, Ribbentrop had a conversation with the Italian Ambassador, Attolico, who told him, according to his (Ribbentrop's) own minutes, that " his compatriots Generals Russo and Pariani and others, who had visited Berlin a short while ago, possibly were of the opinion that France would not intervene militarily in a German-Czech conflict. He, Attolico, did not know what his own government thought about it, but he himself was of the opinion that these compatriots mentioned by him were mistaken, because France in the assumed case would have only the choice between intervention and complete resignation as a great power. The latter would not take place, however."

To this Ribbentrop adds : " Attolico further remarked that we had indeed revealed to the Italians our intentions against the Czechs unmistakably. Also as regards the date, he was informed that it was safe for him to go on leave for two months, but certainly not for longer than that. As an indication of the attitude of other governments, Attolico pointed out that the Rumanian Government had refused to its ambassador in Berlin the leave he had applied for."

Attolico's view that France would intervene was shared by Hitler and the German Supreme Command. A secret Directive issued by the General Staff of the German Air Force on August 25th, 1938, regarding the planned " Case Green " (the invasion of Czechoslovakia) is based on " the assumption that France will declare war during Case Green," and " Italy, Nationalist Spain, Hungary, and Japan are regarded as benevolent neutrals." On August 27th, 1938, Ribbentrop reports a further visit from Ambassador Attolico who communicates the following : " He had received another written instruction from Mussolini asking that Germany communicate in time the probable date of action against Czechoslovakia. Mussolini asked for such notification, as M. Attolico assured me, in order ' to be able to take in due time the necessary measures on the French frontier '." Under the date of September 2nd, 1938, Ribbentrop adds a footnote to this memorandum. " I replied to Ambassador Attolico just as on his former *démarche*, that I could not impart any date to him, that, however, in any case Mussolini would be the first to be informed of any decision."

The story of the Munich Agreement is known in many, if not all, its details, and the Nuremberg documents contain nothing that might serve to clarify in particular the part Mussolini played in bringing about this compromise. Hitler's own utterances, at later stages, indicate that he did not care very much for this compromise solution, since it spoilt his chance of parading his new army before an overawed world, and that he was more or less tricked into it by Mussolini. When the parallel situation arose over Poland a year later, he certainly expressed himself very frankly when he said he was " only afraid that at the last moment some ' dirty pig ' will make a proposal for mediation." Mussolini obviously tried his utmost to exercise a retarding influence on Hitler, on this and other occasions, knowing full well that he was not ready, and would not be ready for some years, to participate in the Führer's adventures on a promising basis, and that in the meantime the risks of being hitched to Hitler's chariot were excessive. On the German side this did not go unnoticed. As the Czecho-slovak crisis draws toward its climax, doubts arise among the military leaders. The expected "benevolence" on the part of at least some of the envisaged neutrals does not seem as fully assured as one had hoped. After a talk with Gen. Stülpnagel on September 8th, Gen. Jodl notes in his diary : " It must be added that Hungary is at least moody and Italy reserved."

The same doubts are found expressed in the secret Hitler Directive of April 11th, 1939, for the preparation of " Case White " (the invasion of Poland) where, in Annexe II, Hitler says : " Hungary is not a certain ally. Italy's attitude is determined by the Berlin-Rome Axis." On April 15th, 1939, Goering has a conference with Mussolini, in the presence of Ciano. Unfortunately only fragments, and not the full text, of the minutes of this conference are available, but the general tenor of what Goering said suggests that Mussolini was again worried and unenthusiastic, and that there was a need for the Germans to reassure the Italians and prove to them that so far all Hitler's calculations had been correct and his actions turned out to the advantage of both Axis partners. Goering is at pains, particularly, to justify the seizure of Czechoslovakia. " The heavy armament of Czechoslovakia," he says, " shows in any case how dangerous that country could have been, even after Munich, in the event of a serious conflict. Because of Germany's action the situation of both Axis countries was ameliorated, among other reasons because of the great armament potential of Czechoslovakia. This contributes toward a considerable strengthening of the Axis against the Western Powers. Further-more, Germany now need not keep ready a single division for its protection against Czechoslovakia, in case of a larger conflict, and this too is an advantage from which both Axis countries will in the last resort benefit." Finally he states bluntly that " the action taken by Germany in Czechoslovakia is to be viewed as an advantage for the Axis in case Poland should finally join the enemies of the Axis Powers "—which is, of course, the Goering way of saying " in case Germany decides to attack Poland," a decision, incidentally, which, by that time, had already been firmly made. " All things considered," Goering concludes, " it has to be stressed that the situation of the Axis is very strong and that it can defeat all possible opponents in a general conflict."

The extracts do not contain Mussolini's views. Was he convinced ? Whatever his misgivings may have been, he authorized Ciano to engage in negotiations with Ribbentrop for a military alliance between Germany and Italy. These took place in Milan on May 6th and 7th, 1939, and the alliance itself was signed in Berlin, on May 22nd, 1939. The very next day, May 23rd, 1939, Hitler held a briefing conference for his military leaders, in which Goering, Raeder, Brauchitsch, Keitel, Warlimont, Halder and several others take part. Hitler surveyed the political and military situation and announced his decision—" to attack Poland at the first suitable opportunity." And he added a little later, when discussing military preparations : " Secrecy is the decisive requirement for success. Our object must be kept secret even from Italy and Japan. The break-through through the Maginot Line is still a possibility for Italy, and must be studied. The Führer considers that such a break-through is possible." The basic idea has remained the same since the days of the Mediterannean Scheme. Italy is to tie down France on the Alpine frontier while Germany gathers another harvest in the opposite direction. One is not surprised that Mussolini remained cautious and reserved.

An interesting side-light, incidentally, on the advantages bestowed on both Axis partners by the seizure of Czechoslovakia, is thrown by the minutes of a conference which Goering held with members of his staff at Westerland on July 25th, 1939, on the question of increasing the German armament potential through exploitation of the armament industries in Bohemia and Moravia. Goering reveals that he offered Italy delivery of 88 mm. anti-aircraft guns from Czech works, but adds that " deliveries are only permissible to a certain extent after reaching the peak of capacity ordered for our own purposes. It is necessary that Italy deliver to us the raw materials required for Italian deliveries, *i.e.*, somewhat more than is necessary for production."

Berchtesgaden Conversations

Hitler's instructions were carried out. The true nature of his intentions and preparations against Poland were kept secret from the Italians. Mussolini was told no more, it seems, than was the rest of the world.

"However," says Ciano in his Diary, "In the summer of 1939, Germany advanced her claims against Poland, naturally without our knowledge. Indeed, Ribbentrop had several times denied to our Ambassador that Germany had any intention of carrying the controversy to extremes. Despite these denials I remained unconvinced. I wanted to make sure for myself, and on August 11th, 1939, I went to Salzburg. It was at his residence at Fuschl that Ribbentrop informed me, while we were waiting to go to eat, of the decision to start the fireworks, in a manner as if he were telling me about a most unimportant and commonplace administrative matter. 'Well, Ribbentrop,' I asked him while we were walking in the garden, 'what do you want? The Corridor or Danzig?'—'Not any longer'. And he fixed on me those cold *Musée Grevin* eyes of his. 'We want war'."

The following day, August 12th, 1939, both Ciano and Ribbentrop proceeded to Berchtesgaden where they met Hitler at Obersalzberg. A long and detailed discussion between Hitler and Ciano ensued of which the complete record is now available. It shows better than any other document the state of relations between the two allies on the eve of the outbreak of the Second World War.

Hitler began, with the help of maps, by outlining the strategic position of Germany with particular emphasis on German fortifications in the West. Describing in detail the vulnerability of Britain from the air, he went on to say that after the destruction of Poland, he would be in a position to assemble " hundreds of divisions along the West Wall, and France would then be compelled to concentrate all her available forces from the Colonies, from the Italian frontier and elsewhere on her own Maginot Line for the life and death struggle which would then ensue. The Führer thought that the French would find it no easier to overrun the Italian fortifications than to overrun the West Wall." In short, Hitler tried to persuade Ciano that Italy was really risking very little, and had nothing to fear. But here, the record notes, " Count Ciano showed signs of extreme doubt."

But Hitler had all Italy's work already cut out for her. In the event of a larger conflict, he pointed out, Poland would in any case side with the enemies of Germany and Italy, and therefore " a quick liquidation at the present moment could only be of advantage for the unavoidable conflict with the Western

Democracies." After that " the best thing to happen would be for the neutrals to be liquidated one after the other. This process could be carried out more easily if on every occasion one partner of the Axis covered the other, while it was dealing with an uncertain neutral. Italy might well regard Yugoslavia as a neutral of this kind. The Führer had told the Prince Regent on his visit to Germany that, with special relation to Italy, he should make a gesture showing that he sided politically with the Axis and was considering a closer connection with the Axis and a withdrawal of Yugoslavia from the League of Nations." Unfortunately, Prince Paul was trying to play the same double-game as Gafencu, the Rumanian Foreign Minister. They went on to London and attempted there to reinsure themselves. In the Balkans, the Axis could trust completely only Bulgaria as being, to some extent, Germany's and Italy's natural ally. Yugoslavia would remain neutral only as long as it was dangerous for her to side openly with the Western Democracies. If matters took a turn for the worse for Germany and Italy, Yugoslavia would openly join the other side.

After thus indicating to Italy the task he had assigned to her, Hitler switched the conversation back to Danzig and gave it a cunning point. It was impossible now for him to withdraw on the Danzig issue for this reason : he had made an agreement with Italy for the withdrawal of the Germans in South Tyrol and " must now take the greatest care to avoid giving the impression that this Tyrolese withdrawal could be taken as a precedent for other areas." In other words, if that were to happen, his whole war would come to nothing, as he would be giving away what were to be the moral grounds for his planned aggressions and territorial expansions. Besides, Hitler went on, there was a psychological side to the Danzig question which Italy would easily appreciate. " To make a comparison with Italy, Count Ciano should suppose that Trieste was in Yugoslav hands and that a large Italian minority was being treated brutally on Yugoslav soil. It would be difficult to assume that Italy would long remain quiet over anything of this kind." Again one is surprised that Hitler should still think it necessary to " propagandize " his own ally and in all seriousness treat him to stories of brutally treated minorities which they both must have known to be fabrications.

Ciano is frankly shocked and appalled. The record notes that " he expressed the greatest surprise on the Italian side over the completely unexpected seriousness of the position. Neither in the conversations in Milan nor in those which took place during his Berlin visit had there been any sign from the German side that the position with regard to Poland was so serious. On the contrary, Ribbentrop had said that in his opinion the Danzig question would be settled in the course of time. On these grounds, the Duce in view of his conviction that a conflict with the Western Powers was unavoidable, had assumed that he should make his preparations for this event, and he had made plans for a period of two or three years. If an immediate conflict were unavoidable, the Duce, as he had told Ciano, would certainly stand on the German side, but for various reasons he would welcome the postponement of a general conflict until a later time."

This is an instructive passage. It shows the extent to which Hitler left Mussolini in the dark about his plans, thus leading him to make preparations on an altogether false assumption. But it shows more than that. It is now quite clear that the difference between Hitler and Mussolini on the eve of the outbreak of war, was not one over aims or policies. It was not one over principles but merely one over the question of timing. Mussolini felt that he could not afford to start the war or take a major share in it for another two or three years ; Hitler was certain he could not afford to wait any longer since the present constellation seemed extremely favourable for him and would not return. The two allies were singularly ill-placed for concerted action at this moment.

Ciano did not hesitate to explain to Hitler Italy's position. With the aid of a map he showed Italy's situation in the event of a general war. " Italy believed," he said, " that a conflict with Poland would not be limited to that country but would develop into a general European war." As has been seen on other occasions, Mussolini's knowledge and judgment of the probable reactions of the Western Democracies was far more accurate and less clouded by delusions and wishful thinking than Hitler's. The Führer " commented that on this point there were differences of opinion. He personally was absolutely certain that the Western Democracies in the last resort would shrink from entering a general war." The overall plans which he had made for the attack on Poland (and for the earlier attacks on Czechoslovakia and Austria), show that he was by no means as certain as all that. He certainly always included at least the possibility, if not the probability, of British-French intervention in his calculations. But on this occasion, when it was a question of dissuading Italy from her justified fears and apprehensions, it obviously suited him to show himself as "absolutely certain." The astonishing thing remains the lack of confidence, sincerity, and frankness between the two partners who were, after all, agreed on their basic principle—namely to divide Europe and the British Empire between them.

Ciano answered he wished the Führer were right, but that he did not think he was. In any case it was necessary to consider the most unfavourable case, that is to say, a general war. He then proceeded to make a clean breast of Italy's difficulties, possibly slightly exaggerating them here and there, in order to drive home his points, but on the whole, it seems, truthfully :

"Since the Abyssinian war Italy had lived in a perpetual state of war and therefore needed a breathing space. Ciano gave figures to show how great the material effort of Italy had been in relation to the Spanish war. Italian supplies of raw materials were completely exhausted, and it was necessary to allow time for their replacement. Italian war industries which were situated on exposed sites must be moved south for purposes of defence. Italian artillery, especially anti-aircraft guns, greatly needed modernization. The long coastline and other exposed places were most insufficiently defended. The naval position was also most unfavourable. At present Italy could only provide two battleships to meet the eleven or twelve battleships of the combined British and French fleets, whereas in a few years she would have eight more ships at her disposal. The long Italian coast was difficult to defend, and the Anglo-French fleets had many bases at their disposal, particularly the harbours of Greece.

"Italy was especially vulnerable in her colonies although Libya was difficult to attack from Egypt, and the Italians might be able to reach Mersa Matruh. On the other hand, in Tunisia the position was very different. The relation between the Italian-Arab and the French-Arab population there was 1 : 20, while the strength of the European troops was 1 : 5 to the disadvantage of Italy. Furthermore, the Italian fortifications on the French frontier were completely insufficient, and new pill-boxes were needed."

Turning to the situation in Abyssinia, the minutes record Ciano as pointing out that "Abyssinia was almost pacified as far as certain areas along the frontier with British territory were concerned. This pacification, however, was only superficial. British gold and propaganda were raising trouble among the population. In a general war it would suffice for a few British aeroplanes to drop leaflets on Abyssinia stating that the world had risen against Italy and that the Negus would come back to cross the Abyssinian frontier. Furthermore, in the case of war Abyssinia would be completely cut off from Italy and the fate of the 200,000 Italians in the country would become most uncertain. Within a few days there would be an army of 4–500,000 men in Abyssinia able to advance successfully. In the event of war against the Sudan, Kenya, and French Somaliland, the islands of the Dodecanese would be in a difficult position owing to the attitude of Turkey. Leros and Rhodes, however, could defend 'themselves for years. Albania was a completely undeveloped country and could not, for some years to come, form a workable basis of operations against the Balkans ; roads would have to be built and it would be necessary to exploit the mineral wealth, iron, copper, chrome and oil, after which a successful advance could be made to Salonika and in other directions in the Balkans.

" In the economic sphere Italy had plans for autarky which would take some years for realization, after which Italy would be in a position to endure a long war without difficulties. An additional reason for the Duce's wish to postpone the conflict, was the question of the Italians abroad who should be brought back to Italy according to plan. There were a million Italians in France of whom about 700,000 could be regarded as still belonging to Italy ; the remaining 300,000, however, in the event of war with France, would be used as hostages, as was clear from the measures taken in France in September, 1938. Finally, the Duce attached great importance to carrying out his plans for the Rome Exhibition of 1942, for which large-scale preparations had been made and from which in the economic sphere and particularly in matters of foreign exchange favourable results were expected."

To conclude his arguments Ciano quoted the international political situation which at the present moment, in the Duce's opinion, was not favourable.

" In addition to these considerations especially affecting Italy, there were other factors of a general political-kind tending to favour the postponement of a general war. According to the Duce's view the encirclement policy of the Western Democracies would certainly function at the present time but, after an interval of time, the points of difference and the fundamental lack of unity between the parties of the encirclement front would make themselves felt and the front would accordingly break apart. Finally the Duce was convinced that the present strong feeling in Britain and France would not last very much longer ; especially in France the ' *union sacrée* ' would break up into party quarrels if sufficient time were allowed on the side of the Axis. At the moment the Axis itself was responsible for the fact that party differences had been set aside in the countries concerned. The position of Japan would also be considerably strengthened in two years' time after the expected conclusion of the China war, while the position of Roosevelt in America would be severely shaken after a period of external tranquillity, so that he would not be elected to the presidency for a third time, whereas his election was certain if war broke out."

Having explained all this at considerable length, Ciano finally submitted to Hitler Mussolini's proposal. The minutes state :

" For these reasons the Duce insisted that the Axis Powers should make a gesture which would reassure people of the peaceful intentions of Italy and Germany. This could be done by means of publication of a communiqué which Ciano had already drafted and given to Ribbentrop." The text of this communiqué is, however, not contained in the record as available, although the record states that it follows at this point. Furthermore, Ciano said, the Duce had in mind a proposal for an international conference. This proposal Hitler turned down on the spot on grounds which are discussed elsewhere in these studies. (Chapter V, Case Barbarossa). Ciano answered that in the Duce's view that party would win at such a conference which was prepared, in given circumstances, to allow the conference to fail and to face the eventuality of war as a result of failure. The Duce had, however, given consideration to the Führer's view and withdrawn his proposal. But since the Western Powers were not really ready for war, he was in favour of a peaceful gesture on the part of Italy and Germany. The Duce, who was obtaining very valuable information about the Democracies, was, however, convinced that the Western Powers would certainly make war at the present time if they were in any way driven into a corner by the Axis and saw no other way out. The proposed German-Italian gesture offered an honourable way out which the Democracies would certainly use in order to avoid war. Wide circles in their own countries were warning them against war, and the position of this anti-war party would naturally be considered strengthened by a peaceful gesture. Poland, from which the Western Powers would certainly draw apart, would be isolated after a certain time and be ready to accept reasonable solutions to the outstanding difficulties."

So much for Mussolini who cannot be said to have altogether misjudged the international situation, nor his own internal position. What Mussolini obviously did not know and what Ciano himself had only just found out, was that Hitler had long ceased to be interested in " reasonable solutions to the outstanding difficulties," if indeed he ever was interested in them. Hitler wanted to invade and conquer, not Danzig, or the Corridor, but the whole of Poland, once and for all. He " wanted war," as Ribbentrop had told Ciano casually just before dinner. Mussolini's schemes for international conferences and peaceful gestures, Ciano must have realized, were a wild goose chase. Nothing could have interested his ally less. Ten days later, in a secret conference with his Commanders-in-Chief, Hitler was to state openly he only hoped that " at the last moment some dirty pig would not make a proposal for mediation."

Ciano obviously realized at this point that he must " catch up with developments " and if possible " get the date," for there could now be little question of anything else. Hitler answered his inquiries bluntly. No time could now be lost; after the middle of September weather conditions would render a Polish campaign impossible. A settlement must be achieved " one way or another," by the end of August. He left no doubt in Ciano's mind which "way" he preferred, and that nothing could inconvenience him more than complete Polish acquiescence in all his demands. But he had already constructed the diplomatic situation in such a manner that it was virtually impossible for the Poles to accept even had they wished to do so. Once again Hitler gives Ciano a dose of anti-Polish atrocity propaganda, and adds that he " had resolved to use the occasion of the next Polish provocation for the invasion of Poland within 48 hours, and in this way to settle the problem. This would mean a considerable strengthening of the Axis just as an Italian liquidation of Yugoslavia would also mean an increase in strength." Ciano, trying once more to obtain precise information, asked how soon " action of this kind against Poland was to be expected because Italy must amply prepare herself for all eventualities." The Führer answered that "in the circumstances a move against Poland must be reckoned with at any minute." But he did not give him the date.

At the end of the conversation, Hitler told Ciano he would consider once more the proposal of a joint communiqué or statement, and that the talks would be resumed the next day. When they were continued, on August 13th, 1939, Hitler began by saying that he had considered the whole position, and that Ribbentrop had meanwhile told him that in the circumstances Ciano had decided not to conclude the conversations with a communiqué. "The Führer agreed with this decision. The door was therefore open. No one was committed, and no course was blocked." It is a fair assumption that this was Ciano's own, free decision and not imposed by Ribbentrop. Whatever communiqué Hitler would have been ready to sign, could, in the circumstances, have hardly met Mussolini's requirements, but merely committed the Italians, directly or indirectly, to a course which they had good reason to fear. It is highly probable that after the discussion with Hitler Ciano decided that Italy, for the time being, must retain her freedom of action and make up her mind independently. He could be certain that Mussolini would approve of this, and Ribbentrop had no choice but to let him go. To both Hitler and Ribbentrop it must have been clear at this stage that Italy would stay out of the war, at any rate during its initial phase.

But Hitler made one more effort to overwhelm Ciano with arguments. In a second lengthy *exposé*, very much on the lines of that of the preceding day, he detailed the reasons which made it imperative for him to strike at Poland now and not to postpone the conflict. He was still doubtful about the intervention of the Western Powers. "If the Western Democracies had already decided to move against the Axis, they would not in any case wait for three or four years before carrying out their plan and attack only at a time when the Axis powers had completed their necessary preparations, but they would press for an earlier conflict. If, however, they had not yet come to a decision in the matter (and the Führer thought that in view of the state of their armaments they had not), the best way of preventing them would be to deal with the Polish matter quickly. In general, however, success by one of the Axis partners meant increased strength, not only strategic but also psychological, for the other partner. Italy had carried out a number of successful operations in Abyssinia, Spain, and Albania, and each time against the wishes of the Democratic Entente. These individual actions had not only strengthened Italian local interests but had also reinforced her general position, and the same was true of German actions in Austria and Czechoslovakia. The strengthening of the Axis by these individual operations was of the greatest importance for the unavoidable clash with the Western Powers." Hitler added that Italy's interests lay in the Mediterranean while Germany "must take the old German road eastwards," and that therefore "the interests of Germany and Italy went in quite different directions and there never could be a conflict between them."

The minutes state that Ciano "thanked the Führer for his extremely clear explanation of the situation. He had, on his side, nothing to add and would give the Duce full details." Having said this, he made a last attempt to obtain the date of the attack on Poland from Hitler.

In order that the Duce might have all the facts before him, Ciano explained, he would ask for more information on one point. It might indeed not be necessary for the Duce to make a decision since the Führer believed that the conflict with Poland could be localized. He (Ciano) quite saw that so far the Führer had always been right in his judgment of the position. If, however, Mussolini had no decision to make, he nevertheless had certain precautionary measures to take, and therefore Ciano would put the following question:

"The Führer had mentioned two conditions under which he would attack Poland; (1) if Poland were guilty of serious provocation, and (2) if Poland failed to make her political position clear. The first of these conditions depended on the decision of the Führer, and German reaction could follow it in a moment. The second condition required certain decisions as to timing. Ciano therefore asked what was the date by which Poland must have satisfied Germany about her political position. He realized that this date depended upon weather conditions."

This time Hitler did not evade the question. He told Ciano that he would need 14 days for the decisive part of the military operations against Poland and another 4 weeks for "final liquidation," and since the whole must be over, for weather reasons, by the end of September or the beginning of October, "it followed that the latest date on which he could take action was the end of August."

This, then, was the date. The Italians had another fortnight in hand. Hitler ended by assuring Ciano that he was " personally fortunate to live at a time in which, apart from himself, there was one other statesman who would stand out great and unique in history. That he could be this man's friend was for him a matter of great personal satisfaction, and if the hour of common battle struck, he would always be found on the side of the Duce."

One does not know what Hitler envisaged as the " hour of common battle." Subsequent events indicate that he continued to reckon with immediate Italian participation, should the Western Powers intervene, although it must have been clear from Ciano's utterances that this would not necessarily be so. However, when the " hour of common battle " did strike for Hitler, the Duce was not found on his side.

Hitler, at this stage, was not altogether blind to the somewhat precarious situation in which Mussolini found himself at home. In his speech to his Commanders-in-Chief on August 22nd, 1939, he indicated as much. After referring to himself as " a factor of great value " and the possibility that he could be " eliminated at any time by a criminal or an idiot," he draws a parallel picture of Mussolini. " His existence is also decisive," he says. " If something happens to him, Italy's loyalty to the alliance will no longer be certain. The basic attitude of the Italian Court is against the Duce. Above all, the Court regards the expansion of the empire as a burden. The Duce is the man with the strongest nerves in Italy." Nevertheless, Hitler probably over-estimated Mussolini's hold on, and popularity with, the mass of the Italian people.

No Second Munich

Mussolini, as is known, did not give up hope for an international conference which would lead to a postponement of the general European conflict. He was certain that Hitler's war against Poland could not be isolated, and that a general war would ensue for which Italy was not ready but into which she would be drawn, sooner or later, and which she would then have to fight at a grave disadvantage. He endeavoured until the last moment, and rather beyond the last moment, to cut the Polish war short and bring it to a standstill. He made an all-out effort to bring about a second Munich, not for love of peace but to save Italy's neck.

The story of Ciano's *démarches* in London, Paris, and Berlin, between August 31st and September 2nd, 1939, with a view to calling a conference on or about September 5th, 1939, is well known from the official British White Paper and the French *Livre Jaune* on the events leading up to the outbreak of war. There is no need to retell it here. But the Nuremberg documents contain two papers—the only two referring to this phase—which add a new facet to this epilogue. They are a letter from Mussolini to Hitler, and Hitler's answer to it.

According to the French official Yellow Book, Ciano called the British and French Ambassadors to the Palazzo Chigi, shortly after noon, on August 31st, 1939, and informed them of the following : Mussolini offered, provided Britain and France accepted, to invite Germany to a conference which would meet on September 5th, 1939, with the aim of examining those clauses of the Treaty of Versailles which were " the cause of the present trouble." The invitation to Germany would be tendered only after Britain and France had given their assent, and immediate replies were desired. Almost precisely 24 hours later, on September 1st, 1939, at 11.45 hours and a few hours after the opening of hostilites by Germany, M. Bonnet, the French Foreign Minister, informed Ciano by telephone through the French Ambassador in Rome that France was favourably disposed towards the proposed conference, but that in the view of the French Government "such a conference could not be held without all interested and affected powers being represented, and that it should not limit itself to finding partial and provisional solutions to limited and immediate problems but should deal with the entire complex of general problems which were at the root of all conflicts, and should lead to a general appeasement which would permit the re-establishment and organization of world peace on a solid basis."

On September 2nd, 1939, at 14.15 hours Ciano telephoned M. Bonnet direct and informed him that he had forwarded to Berlin what he called " *notre projet de réunion d'une conférence*," without exercising any pressure and for information only. The Italian Ambassador in Berlin, Attolico, had just given him Ribbentrop's reply which was to the effect that Hitler was not opposed to considering the project but that he had before him a British and a French note which had been handed to him the previous evening. If these notes had the character of an ultimatum, his answer would be a categorical " no," and as a consequence he would be unable to consider the conference plan. Ciano wished

M

to know whether the French note was in fact to be regarded as an ultimatum. The British Ambassador had already assured him that the British note was not to be so regarded. M. Bonnet thereupon told Ciano over the telephone that the French note bore in no way the character of an ultimatum. Ciano, on his part, added that Poland would be invited to the proposed conference.

Five hours later, at 19.25 hours, on September 2nd, 1939, the French Ambassador in Rome, François-Poncet, telegraphed M. Bonnet (the message was received in Paris at 22.00 hours) that Ciano had also been in touch with Lord Halifax, the British Foreign Secretary, who had told him that in his view it would not be sufficient for the German troops to be halted in their present positions, as a prerequisite for an armistice and the basis for a conference, but that the territory already occupied should be evacuated. In these circumstances, Ciano had told Lord Halifax, he saw little prospect of obtaining German consent. But he would go on with his consultations and had asked the Ambassador to see him again a few hours later.

According to a second message from M. François-Poncet to M. Bonnet, despatched from Rome on September 2nd, 1939, at 23.10 hours, and received in Paris on September 3rd, 1939, at 03.10 hours, the British and French Ambassadors saw Ciano again at 19.20 hours when they were told that Lord Halifax had accepted the Italian suggestion on condition that the German troops were withdrawn to the Reich frontiers. Ciano declared that he did not feel he could address such a demand to Germany, and that this view was shared by Mussolini. He had, therefore, advised his ambassador in Berlin, Attolico, that in the circumstances Mussolini did not believe he could follow up his suggestion and that the Italian plan had to be abandoned. Before this message had actually reached him, M. Bonnet had telephoned Ciano direct, at 21.00 hours, on September 2nd, 1939, informing him that the French Government associated itself with Lord Halifax's stipulation. To this Ciano replied that he did not think this condition would be accepted by the Reich Government.

The plan for the conference, the second Munich, was thus definitely abandoned and dead, on September 2nd, 1939, at 19.25 hours, or at the very latest at 21.00 hours. Final confirmation that Ciano had informed Berlin that he did not propose to go ahead with the plan was received by M. Bonnet at 03.10 hours, on 3rd September, 1939. This is the point where the two new documents, published at Nuremberg, come in.

On September 3rd, 1939, at 02.50 hours, Woermann, Ribbentrop's assistant in the Foreign Office, sent a coded, top-secret telegram to the German Ambassador in Rome, for his " personal and confidential information." This telegram reached Rome at 03.00 hours and the German Embassy at 06.30 hours. It runs as follows :

" The Italian Ambassador (Attolico) handed to the State Secretary at the Duce's order the following message for the Führer and Reich Chancellor and for the Reich Minister for Foreign Affairs :

' Italy sends the information, leaving, of course, every decision to the Führer, that she still has a chance to call a conference with France, Britain, and Poland on the following basis : (1) Armistice which would leave the Army Corps where they stand at present ; (2) Calling the conference within 2-3 days ; (3) Solution of the Polish-German controversy which would be certainly favourable for Germany as matters stand today. The idea which originated from the Duce has its foremost exponent in France. Danzig is already German, and Germany is already holding securities which guarantee most of her demands. Besides, Germany has already had her " moral satisfaction." If she were to accept the plan for a conference, it would achieve all her aims and at the same time prevent a war which already today has the aspect of being universal and of extremely long duration. The Duce does not insist on it, but he particularly emphasises that the above be brought to the immediate attention of von Ribbentrop and of the Führer ! '

" The answer to the Italian Ambassador was promised by September 3rd, 1939. Signed : Woermann."

The document does not indicate precisely at what hour Mussolini's message was received in Berlin. But communications between Rome and Berlin were excellent, and it can be assumed that it was despatched from Rome during the late hours of the night of September 2nd, 1939. Even allowing for the time necessary for coding and decoding, there is every reason to believe that it went out from Ciano's office after his last telephone conversation with M. Bonnet which was at 21.00 hours. The contents of the message seem to bear out this assumption.

It is Mussolini's last, desperate bid for a conference, and in order to achieve his aim he does not shrink from telling Hitler a manifest untruth, or rather several untruths. At a time when he knew that Britain and France would accept nothing short of a complete withdrawal of the German armies to the frontiers of the Reich, he tells Hitler that " the armistice would leave the Army Corps where they stand at present." At a time when he knew from M. Bonnet that France was not prepared to be a partner to such an arrangement, he tells Hitler that " the idea has its foremost exponent in France."

The manoeuvre is transparent. Mussolini tried to obtain Hitler's consent to a conference at all costs, even under wholly false pretences, obviously in the hope of being able to induce Britain and France afterwards, in the light of Hitler's consent, to modify their conditions. He tried to trick all three powers (or all four, if one includes Poland), into an arrangement which had no basis in reality at all but which he hoped to establish, once he had them round the conference table. It is an extra-ordinary performance. But if Mussolini misjudged the Western Powers, he also misjudged Hitler. He was either still unaware or deliberately ignored the fact that there was no longer a question of Danzig. Ribbentrop had told Ciano that in all bluntness on August 11th. Did he still believe that all Hitler was after was " moral satisfaction". It is hardly credible, after what Hitler had told Ciano. Why then does he use this out-dated argument ? It is clear that he was terrified at what he saw was happening. His worst fears were coming true. He foresaw— and this is the one point where his clear judgment did not desert him—that the war already had " the aspect of being universal and of extremely long duration," and he knew that it would be his undoing. In his desperation he tried to lie and cheat himself out of it. But the last sentence of his message shows that he had not too much confidence in the success of his trick. He " does not insist on it " ; his main fear is, after all, lest he annoy his ally, arouse his genuine anger. And that, too, must be the reason for the pedestrian and old-fashioned way in which he despatches his message. Why, when Ciano can telephone personally and direct to M. Bonnet and Lord Halifax in a matter of such supreme importance to Italy, does not the Duce pick up the telephone and speak personally to his ally Hitler, or to Ribbentrop? Why, when the sands were running out and every hour was beginning to count, has he recourse to a written message which has to be coded and decoded and which has to go through the Italian Embassy in Berlin, thus involving a further loss of several hours ? It is possible that either he or Ciano tried to speak to Hitler or Ribbentrop over the telephone and that their partners in Berlin evaded the call by pretending not to be " at home." It is more likely that both Mussolini and Ciano were afraid to telephone, since Hitler or Ribbentrop might challenge their manifestly false assertions or begin to argue and haggle. The Italians were presumably quite prepared to lie to the Germans on paper and through their ambassador, but they had not the heart to do it, so to speak, to their ally's face.

But in any case, Hitler wasn't having a conference. Woermann's telegram promised a reply in the course of September 3rd, 1939. Hitler's letter, " to be forwarded to the Duce personally," was despatched to the German Ambassador in Rome on that day, at 20.51 hours. Hitler was in no hurry to answer. He let the whole day pass until he settled down to write his very illuminating message.

" Duce—First of all let me thank you for your last attempt at mediation. I should have been ready to accept, but only on condition that there would be a possibility of my obtaining certain guarantees that the conference would be successful. For during the last two days the German troops have been engaged in an extraordinarily rapid advance in Poland. It would have been impossible, by diplomatic intrigues, to render valueless the sacrifices in blood already made. Nevertheless, I believe that a way could have been found if Britain had not been determined to wage war in all circumstances. I have not given in to the British because, Duce, I do not believe that peace could have been maintained for more than six months or a year. In these circumstances I felt that, in spite of everything, the present moment was more favourable for resistance. At present the superiority of the German armed forces in Poland is so overwhelming in all fields that the Polish Army will collapse in a very short time. I doubt that so rapid a success could be achieved in a year or two from now. Britain and France would have armed their allies to such an extent that the crushing technical superiority of the German armed forces would no longer have been so apparent. I am aware, Duce, that the fight which I enter is one for life and death. My own fate is of no importance in it at all. But I am also aware that one cannot permanently avoid such a struggle and that one has to choose, after cold deliberation, the moment for resistance in such a way that the probability of success is guaranteed, and I believe in this success, Duce, with the firmness of a rock. Recently you have given me the kind assurance that you think you will be able to help me in a few respects. I acknowledge this in advance with sincere thanks. But I believe also—even if we march now over different roads—that fate will finally join us. If National Socialist Germany were destroyed by the Western Democracies, Fascist Italy would also have to face a grave future. Personally, I was always conscious of this common future of our two governments and I know that you, Duce, think the same way. Regarding the situation in Poland, I should like to say briefly that we should, of course, put aside all unimportant things, and not waste a single man on unimportant tasks, but concentrate everything on action in the light of overriding operational considerations. The Northern Polish Army which is in the Corridor, has already been completely encircled. It will either surrender or be wiped out. Otherwise all operations are proceeding according to plan. The daily achievements of the troops are far beyond all expectations. The superiority of our air force is complete although scarcely one-third of its strength is committed in Poland. In the West I will be on the defensive. May France here sacrifice her blood first. Later the moment will come when we can confront the enemy, also on this front, with the full power of the nation. Accept my thanks, Duce, for all your assistance which you have given me in the past, and I ask you not to deny it to me in the future. (Signed) Adolf Hitler.''

It is not necessary to analyse the jumbled and disconnected argument of this letter. It is not a carefully phrased diplomatic document but rather a careless, slapdash piece of writing which betrays Hitler's impatience with being bothered with '' unrealistic '' schemes. Its object is not to convince Mussolini but merely to tell him, without hurting his feelings too much, that the decision has been made without him and that he is in this war together with Hitler to the bitter end whether he knows and likes it or not. It tells him candidly and without much nicety that if Nazi Germany falls, Fascist Italy will fall with it, and that even if Mussolini now thinks he can branch off into a side-road, away from the war, the war will catch up with him and '' fate will finally join us,'' as indeed it did, in a most spectacular manner. Again Hitler does not trouble to telephone his friend and tell him so personally, but he sends the rude letter through the Embassy. The days when Prince Philip of Hesse was despatched to Rome and his reply anxiously awaited over the telephone, are gone.

One sentence in the letter, however, is of interest. Hitler says he does not, for the time being, intend to attack in the West, and will leave the initiative to the French while remaining himself on the defensive. At the appropriate moment, however, he will hurl his full forces against France, but there is no indication here that he expects Mussolini to join him when that moment arrives. In his speech to his Commanders-in-Chief of November 23rd, 1939, he reveals that he does not expect Mussolini to act until after Germany has seized the initiative in the West. In this secret briefing address which contains a general appreciation of the military and political situation as it presented itself after the conclusion of the Polish campaign, Hitler says :

" Much depends on Italy, above all on Mussolini, whose death could alter everything. Italy sees her great goal in the consolidation of her empire. Those who carry this idea are fascism and the person of the Duce. The Court is opposed to it. As long as the Duce lives, we can rely on it that Italy will seize every opportunity to reach her imperialist goal. However, it is too much to ask of Italy to join in the battle before Germany has gone over to the offensive in the West. In the same way Russia did not march into Poland until we had attacked. Otherwise Italy would feel that France has only to deal with her while Germany is sitting behind her West Wall. Italy will not attack until Germany has taken the offensive against France. As long as Italy maintains her present position no danger from Yugoslavia need be feared."

Presumably Hitler did not expect Mussolini to wait until the very last moment when, for all practical purposes, he had already crushed France and Italy's intervention, so far from affording Germany any assistance, reduced itself to a purely opportunist stab in the back. Nor, probably, did Hitler expect France to succumb so quickly. In the upshot he may have been satisfied with the way things went since he disliked sharing his laurels and could now claim the entire success for himself. Whether there existed a precise time table, pre-arranged between Hitler and Mussolini, and what the arrangement was, the Nuremberg documents do not tell us.

Hitler to the Rescue

From now on, German-Italian relations, as seen through the Nuremberg documents, become a long drawn-out story of Italian failures and increasingly frantic and less successful attempts on the part of Germany to rescue her from her difficulties, until in the end the ally deserts the floundering ship and jumps overboard. The Nuremberg documents do not provide a consecutive account, for which we shall have to wait until the captured archives are published in their entirety, but they do supply the documentation for certain important incidents along the road of Italian miscalculations and misfortunes. Every single one of them bears out the lugubrious forecasts made by Mussolini and Ciano before the start of the Polish campaign. The Italians knew how they stood and that they could not afford this war if it meant pulling their weight and really fighting it. Their only hope was to join in when their contribution was no longer required and to obtain a share in the victory without having to go and get it themselves. That moment seemed to have come when France fell and the war seemed over. When it turned out that Britain held and the struggle was really only just beginning, the Italians knew that they had not got a chance. Mussolini knew it, and Ciano had told Hitler so. A long war spelt the end of Mussolini. He knew what his position in Abyssinia and elsewhere in Africa was ; he had no illusions about his Navy ; he was painfully conscious of the poor state of his anti-aircraft defence and his dependence on German deliveries of arms and munitions ; he was fully aware that he lacked the support of the Court— he had told Hitler all that. He probably over-estimated his popularity with the Italian people, and he certainly had too high an opinion of the fighting qualities of his soldiers. These were two additional disillusionments still to come.

Hitler, it seems, at least in the early stage, believed that the Italian armies would do their part, strictly limited as it was. He certainly does not seem to have anticipated their spectacular failure in North Africa. In his War Directive No. 18, issued on November 12th, 1940, he states with regard to an " Italian Offensive against Egypt : "

" If at all, the use of German forces comes into consideration only after the Italians have reached Mersa Matruh. Even then the use of units of the German Air Force will be considered only if the Italians place at our disposal the air bases necessary for this. The preparations of the branches of the armed forces for use in this or any other North African theatre of war are to be carried out as follows : *Army*—holding an armoured division ready for use in North Africa ; *Navy*—fitting out of such German ships lying in Italian ports as are suitable as transports for the transfer of the strongest possible forces either to Libya or to North West Africa ; *Air Force*—preparations for attacks on Alexandria and on the Suez Canal, so as to deny the British the use of the latter."

The calculation was obviously that the Italians would be strong enough to break through at the frontier and capture the rail-head at Mersa Matruh but that they might need armoured support and assistance from the air to crack the hard nut of Suez. One knows how this calculation was confounded. In his Munich speech of November 7th, 1943, Gen. Jodl, looking back on the winter 1940-41, says :

" To the degree in which the weakness and failure of Italy became more and more manifest, North Africa became more and more a German theatre of war. Employing our forces in this way—incidentally, no great force was involved—appeared to be all the more justified since by this means strong British land, sea, and air forces, and a very considerable tonnage in the way of sea-transport would be kept tied down away from German ' living space '."

This was making the best of an avowedly ugly business which Hitler would have liked to see avoided. Jodl certainly minimized deliberatedly, for the sake of his audience, the volume of German commitments, but his appreciation of the effects of German intervention on British strategy was basically sound and correct.

But the really bad business began with the Italian attack on Greece.

Contrary to All Agreement

In this same confidential speech of November 7th, 1943, Jodl says : " What was however less acceptable was the necessity of affording our assistance as an ally in the Balkans, in consequence of the ' extra turn ' of the Italians against Greece. The attack which they launched in the autumn of 1940 from Albania with totally inadequate means was contrary to all agreement, but in the end led to a decision on our part which—taking a long view of the matter—would have become necessary in any case sooner or later. The planned attack on Greece from the North was not executed merely as an operation in aid of an ally. Its real purpose was to prevent the British from gaining a foothold in Greece and from menacing our Rumanian oil area from that country."

This is more or less the truth. Hitler had planned a campaign against Greece, based mainly on Bulgaria, and to be carried into Greece from the North, after most careful preparation and under favourable weather conditions. Italian assistance was probably envisaged but its main purpose would have been—as Hitler indicated many times—to hold off and neutralize the uncertain neutral Yugoslavia. The Italian "extra turn," sprung on Hitler as a surprise, achieved the opposite effect. It brought the British into Greece, and so far from neutralizing Yugoslavia, set the spark to that powder barrel. Small wonder that Hitler was annoyed. A long letter which he wrote to Mussolini towards the middle of November 1940, and of which portions have been made available, shows it.

"Duce! Allow me at the beginning of this letter to assure you that my heart and my thoughts have been, in the last fortnight, more than ever with you. Be further assured, Duce, of my determination to do all I can in the present situation to be of aid to you. When I asked you to receive me in Florence, I undertook that journey in the hope that I could make my thoughts known to you before the threatening conflict with Greece, of which I had received only general knowledge. I had wanted to ask you, first of all, to postpone the campaign, if possible, until a more favourable time of year, in any case, however, until after the American presidential elections. Above all, however, I had wanted to ask you, Duce, not to undertake this campaign without a previous lightning-like occupation of Crete, and for this purpose I had wished to bring along for you some practical suggestions for the commitment of a German parachute division and a further airborne division."

Later on in his letter, he refers to Yugoslavia.

"Yugoslavia must become disinterested. If possible she should become even positively interested in our point of view and co-operate in cleaning up the Greek question. Without security from the side of Yugoslavia, no successful operation in the Balkans can be undertaken."

And finally, at the end of his letter :

"I must, therefore, unfortunately, observe that conducting a war in the Balkans is not possible before March. Therefore any threatening move toward Yugoslavia would be useless, since the Serbian general staff know very well that it is impossible materially to back up such threats before March. Therefore, Yugoslavia must be won, if at all possible, by other ways and means."

Clear notice is here served on Mussolini that he must not expect any help from Germany before March, and that meanwhile, he must try to get along as best he can. If things go wrong for the Italian armies, he has only himself to blame for it. Hitler, however, loses no time in adapting his own plans to the awkward situation created by his ally. On December 13th, 1940, he issues War Directive No. 20 " Operation Marita." This was the code-word for the German campaign in Greece while the invasion of Yugoslavia was known under the code-name " Operation 25." At a later stage the two were combined and dove-tailed in a joint directive.

Directive No. 20 opens with this sentence :

" The result of the battles in Albania is not yet decisive. Because of a dangerous situation in Albania it is a double necessity that British attempts to create air-bases under the protection of a Balkans front be foiled, for this would be dangerous above all to Italy as well as to the Rumanian oil-fields."

Hitler then outlines his plan. He intends to form a " slowly increasing task force in Southern Rumania within the next months," and after the arrival of favourable weather in March to send this task force south through Bulgaria in order to occupy the Aegean North coast and " if necessary the entire Greek mainland." The support of Bulgaria is expected. The entire operation is based exclusively on German troops. Italy is mentioned only in the opening paragraph and briefly towards the end of the plan where it is said that " the question in which way ' Operation Marita' is to be supported by Italian forces, and how co-ordination of the operations is to be effected, awaits a later decision." Hitler had another three months in hand before he was going to strike, and he preferred to wait and see what Mussolini was able to do in the meantime.

But the Italians were in a bad way not only in Albania but also in North Africa. Hitler had to do some more quick planning. The outcome was War Directive No. 22 (" Participation of German Forces in the Fighting in the Mediterranean Theatre of Operations"). It is dated January 11th, 1941, and begins :

" The situation in the Mediterranean Theatre of Operations

demands for strategical, political, and psychological reasons, German assistance, owing to the employment of superior British forces against our allies. Tripolitania must be held and the danger of a collapse of the Albanian front must be removed. Beyond that, the Army Group Cavallero, in connection with later operations of the 12th Army, shall be enabled to start an attack also from Albania."

Two separate support actions are planned, one in Tripolitania, and another in Albania. The first bears the code-name "Operation Sunflower," while the second is called "Operation Cyclamen." The latter, as will be seen, was subsequently abandoned. Hitler now ordered a "blocking unit" to be recruited by the Army High Command, which "will be in a position to render valuable service to our allies. in the defence of Tripolitania especially against the British armoured divisions." This unit was to be transferred immediately following the transport of an Italian armoured division and a motorized division to Tripoli, which was then under way. The date envisaged was approximately February 20th, 1941.

Further, the Tenth German Air Corps was to retain Sicily as its base of operations. Its chief task was to combat British naval forces and interfere with their communications between the Western and Eastern Mediterranean. Besides, provision is also to be made, with the help of temporary landing fields, for attacking British unloading harbours and supply bases along the coast of Western Egypt and Cyrenaica and "thus give immediate support to the Army Group Graziani." The Italian Government had been asked to declare the area between Sicily and the North African coast a "restricted area" in order to "facilitate the operations of the Tenth Air Corps and avoid incidents against neutral ships."

Concerning Albania, the Directive orders German units "in the approximate strength of one corps, among them the 1st Mountain Division and armoured forces" to be held in readiness for transfer. "The transport of the 1st Mountain Division is to commence as soon as the approval of the Italians is received by the High Command of the German Armed Forces. In the meantime, it must be examined and determined in conjuction with the Italian High Command in Albania whether and how many more forces for operational attacks could be employed to good advantage and could also be supplied apart from the Italian divisions."

The duties of the German forces in both theatres are then defined. They are, to serve in Albania " for the time being as a reserve for an emergency case " and to " ease the burden of the Italian Army Group when later attacking with the aim of (a) tearing open the Greek defence front on a decisive point for a far-reaching operation ; (b) opening up the straits west of Salonika from the rear in order to support thereby the frontal attack of List's army." Directives regarding " the authority over the German troops to be employed in North Africa and Albania, and the restrictions which are to be imposed with reference to their employment " are to be settled between the German and Italian High Commands. Finally it is ordered that " every effort should be made to complete the transfer of the bulk of the German forces to Albania before the transfer of the blocking unit to Libya starts and the use of all German shipping becomes necessary for this purpose."

What is here referred to as a " blocking unit " was in fact the nucleus of Rommel's Africa Corps which was to grow into a very large and formidable army before it was finally defeated.

And What Will Happen to Us

A week after the issue of this Directive, on January 19th and 20th, 1941, Mussolini visited Hitler at his headquarters. He was accompanied by Ciano and Generals Guzzoni, Marras, and Gandin. On January 19th a military conference was held with General Guzzoni in which the latter developed his appreciation of the situation. On the following day Hitler, in what appears to have been a lengthy speech, gave his thoughts and views based on the staff conversations. Among those present were Mussolini, Ciano, and the three Italian generals as well as Ribbentrop, Keitel, Jodl, Gen. von Rintelen, Ambassador Schmidt and a number of other German officials. The minutes of both conferences are available. They bear the signature of Gen. Jodl.

General Guzzoni gives a somewhat coloured picture of Italy's military situation which the Germans receive with apparent scepticism.

Albania, Guzzoni declares, is the most important Italian theatre of war. " Although the front is not sufficiently secure to make it certain that the present line can be held against Greek attacks in all circumstances, there is no danger of Valona or Berat being lost." There are 21 Italian divisions now

Albania, and it is intended to send another three divisions from Italy. It is further intended " to form a group for attack on the northern flank, with the strength of about 10 divisions. These would include the three divisions still to be brought from Italy and 4 Alpine divisions." But this group will " not be ready for attack for another 2½ months, since transport facilities do not allow the 3 divisions or the personnel and equipment required for the reinforcement of the remaining divisions to be shipped any faster." Guzzoni intends to attack with this group in the direction of Korika. From there some units are to carry out a flanking movement to Erseke in order to cause the collapse of the northern part of the Greek front, the main body to continue the attack in the direction of Florina as soon as supplies are safe-guarded beyond Korika, where there is only one road available. Guzzoni explains that he has abandoned the intention of launching an attack with a limited objective along the coast in the near future.

These strategic details are now of no particular interest but for the reaction they provoke on the German side. Under the heading " Views on the Italian Appreciation of the Situation " and included in the minutes, the German Supreme Command remarks : " Very unlikely that the Italians will be able to muster the forces required for an attack within the time provided. Their support of a German attack from Bulgaria against Greece must therefore be discounted. The German attack will, however, bring strong relief to the Albanian front."

Guzzoni goes on to outline his intentions for the continuation of the campaign in Libya. He proposes to hold Tobruk as long possible and to concentrate on the defence of Derna, using the armoured units stationed at Mekili for offensive action. Reinforcements from Tripoli are to be sent to Cyrenaica in order to strengthen the defence planned there, in case the situation in Cyrenaica continues to develop favourably, thus making it possible to hold the western part of Cyrenaica. The minutes continue : " If Cyrenaica cannot be held, defence of Tripoli. The Italians believe that Tobruk can hold out for some time, and that the British will not advance upon Benghazi-Agedabia before the fall of Tobruk. The following reinforcements are earmarked for Libya—bringing the 3 divisions stationed in Tripoli up to full strength, transferring one armoured division and one infantry division (motorized) from Italy to Tripoli. Completion of these transports about February 20th, 1941."

The Germans comment on this as follows : " Whether or not Cyrenaica can be held cannot yet be determined. Unless the situation is basically changed, a loss also of Tripoli need not be feared, all the more since from May onward large-scale operations will no longer be possible, owing to the heat." A hand-written marginal note adds : " The loss of Morzuk is evidently considered trifling. *Conditio sine qua non :* no complications out of Tunis."

On East Africa Guzzoni is not too hopeful. " The situation will be difficult in case of a British attack which is expected in the near future. Defence to the utmost is intended. It is desirable to divert British forces from Libya to East Africa, even though it may render the situation in East Africa more difficult." German comment is contained in one sentence. " Duration of resistance in the case of a British attack cannot be estimated."

Finally the Dodecanese which have a strong bearing on the intended Greek campaign. Guzzoni says that " the expected attack on the Dodecanese has not yet taken place. Supplies are in hand for about 3 months. Forces in the Dodecanese are weak, nevertheless a certain offensive power in the case of a German attack upon Greece from Bulgarian territory, especially against British transports from Egypt into the Aegean, can be counted upon." The Germans think little of this. Their comment is : " No resistance of any significance is to be expected in the case of attack. Offensive action of the Italian forces stationed there against British transports to Greece cannot be counted on." A handwritten marginal note adds : " These ought to be built up to form an important complementary operation during the occupation of Greece."

So much for General Guzzoni. The German comment adds a note on the " Employment of German Units in Libya and Albania." In Libya " the Italians warmly welcome the despatch of the 5th Light Division (motorized). Shipment to Tripoli can begin approximately between February 15th and 20th. It will, however, be possible to carry out transport of equipment before that date." As for Albania " the despatch of a German unit is described by the Italians as desirable but not necessary. The despatch of a corps is impossible as transport facilities are inadequate. For reasons of transport, the despatch of only one mountain division with light equipment could be considered. A decision on this is not urgent at the moment.

An Italian attack—unless strong Greek forces are moved from the Albanian front to the Bulgarian frontier—is impossible in any case before the beginning of April, therefore the German unit need not be sent before March. Consequently, a new decision whether this unit is to be sent, at the beginning of March. Preparations for making a unit available will, however, continue."

The following day Hitler gives his decisions, based on the staff conversations. He explains that he is massing troops in Rumania for the intended operation against Greece, stating that it is " desirable that this deployment is completed without interference from the enemy. We must therefore disclose the game as late as possible. We shall cross the Danube at the last possible moment, and line up for attack at the earliest possible moment. For this reason, as well as owing to the difficulties of transport which came to light during yesterday's military discussions, it is not advisable at present to despatch a German unit to Albania. If it remained stationary behind the front, psychologically undesirable reactions would result, with the Italians in heavy fighting and the Germans looking on from the rear. On the other hand, if the German unit were employed, the war in the southeast, too, would be prematurely started."

Hitler then turns to Libya. " In no case must we despatch valuable units to places where they will remain inactive. We shall, therefore, send to Libya not an armoured, but an anti-tank unit which can be transported more quickly, and can still be employed before the hot weather sets in. For employed it shall be. We do not want to act like the British in France. The tanks and anti-tank guns in this unit penetrate any British tank which is in action there."

Finally, after a rambling dissertation on tank warfare in general and the excellence of German units, and passing references to Britain, the Soviet Union, and Rumania, Hitler has one more word about Italy. " The blocking of the straits of Sicily by the Air Force," he says, " is only a poor substitute for the possession of Gibraltar. We had made such preparations as would have ensured success. Once in the possession of Gibraltar, we would be in a position to gain a foothold with strong forces in North Africa, and thus put an end to Weygand's blackmail. If, therefore, Italy were after all to succeed in getting France into the war, this would be a great success and would basically change the situation in the Mediterranean within a short space of time."

What lies behind this rather cryptic remark, we do not know. The Nuremberg documents contain no further reference to it. How was Italy supposed to manoeuvre Vichy-France into the war on the side of the Axis? We know something about Hitler's preparations for seizing Gibraltar with or without the help of Franco (Chapter IV, Felix and Isabella), and we have been given to understand by Jodl that this operation was finally frustrated by Suñer. The seizure of parts or the whole of French North Africa with the help or connivance of Vichy and the elimination of Gen. Weygand was apparently planned as an alternative scheme. But what was Mussolini supposed to contribute to it?

Apparently everything here depended on whether or not he would succeed. The Nuremberg documents do not contain the answer.

Was Mussolini satisfied with the conference? Apparently he was. Ciano notes in his Diary on January 20th–21st, 1941:

" Mussolini says he brought him (Hitler) up to date on Italian affairs, and talked to him about the unenthusiastic but not actively antagonistic attitude of the King, and finally told him of the Badoglio affair which Hitler compared to the Fritsch affair. The Duce is on the whole pleased with the conversation. I am less pleased, particularly as Ribbentrop, who in the past had always been so boastful, told me, when I asked him outright how long the war would last, that he saw no possibility of it ending before 1942. And what will happen to us? "

The war lasted considerably longer than 1942, and what happened to Mussolini's and Ciano's Italy both Mussolini and Ciano had foreseen with great accuracy already in August, 1939.

A Pistol to Italy's Head

A fortnight later, the Italian situation in the Mediterranean, as seen by the German Supreme Command, has deteriorated still further. Besides, " Operation Marita " (the conquest of Greece) and " Case Barbarossa " (the invasion of the Soviet Union) are approaching and command all the attention of the Führer. The *coup d'état* in Yugoslavia is an additional complication, undoing much of Hitler's preparatory work in the political field.

On February 3rd, 1941, he holds a secret conference with his chief military advisers. " Barbarossa " (Soviet Union) and "Sunflower " (North Africa) are discussed. Keitel, Jodl, Brauchitsch

N

are present. The forthcoming invasion of the Soviet Union overshadows all other planning. But Hitler is seen to be most conscious of the dangers pointing from the south. He tells his advisers that " the loss of North Africa could be withstood in the military sense but must have a strong psychological effect on Italy. Britain can hold a pistol to Italy's head and force her either to make peace and retain everything or, after the loss of North Africa, to be bombarded. This would be to our disadvantage. British forces in the Mediterranean area will not be tied down. We ourselves have a weak base there through Southern France. The British have the free use of a dozen divisions and can employ them most dangerously, *i.e.*, in Syria. We must make every effort to prevent this. Italy must be given support."

For the first time, at any rate in the documents available, Hitler clearly states that his ally has ceased being able to stand on his own legs and has become a liability. To prop him up and keep him in the fight is now a vital necessity for German strategy. Italy must be given support. But how, in view of all the other commitments and the operations looming ahead?

" We are already supporting Italy with ' Marita '," Hitler continues. " We must, however, attempt to render effective assistance in North Africa. The Italians are of the opinion that they can put up a defence now only at Tripoli. This is not feasible. The Air Force cannot operate there. Therefore the position cannot be held. There must be some larger protection zone. Our blocking units can also be effective only in larger protection zones. What can be done? Land units will arrive late, if not too late. Graziani must receive some kind of support. Therefore the Air Force must be employed if possible with Stuka groups, with jumping-off bases and home-fields in Libya. If this can bring the British advance to a standstill, the intended blocking unit is still insufficient and must be reinforced by a mobile unit, *i.e.*, a strong armoured division. The British personnel and material must have been exhausted during the advance. If the British encounter fresh and well-equipped German forces, the situation will soon alter. The question is : Can we spare an armoured division for this purpose ? "

The Commander-in-Chief of the Army answers that he would do so only unwillingly from " Marita," and Hitler replies immediately that that is out of the question. The Army Chief adds significantly : " If it comes to that, ' Barbarossa ' is also in need."

What, then, is to be done ? " If we send help to North Africa," Hitler continues, " we must do so at once before the Italians lose heart. After all, we have made the offer to the Italians. The primary consideration is : can the Air Force intervene now ? The time required for the transport of Air Force supplies, blocking units and armoured divisions must be established at once. Then, what are the climatic conditions ? " The C-in-C. of the Army intervenes. " It is important that British supplies by land and sea are stopped. This can be done only by the German Air Force." Once again Hitler probably moans : If only we had Gibraltar ! The Chief of the Air Force General Staff points out the position of the ground organ- ization in North Africa. " Only in Benghazi are Stuka forces ready within range for operations. Fighter forces will naturally be sent there also, or Italian fighters be placed under German orders. It is most important that the air base of Malta be subdued."

The Führer agrees. But Malta is not discussed any further at this point. We know from the preparations for " Case Barbarossa " what high priority Raeder placed on the seizure of Malta before the war against the Soviet Union was begun, and that he was finally overruled by Hitler. All Hitler can suggest at this point is that " the Italians are to withdraw their fighters from the Channel coast." He will speak to the Duce about that. He knows what this Italian fighter force is worth. It showed itself but once above the Thames Estuary and was shot out of the sky. Nevertheless, Mussolini, who not so long ago asked for permission for his Air Force to take part in the Battle of Britain, must now swallow the bitter pill. " The Air Force," Hitler continues, " must test immediately the possibilities of intervening in North Africa. The Army is to see to the transport of the blocking unit. The transport must be speeded up. Reinforcement by an armoured regiment, further reinforcement up to an armoured division will be withdrawn from Marita." A little while ago this was still " out of the question," and the C-in-C. Army had shown himself " unwilling." Now the C-in-C. Army makes his condition. He proposes " a united command of all mobile forces under First General Headquarters and co-operation with the Air Force which also commands the Italian naval air forces."

It is a momentous meeting. The following conclusions are reached and recorded in the minutes :

" The Air Force must intervene as soon as possible with Stuka and fighter forces. Bases and jumping-off bases in accordance with decisions made in North Africa. It is desired that the Italian fighter forces be placed under German orders. The Tenth Air Corps is to take over the task of protecting the transports to North Africa, in closest co-operation with the Italian Air Force and Naval Command in Catania. The Tenth Air Corps is to strike a strong blow against the British troops in Cyrenaica as soon as possible, using heaviest bombs. Its main task is to disrupt British supplies by land and sea ; next, to combat the British fleet. But first of all, attempts must be made to subdue the air base of Malta. The Army is to continue the transport of the blocking unit. This, however, is to be reinforced at once with armour. Preparations for adding one armoured division (Staffel II from Marita). Anti-aircraft forces to move on ahead. First General Headquarters to be established immediately. United German Supreme Command over all mobile forces will be proposed to the Italians."

It is the end of Mussolini's Italy as an independent military ally.

Three weeks later, on March 27th, 1941, the *coup d'état* in Yugoslavia confronts Hitler with an entirely new situation, and he holds a secret meeting with his military leaders to discuss the position. Goering, Ribbentrop, Keitel, Jodl, Brauchitsch and a number of other officers are present. Hitler declares that Yugoslavia had always had to be considered an uncertain factor with regard to the coming " Marita " and " Barbarossa " operations, and that there was an advantage for Germany in having this revolution now rather than later when the consequences, particularly for the " Barbarossa " action, would have been considerably more serious. He is " determined, without waiting for possible loyalty declarations from the new government, to make all preparations in order to destroy Yugoslavia militarily and as a national unit. No diplomatic inquiries will be made nor ultimata presented."

What is Italy's part going to be ?

" It is important that action is taken as rapidly as possible," the minutes record Hitler as stating. " An attempt will be made to let the bordering states participate in a suitable way. An actual military support against Yugoslavia is to be requested of

Italy, Hungary, and in certain respects, of Bulgaria too. The Hungarian and Bulgarian Ambassadors have already been notified. During the day, a message will be addressed to the Duce. The war against Yugoslavia should be very popular in Italy, Hungary and Bulgaria, as territorial acquisitions will be promised to these states, *i.e.*, the Adriatic coast to Italy, the Banat to Hungary, and Macedonia to Bulgaria."

At the end of the conference Hitler " orders the immediate start of all preparations. He expects the plans of the different branches of the Armed Forces during the evening of March 27th (*i.e.*, the same day). General von Rintelen (who acts as military liaison officer with Mussolini) is ordered to receive the message and verbal orders from the Führer during the night of March 27th, 1941."

Attached to the minutes of this meeting is a " Tentative Plan for the Co-ordination of the German and Italian Operations against Yugoslavia." It is dated March 28th, 1941. It outlines the strategic plan for the German attack on Yugoslavia and states that " the following tasks result for the participation of the Italian armed forces : (a) Flank protection for the German attack group Graz by advancing towards the line Split-Yajele, with forces as strong as possible ; (b) shifting to the defence on the Greek-Albanian front and deployment of an attack group, in order to join with the German forces committed around Skoplje and in the South ; (c) elimination of the Yugoslav naval forces ; (d) at a later date, resumption of the attacks against the Greek front in Albania." Hitler adds that it is intended to favour the Croat independence movement in every respect and to treat the Croats as friends of the Axis. For this reason the Italians are warned to avoid air attacks on Croat territory. The time schedule is attached—attack against Greece April 2nd–3rd ; attack from the area south of Sofia April 3rd or 4th ; attack from the area around Graz and east of it April 12th. The plan bears a note in pencil : " Handed to Gen. von Rintelen on March 28th, 1941, at 4 p.m."

I Cordially Request You, Duce

The same day, March 28th, 1941, the letter to Mussolini is despatched through the German Ambassador in Rome. It is, coming from Hitler, a comparatively brief document but full of interest, and is, therefore, quoted in full.

" Duce—events force me to give you, Duce, by this, the

quickest means, my estimate of the situation and the consequences which may result from it.

(1) From the beginning I have regarded Yugoslavia as a dangerous factor in the controversy with Greece. Considered from the purely military point of view, German intervention in the war in Thrace would not be at all justified as long as the attitude of Yugoslavia remains ambiguous, and she can threaten the left flank of the advancing columns on our enormous front.

(2) For this reason I have done everything, and honestly have endeavoured to bring Yugoslavia into our community bound together by mutual interests. Unfortunately, these endeavours did not meet with success, or they were begun too late to produce definite results. Today's reports leave no doubt as to the imminent change in the foreign policy of Yugoslavia.

(3) I do not consider this situation as being catastrophic, but nevertheless it is a difficult one, and we, on our part, must avoid any mistake if we do not want, in the end, to endanger our whole position.

(4) Therefore I have already arranged for all necessary measures to be taken in order to meet a critical development with the required military means. The change in the deployment of our troops has been ordered also in Bulgaria. Now I would cordially request you, Duce, not to undertake further operations in Albania in the course of the next few days. I consider it necessary that you should cover and screen the most important passes from Yugoslavia into Albania with all available forces. These measures should not be considered as designed for a long period of time, but as auxiliary measures designed for at least two or three weeks to prevent a crisis from arising. I also consider it necessary, Duce, that you should reinforce your forces on the Italian-Yugoslav frontier with all available means and with utmost speed.

(5) I also consider it necessary, Duce, that everything which we do, and order, be shrouded in absolute secrecy, and that only persons who necessarily must be informed, know anything about it. These measures will completely lose their value should they become known.

(6) Today I called in the Bulgarian and Hungarian Ministers, and outlined to them my thoughts on the situation, and, with a view to military developments, tried to arouse their interest by explaining to both of them the negative and positive effects that would arise for them in this case. For without the aid of

Hungary and Bulgaria operations cannot develop with the swiftness which might be necessary under the circumstances. If possible, I will inform you, Duce, more thoroughly about all this in the course of tomorrow.

(7) If the weather is suitable for flying, General von Rintelen will therefore report to you, Duce, tomorrow, and will tell you the military dispositions which are being prepared and which we shall carry out. Duce, provided secrecy is observed regarding these measures, I have no doubt that, in case action on our part should become necessary, we shall both achieve a success which will not be smaller than the success in Norway a year ago. This is my unshakable conviction."

It is a stern and serious letter, but it is not as peremptory as one might have expected in view of the general state of German-Italian relations at this juncture and the heavy obligations under which Mussolini found himself to Hitler in Albania and North Africa. But for the first time in a long period, Hitler finds himself dependent on others, and not others on him. He is faced with a most awkward situation which he knows he cannot resolve without the help and loyalty of his friends and allies. The aid of Hungary and Bulgaria is urgently required, and Hitler is apparently hard put to "arouse their interest." Without Italian assistance, the entire operation would be jeopardised, and Hitler trembles lest Mussolini does another of his "extra turns" in Albania, and thereby endangers "our enormous front." But above all, he is afraid of Italian indiscretions, and exhorts Mussolini twice to keep the vital secret to himself, as otherwise his measures "will completely lose their value." He must have had some unpleasant experiences in the past. But if Mussolini, to some extent, has Hitler in his hand, Hitler in his turn has Mussolini by the throat. Neither can afford to drop the other. It is a curious situation.

On March 30th, 1941, the High Command of the German Army issues operational directions for the attack on Yugoslavia which bears the code-name "Operation 25." They begin with the sentence : "The Führer and Supreme Commander has decided to smash Yugoslavia as quickly as possible." It stipulates in precise military terms the details of Italian and Hungarian participation, stating that active Rumanian participation is expected, since Rumania's main task is protection against Russia, and that Bulgarian participation will be determined later. The order is signed by Brauchitsch.

Operation Alaric

This is as far as the Nuremberg documents take the inside story of the German-Italian alliance. There is nothing, so far, to illuminate the crucial period between the spring of 1941, and the Italian collapse in the summer of 1943. But there is one document which throws a good deal of fresh light at least on this last phase. It is the speech on " The Strategic Position at the Beginning of the Fifth Year of War " which Gen. Jodl made to a confidential meeting of German Gauleiters in Munich on November 7th, 1943.

Referring to the end of the winter campaign 1942–43 in Russia and North Africa, Jodl says :

" The complete failure of Italy in all domains and the absence of any munitions production worthy of the name among our other allies could not be adequately compensated by the tremendous efforts made by Germany."

And he goes on to analyse the subsequent Italian collapse.

" It was at this stage of the war that the Italian betrayal took place. Its main features will be known to you from what appeared in the press. Actually it was even more dramatic than the newspapers showed. For the Supreme Command it was perhaps one of the hardest problems which it had as yet to master. It was completely clear to the Führer from the first, that the removal and arrest of the Duce could not end otherwise than by the defection of Italy, although many politically less well-trained eyes thought to see in it rather an improvement in our position in the Mediterranean and our co-operation with the Italians. There were many people at this time who failed to understand the Führer's Headquarters in its political and military actions. For these actions were directed towards the overthrow of the new Government and the liberation of the Duce. Only the smallest possible circle could be allowed to know of this plan. On the military side, in the meantime, everything was to be done to stop enemy penetrations of the Southern front as far south as possible, namely on Sicily."

This German rush to Sicily, in a last-minute desperate attempt to stop the rot and establish a solid front, was known under the code name "Operation Alaric", obviously a deliberate allusion to the barbarian king of the Visigoths, who some 1,500 years earlier had invaded Italy from the North, sacked Rome, and made an unsuccessful attempt to cross the straits to Sicily and reach for North Africa.

" There was not the slightest doubt," continues Gen. Jodl, " that the enemy would bring his point of gravity to bear on some point further West in the Mediterranean. The distribution of his shipping and landing space made this clear. Where, however, would this point be? On Sardinia, on Corsica, in Apulia, in Calabria or—if the thesis of the betrayal were true— why not in Rome itself, or near Leghorn or Genoa? Unless he did this, our task was to hold as much of Italy as possible in order not to let the base of the enemy succeed in landing in Northern Italy. In that case all German formations in Central and Southern Italy would be lost. Moreover, no grounds must be given which might serve the Italians as a moral pretext for their betrayal, or by premature hostile action to commit the betrayal ourselves. In the meantime, the traitors simply over-flowed with amiability and assurances of faith. They even succeeded in making some of our officers who were in daily contact with them, doubtful of the truth of the betrayal hypothesis. This was nothing to be wondered at, for to the German officers such depths of infamy were simply incompre-hensible.

" The situation became more and more difficult. It was perhaps the only time in this war when at times I myself hardly knew what to suggest to the Führer. The measures to be taken in the event of open betrayal had been decided in every detail. The watchword ' Axis ' would set them in motion. In the meantime, however, all the divisions which the Führer at once caused to be moved from the West to Upper Italy, were operatively idle there—and that at a time when the East front, subjected to severe assaults, was clamouring for reserves more urgently than ever.

" How much meanwhile we had been able to find out through our troops and through the bordering ' gaus ', which were keen as sleuth-hounds on the track of Italian machinations, in the matter of manifestly hostile actions and preparations, is known to you all. However, somehow or other the Italians explained it all away, either as a misunderstanding or with excuses.

" In this unbearable situation the Führer agreed to slash through the Gordian knot by a political and military ultimatum. Then, on the morning of September 7th, the enemy landing fleet appeared at Salerno, and in the afternoon of September 8th, news of the Italian capitulation flew through the ether. Even now, however, at this last moment, the freedom of action

of the Command was still held up : the Italians refused to admit
the authenticity of the wireless message. The pass-word itself,
therefore, was not given, but only the 'stand by' for the troops,
until at last, at 19.15 hours, this most monstrous of all betrayals
in history was confirmed by the Italian political authorities
themselves.

" What followed was both a drama and a tragedy. Only
at a later date will it be possible to gather together and set forth
all the grotesque details."

But the story of German-Italian relations does not end here.
it had, as we know, a bitter and cruel sequel. Even from the
defeat of his ally Hitler extracted an advantage. Dealing with
Germany's most pressing problem at the end of 1943, the man-
power and labour shortage, Gen. Jodl says, later in his speech :

" Fortunately Italy's betrayal has its good side in this respect.
The flow of military internees and workers from Italy will afford
considerable relief in this domain."

III

Operation Sea-Lion
The Planned Invasion of Britain

" Our aim will always be to force Britain to her knees."

Thus Hitler in his secret speech to his Commanders-in-Chief on May 23rd, 1939, three months before the outbreak of war.

How was it going to be done ?

" A country cannot be brought to defeat by an Air Force," Hitler said in the same speech. " It is impossible to attack all objectives simultaneously, and the lapse of time of a few minutes would evoke defensive counter-measures."

Nevertheless, Hitler's strategy to " force Britain to her knees " begins with a bombing plan.

Bombs on England

On August 25th, 1938 when preparations for a German invasion of Czechoslovakia were going ahead at full speed and the Munich Conference was still five weeks away, the General Staff of the German Air Force issued to all commanders a top secret Directive on the subject " Extended Case Green." " Case Green " was the code-name for the invasion of Czechoslovakia, and its "extension", which at one time had the separate code-name " Case Red," signified simultaneous war in the West as a result of France, with active military assistance from Britain, opening hostilities against Germany in fulfilment of her treaty obligations toward Czechoslovakia. Operational plans for the German Air Force were made on this assumption. But the *Luftwaffe* in 1938 was not yet an overwhelmingly powerful force. It had to husband its resources carefully, and concentrate on the most important targets in order to achieve maximum results.

The chief target area was, of course, France. But Britain was an immediate second. In a special chapter dealing with " preparation of target data," the Directive states :

" Basic target maps of British ground organization (airfields) are approximately 90 per cent. ready. They have been passed on to Air Force Group II for printing and for the adding of sectional excerpts of maps. They have been ordered to be ready by September 15th, 1938. As far as essential industrial targets are concerned, work has been carried out on the food and crude oil supply systems and docks in the London and Hull areas, *i.e.*, basic target maps, sector maps, partly covered also by aerial and ground panoramas. These will be reproduced after the ground organization targets have been printed. They cannot be expected to be ready before October 20th, 1938. Tactical maps of London and Hull will be issued to the Command authorities prior to the end of September."

That was in August 1938. The bombing of London, as can be seen, had even then a high priority, at least in the planning. As to execution of these plans, there were serious difficulties which the Directive points out. The following section, "Recommendations for our own Prosecution of the Air War," states :

"A negative answer must be given to the question as to whether it is appropriate to postpone the massed commitment of our striking power until the spring. The balance of forces would probably have altered by that time to our disadvantage owing to further progress of French and British aircraft industry and imports from North America."

We are still two years away from the Battle of Britain which actually just tipped the balance to Germany's disadvantage, yet so conscious was Goering's Air Staff of their own short-comings that even then they did not think they could afford to wait six months for fear of losing their superiority. The Directive continues :

"As our forces must be regarded as small, even if we accept the figure of 5 Air Fleets as a basis, the task can only be fulfilled by concentrated blows directed against the enemy's weakest points. For this purpose the choice of targets must be made with the greatest care and must be limited to the decisive points." After stating that "attacks on Paris should only be carried out as a reprisal." the Directive lays it down that "attacks against objectives in the British Isles are to be regarded as unjustifiable in view of the small numbers of our combat forces."

Later, after having emphasized once more that in addition to the tasks allotted to the Air Force in France "no large-scale operations against targets in the British Isles could be carried out," the Directive goes on to say :

"Everything should, however, be prepared to make reprisal attacks against London possible at any time. Considering the strength of the air defences in and around London, success in such attacks is only likely if strong forces are committed. In addition, occasional harassing attacks against targets in Southern and South-eastern England may be worthy of consideration, particularly if the weather enforces a lull in France. A secondary aim of such attacks would be to pin down strong defence forces in Great Britain. Should still stronger war plane forces—at least 3 Air Fleets—be available after the French targets have been attacked successfully, they might be committed to advantage in attacks against the food supply of Britain, notably of London. It must, however, be emphasized that it is only regarded as possible to achieve decisive successes if considerably stronger forces are committed, and if the western ports are also subjected to air attacks."

Those were the days, apparently, when Goering was still comparatively modest ; when he still showed a sober and realistic appreciation of what his own, limited forces could achieve in addition to what would today seem a rather exaggerated estimate of British defensive capacity at that time. If one looks back on this plan today, in the light of what actually happened during the air war over Britain, the entire picture strikes one as somewhat askew and out of focus. But it does contain already all the elements of later happenings, and in the two years that were still to pass, the discrepancies, at least on the German side, reduced themselves considerably.

Lessons of the Last War ?

With the whole of Czechoslovakia in his pocket, Hitler at once considered all factors which would come into play were he involved in war against Britain and France as a result of his planned attack against Poland. In his briefing conference with his Commanders-in-Chief on May 23rd, 1939, he dwells at length on Britain. He comes to the conclusion that " England is the main driving force against Germany " and determines that her strength resides in the following factors :

" The British are proud, courageous, tenacious, firm in resistance and gifted as organizers. They know how to exploit every new development. They have the love of adventure and bravery of the Nordic race. Quality is lowered by dispersal. The German average is higher.

" World power as such. It has been constant for 300 years. It has been extended by the acquisition of allies. This power is not merely something concrete, but must also be considered as a psychological force embracing the entire world. Add to this immeasurable wealth, with the resultant financial credit.

" Finally, geo-political safety and protection by strong sea power and a courageous air force."

It cannot be said that this is a superficial or inaccurate analysis. This time war is near, and Hitler does not believe in another compromise. It is in this speech that he declares his aim to be " to force Britain to her knees," that he admits that by air power alone it cannot be done.

How then can it be achieved ? Hitler analyses Britain's weaknesses.

" If in the First World War we had had two battleships and two cruisers more, and if the Battle of Jutland had begun in the morning, the British fleet would have been defeated, and England brought to her knees. It would have meant the end of that war. In the old days it was not sufficient to defeat the Navy ; landings had to be made in order to defeat England. In those days England was able to provide her own food supplies. Today this is no longer possible." It follows, for Hitler, that " the moment Britain's food supply routes are cut, she is forced to capitulate. Her imports of food and oil depend for their protection on the Navy. If the German Air Force attacks British territory, Britain will not be forced to capitulate in one day. But if the Navy is destroyed, immediate capitulation will be the result. There is no doubt that a surprise attack can lead to a quick decision. It would be criminal, however, for the government to rely entirely on the element of surprise. Experience has shown that surprise may be nullified by (1) disclosure outside the military circles immediately concerned ; (2) mere chance which may cause the collapse of the whole enterprise ; (3) human failings ; (4) weather conditions."

It is interesting that, at this date, Hitler considered actual landings in Britain an antiquated and unnecessary method of forcing her into capitulation. Many people would probably have agreed with him at that time, not only in Germany. But what is more interesting and considerably more odd than the fact that finally he was reduced to trying this antiquated method, is his apparent confidence that the combined Nazi Navy and Air Force would be able to knock out the combined British Navy and Air Force. For that is obviously his plan, although he makes it clear that he envisages it as a surprise stroke out of the blue, an isolated, wholly unexpected action. And this " will only be possible if we are not involved in a war with England on account of Poland."

Assuming then, that it would be possible to keep clear of Britain at least in the initial stages of the war, he lays down that " the final date for striking must be fixed well in advance. Beyond that time the tension cannot be endured for long. It must be borne in mind that weather conditions can render any surprise intervention by Navy and Air Force impossible. An effort must be made to deal the enemy a significant or the final and decisive blow. Considerations of right or wrong, or treaties do not enter into the matter." In order to achieve this, " the Army will have to hold positions essential to the Navy and Air Force. If Holland and Belgium are successfully occupied and held, and if France is also defeated, the fundamental conditions for a successful war against Britain will have been secured. Britain can then be blockaded from Western France at close quarters by the Air Force while the Navy with its submarines can extend the range of the blockade."

Here then is the precise pattern of things to come. What will be the outcome of this position ? Hitler explains :

(a) Britain will not be able to fight on the Continent.
(b) Daily attacks by the Air Force and Navy will cut all her lifelines.
(c) Time will not be on Britain's side.
(d) Germany will not bleed to death on land.

This strategy, Hitler declares, " has been shown to be necessary by the First World War and subsequent military operations. The First World War is responsible for the following strategic considerations which are imperative :

(1) With a more powerful Navy at the outbreak of the war, or a wheeling movement by the Army towards the Channel ports, the end would have been different ;
(2) A country cannot be brought to defeat by an Air Force. It is impossible to attack all objectives simultaneously and the lapse of a few minutes would evoke counter-measures ;
(3) The unrestricted use of all resources is essential ;
(4) Once the Army, in co-operation with Air Force and Navy, has taken the most important positions, industrial production will cease to flow into the bottomless pit of the Army's battles and can be diverted to the benefit of Air Force and Navy.
(5) A weapon will only be of decisive importance in winning battles as long as the enemy does not possess it. This

applies to gas, submarines, and the Air Force. It would be true of the latter, for instance, as long as the British Navy had no counter-measures. This will no longer be the case in 1940 and 1941."

The Pattern Changes

So far the basic assumption underlying Hitler's strategic planning against Britain had been that he would succeed in keeping Britain out of the war altogether, and pounce upon her with all his might and without warning at a moment chosen by him. This lightning stroke would have been preceded by a surprise invasion of France and the Low Countries and an occupation of the Channel and Atlantic coasts.

Things did not work out that way. When Britain and France declared war following the invasion of Poland, Hitler immediately revised his strategic pattern and did the next best thing. If he could not keep Britain out of the war, he would refuse to fight her (and France), and remain entirely on the defensive.

" Directive No. 1 for the Conduct of the War " issued and signed by Hitler on August 31st, 1939, states emphatically : " In the West it is important that the responsibility for the opening of hostilities should rest unequivocally with Britain and France. The German land frontier in the West is not to be crossed at any point without my express consent. The same applies to warlike actions at sea or any which may be so interpreted."

There is, however, an important exception. " In its warfare on merchant shipping the Navy is to concentrate on Britain. To intensify the effect of this, a declaration of danger zones is to be expected." And further on, " in waging war against Britain preparations should be made for the use of the Air Force in causing damage to sea transport, the armament industry, and troop transports to France. Full use should be made of favourable opportunities to make an effective attack on massed British naval units, especially battleships and aircraft carriers." The Directive ends with these words :

" The decision regarding attacks on London rests with me. Attacks on the English mother country should be prepared, bearing in mind that whatever happens, inadequate success with part forces is to be avoided."

On November 23rd, 1939, after the conclusion of the Polish campaign, Hitler called his Commanders-in-Chief together and reviewed the situation for them. The record of this speech was found among the archives of the German Supreme Command at Flensburg.

" I am disturbed by the increasingly strong appearance of the British," Hitler declared. " The British are a tough enemy, above all in defence. There is no doubt that Britain will be very much represented in France at the latest in six to eight months." Very little, if anything is left of the original Anglo-German constellation as Hitler had imagined it. Not only has he not been able to keep the British out of the war until the moment chosen by him, but his second-best calculation, namely, of not having to fight them on the Continent, seems equally to turn into a miscalculation. In the circumstances his main attention is concentrated on cutting Britain's life-lines and paralyzing her food supplies. But the difficulty is still how to get at Britain. " U-boats, mines, and the Air Force could strike against Britain effectively if we had a better base to start from. At present a flight to England requires so much fuel that sufficient bomb loads cannot be carried. The invention of a new type of mine is of the greatest importance for the Navy. From now on aircraft will be our chief mine-layers. We shall sow the English coast with mines which cannot be cleared. But this mine warfare which makes use of the Air Force, demands a different starting base. England cannot live without her imports. We can feed ourselves. The permanent sowing of mines along the English coasts will bring Britain to her knees. However, we can achieve this only if we occupy Belgium and Holland ! "

Some months later, in his Directive for the occupation of Denmark and Norway, dated March 1st, 1940, Hitler amplified this by ordering that " the Air Force, after the occupation has been completed, will ensure air defence and will make use of Norwegian bases for air warfare against Britain."

The " better starting bases " were secured in the spring and early summer of 1940. After the unexpectedly rapid fall of France, Belgium, and Holland had placed Hitler in possession of the entire Channel and French Atlantic coast, the situation envisaged in his earlier planning had at last come about. But was he ready to exploit it ? There still exists a good deal of obscurity on this point, and the Nuremberg Documents contribute little toward its clarification. Hitherto, the generally accepted assumption had been that Hitler himself had been surprised by the rapidity of his success in the West and was not

O

ready for the next stage when it presented itself ; it was believed that in the face of the total collapse of France and the Dunkirk calamity, he expected Britain to give up the fight and ask for an armistice ; that he waited for this British move which he was certain was the only one possible for Britain, and waited too long ; that finally when he realised he had miscalculated, it was too late to revise his plans.

There is nothing in the Nuremberg Documents to support this assumption. Nowhere in his several briefing speeches to his Commanders-in-Chief, nor in his conversations with Jodl, Raeder, and others, of which we possess the records, is there an indication that Hitler expected the automatic surrender of Britain after the fall of France. If he did so, he refrained from hinting at it. It is helpful here to bear in mind the relevant dates. The Germans entered Paris on June 13th, 1940, and the French asked for an armistice on June 17th, 1940. Fighting actually ceased in France a day or two later. Yet already a fortnight earlier, on June 4th, 1940, Hitler described to Raeder his next objectives, following the end of the French campaign. He planned to reduce the strength of the Army, discharge the older age classes, especially skilled workers, and to concentrate all his efforts on strengthening the Navy and Air Force. The only meaning this redeployment and shift of emphasis could have, was an all-out effort against Britain. For this battle Hitler would indeed require every ship and every aircraft he could lay his hands on. His remarks to Raeder indicate that he was fully aware of these necessities as early as a fortnight before the final collapse of France.

But this still does not give us the whole answer. If Hitler expected having to meet Britain in a straight fight across the Channel in order to " force her to her knees," it remains unclear why he allowed several precious summer weeks to pass without action before actually setting fresh plans in motion. We have seen Hitler, on other occasions, issuing detailed War Directives for emergency operations with as little as 48 and 24 hours' notice, and putting them into operation. The fighting in France ceased on June 17th, 1940, and systematic attacks on Britain by the German Air Force did not begin until August 8th, 1940. The first operational order for the invasion of the British Isles, of which we have knowledge, was not issued until August 17th, 1940, when the air battle over Britain had been under way for just over a week and Hitler was presumably still confident that he would win it. What happened during the intervening weeks? Was it Hitler's belief, during a few weeks, that a combined big effort by Navy and Air Force, making full use of U-boats, mines and other naval weapons, would after all suffice to cut Britain's life-lines and force her into surrender, thus rendering a physical invasion by the army superfluous? One does not know. If he had this idea, he did not adhere to it very long, nor did he pursue it very vigorously. At what point between the French Armistice and August 17th, 1940, did he realize that the physical invasion of Britain—the one solution he had originally considered utterly antiquated and unnecessary—was after all required? The Nuremberg Documents fail to furnish the answer.

In his secret speech before an assembly of Gauleiters in Munich on November 7th, 1943, Gen. Jodl, then German Chief of Staff, gives us his own version—more than three years after the event. He says:

" The decisive success of this campaign (in France and the Low Countries) improved our position in the best possible way. We gained possession not only of the French armaments poten-tial—destined to render important service to us in the further course of the war—but above all the entire Atlantic coast fell into our hands with its naval ports and air bases. A direct threat to the British mother country had by this means become possible. The question now arose whether or not we should carry the war into Britain by a landing on the grand scale."

Jodl apparently wishes his audience of Gauleiters to believe that at the time of the fall of France Hitler had not yet made up his mind as to what to do next with Britain. He leaves it to be inferred that a "landing on the grand scale" was but one of several possibilities of creating "a direct threat to the British mother country," and that other courses were open to Hitler. This is wisdom after the event, dispensed deliberately for special purposes by one who knew better. Indeed, Jodl goes on to elaborate this argument, and we shall return to it presently.

Operation Sea-Lion

The code-name for the planned invasion of Britain was "Operation Sea-Lion." The actual operational Directive, bearing this code-word, is in Allied possession but did not form part of the documents released at Nuremberg. It was released by the British military authorities in Berlin, in a paraphrased form, on September 25th, 1945. The original text was not made available. The Directive is dated August 17th, 1940. One of the Nuremberg Documents, however—the war diary of Raeder's Chief of Staff—contains a reference note, inserted by the translator and drawing attention to the "Directive of the Supreme Command of the Armed Forces (OKW) of August 27th, 1940, in documents 'Seelöwe' (Sea-Lion), directives of OKW I, Volume I," in connection with the transfer of German army units from the West to the East in August, 1940. As these documents are not at present accessible, it has not been possible to establish whether the difference in the dates is due to a clerical error or whether there are, in fact, two separate "Sea-Lion" Directives, issued on August 17th and 27th respectively, and showing the invasion planning at two different stages. The following notes are based on the Directive dated August 17th, 1940, as paraphrased by the issuing authorities in Berlin.

In broad outline the plan was, first, for the German Air Force to gain command of the daylight air over Southern England and the Channel. On August 8th, 1940, therefore, the Battle of Britain began. When that battle had been won, and not until then, the narrow seas would be barred to the British Navy, and the invasion of Britain would become a practical proposition.

The following troops were to be employed : on the right was to be Army Group "A" comprising the Ninth and Sixteenth Armies ; on the left Army Group "B", a reinforced Sixth Army. These two groups had available for the initial assault 11 infantry and two mountain divisions. Thus the force which would have landed on the first day would have been of much the same strength as the nine Allied divisions which landed in Normandy in 1944, with the important difference that whereas in Normandy the Allies possessed a bigger reserve, German strength in the West in 1944 was incomparably superior to that of Britain at home in 1940. The two German Army Groups in 1940 had a reserve, with which to follow up the initial landings, consisting of six armoured divisions, two motorised and one SS division. In addition there were to be nine infantry divisions in Army and Army Group reserves, and eight infantry divisions in G.H.Q. reserve, making a total of 39 divisions earmarked for the operation.

Two main landings were to be carried out. The Sixteenth Army was to sail from Ostend, Calais and Boulogne, and land in Kent and Sussex, between Margate and Hastings. The Ninth Army was to sail from Dieppe, Le Havre and Caen, and land in Sussex and Hampshire, between Brighton and

Portsmouth. Airborne troops were to clear the exits from the Romney Marshes, the defiles through the South Downs behind Brighton, and other key points in the Brighton beach-head. Army Group " B " was not to come into battle until after Army Group " A " had landed. It was to sail from the Cherbourg Peninsula and to land west of Bournemouth in Weymouth Bay. By that time, so the Germans doubtless calculated, Army Group " A " would have drawn Britain's central reserves towards Kent.

The first objective of Army Group " A " after the Kentish and Sussex landings had been linked, was a line from the Thames estuary about Tilbury, south-westward through Caterham, Leatherhead and Aldershot to Southampton Water and Portsmouth. Army Group " B"'s first objective is not stated. Probably it was expected to have a more or less clear run northward across the Hampshire and Wiltshire Downs. The second objective of both Army Groups was a line from Colchester to the mouth of the Severn. London was to be encircled and mopped up. Beyond that, strong mobile forces were to overrun the industrial areas of the Midlands, South Wales, Lancashire and Yorkshire, and occupy the important ports.

There is no absolute certainty about the date for which the invasion was fixed. It appears from the paraphrased Directive that a date on or about September 20th, 1940, was envisaged. The Battle of Britain was won on September 15th, the day 185 German aircraft were lost, and it was won by the R.A.F. Command of the daylight air over Southern England and the Channel, the indispensable prerequisite for the launching of the invasion, was never achieved. Had the Battle of Britain gone in Goering's favour—and we know that the margin was perilously slender—and the landings been carried out, there is today no doubt that nothing could have saved the British Isles.

Jodl Explains

How did all this look to the German High Command ? It is their point of view, and their interpretation of the situation which interests us primarily in these studies.

Gen. Jodl stated in his Munich speech of November 7th, 1943, that it was a question of " whether or not we should carry the war into England by a landing on the grand scale." The Directive for " Operation Sea-Lion " has shown how this question was answered by the German Supreme Command. Hitler was definitely determined to have his armies cross the

Channel. But Jodl, in retrospect, tries to make out that the situation was not as clear-cut and easy as that. He continues :

" Furthermore—in view of the possibility of the U.S.A. entering the war—it was necessary to take into consideration the occupation of a number of advanced support points in the Atlantic, for instance Iceland and the Azores. From these islands we should be able to carry on particularly effectively the fight against British supplies, and to defend the territory of Europe in exactly the same way as Japan now holds Greater East Asia secure by means of her advanced island bases in the Pacific."

This statement is meant to deceive, but it doesn't. It makes no sense. At the time Hitler had to make his decision whether or not to invade Britain, there was no question at all of the U.S.A. entering the war, and the possibility, utterly remote as it then was, certainly did not enter into Hitler's calculations. The parallel between the Azores, Iceland, and the British Isles— all highly technical combined sea, land, and air operations fraught with great difficulties and dangers—is artificial and false. If on the other hand Hitler decided to invade Britain almost immediately, as we know he did, then the second part of Jodl's argument falls to the ground as well—namely that these Atlantic bases were needed in the fight against British supplies. In the case of a successful invasion there should have been no further need to fight Britain's supply lines. What Jodl does is to telescope the situation of 1940 into the later war years and to draw a joint conclusion. One wonders how many of the Gauleiters noticed the red herring. But then it was the purpose of this confidential speech, made at the beginning of the fifth year of war, to rebuild waning morale and supply the Gauleiters, after taking them into his confidence up to a point, with usable arguments to combat defeatism and confirm belief in the correctness of all Hitler's decisions. The next sentence in Jodl's speech shows this.

" However," he continues, " very wisely the Führer refrained from adopting these objectives. Not alone their initial execution but the subsequent maintenance of communications by sea would have involved a measure of strength which our naval and air equipment could not have provided permanently."

The blame is thrown on what Jodl calls " our hopeless inferiority at sea," and he goes on to explain that " the landing in England, prepared for down to the smallest detail but with improvised transport resources only, could not be dared as long as the British Air Force had not been completely beaten. And this we were never able to do, just as we have not been able completely to shatter the Soviet armed forces. Later generations will not be able to reproach us with not having dared the utmost, and spared no effort to achieve these aims which would have decided the war. But one could not take it upon oneself to allow the German air arm to bleed to death in the Battle of Britain in view of the struggle which lay before us against the Soviet Union."

Except for the last sentence Jodl here approaches the truth as far as he dares with his Gauleiters. It is in the last sentence that he draws another red herring across the path. Once again he telescopes 1940 with a later period of the war, this time 1941. To suggest that Hitler had to be economical with his aircraft " in view of the coming struggle against the Soviet Union," is, of course, nonsense. At the time of the Battle of Britain the war with Russia was not yet " in view." Hitler was planning the invasion of the Soviet Union—in fact, we know that he made his first tentative moves in August 1940—but not even a tentative date was set, and he had it entirely in his own hands when he wished to start it. No one need believe that he would not have thrown in his last aircraft if he could have been certain thereby to tip the balance and knock Britain out. But he could not be certain. Had he conquered Britain, as he would have done if he had won the Battle of Britain, the danger of a Soviet attack against Germany would have been even more remote than it was even so ; on the contrary Hitler would have had all the time he needed and more than that, to prepare what would then have been an entirely new and separate war which he could have started where and when he pleased. We do not possess precise figures regarding the reserves in aircraft which Britain and Germany respectively still held at the end of the Battle of Britain, and one ventures to guess that on balance Goering was still better off than the Royal Air Force, both in actual reserves and production capacity. Goering certainly had plenty of aircraft to waste and squander away over Britain during the following winter in a bombing campaign which, tactically and strategically, got Hitler nowhere.

Raeder Explains

We possess a document which provides an interesting foot-note to this question. It is a memorandum prepared for Admiral Assmann " for his own information and not to be used for publication," which bears the signature " Raeder " and is dated January 10th, 1944. It deals with the same period, also in retrospect, and its purpose is obviously to familiarize Admiral Assman with the views held and expressed by his Chief at this crucial period. It should be noted that Raeder always made a special point of insisting that no action against the Soviet Union should be undertaken, as long as Britain was not beaten and the front in the West liquidated.

" At this time," Raeder says, " the Führer had made known his ' unalterable decision ' to conduct the Eastern campaign in spite of all remonstrances. Experience has shown that, after this, further warnings were completely useless, unless entirely new situations arose. As Chief of Naval War Staff I was never convinced of the ' compelling necessity ' for ' Barbarossa ' (the invasion of the Soviet Union).

" During the campaign in France and also during the beginning of preparations for ' Sea-Lion '—while the Führer still had hopes of gaining control of the air (which he too recognized as being an essential prerequisite to ' Sea-Lion ')— it was doubtless his intention after the fall of France to concentrate on the Navy and Air Force. The Führer described to me the movement of troops to the Eastern frontier in August, 1940, as a large-scale camouflage measure for ' Sea-Lion '.

" The fear that air superiority over the Channel could no longer be attained in the autumn of 1940—a realization which the Führer no doubt gained earlier than the Naval War Staff who were not so fully informed of the true results of our own losses during the air raids on England—must undoubtedly have caused the Führer, as far back as August and September, to consider whether, even prior to victory in the West, an Eastern campaign would be feasible, with the object of first eliminating our last serious opponent on the Continent."

It is a very ugly sentence, but it makes interesting reading when held against Jodl's contention. What Jodl said was, in essence : " We cannot afford to waste any more aircraft on this battle against Britain, since we shall presently need them against Russia. Therefore, we must call the battle against Britain off." Whereas Raeder says, in essence : " Since we do not seem to be getting anywhere in this battle against Britain this autumn, we might as well call it off for the time being and start a war against Russia in the meantime. We can come back to it after we've won in the East." Two rather different interpretations of which the second is undoubtedly the less incorrect and fanciful.

It is worth noting, in passing, that Hitler tried to deceive even his own Naval Chief, and not without success, with regard to the alleged camouflage purpose of the troop movements in August, 1940. Raeder seems to have had his doubts, for he adds in brackets that " a statement from the Supreme Command of the Army would have to be obtained on this point." But the fact remains that Hitler, who was aware of Raeder's opposition to the " Barbarossa " plan, tried to tell him that the preparations for " Barbarossa " were merely a large-scale camouflage of " Sea-Lion," while in fact it was given out to be such a camouflage for the very real " Barbarossa " preparations. The " Barbarossa " Directive itself says so. What Hitler did, was to sell his own Naval Chief a Counter-Intelligence propaganda story.

Ribbentrop Explains

When was the decision taken to cancel " Operation Sea-Lion," at least for the 1940 season? It seems that it must have been shortly before September 19th, 1940. For on that day Ribbentrop had a conversation with Mussolini in Rome, at which Ciano and the ambassadors von Mackensen and Alfieri were also present. Only extracts of the minutes of this discussion have been made available, but they make it clear that Ribbentrop was at pains to explain to Mussolini (who had hoped to get in and out of the war within a fortnight in June 1940), that the subjugation of Britain was a rather more protracted affair than had been anticipated, and that the war would last through the winter—a prospect which Mussolini abhorred and knew why.

" All the same," the record notes Ribbentrop as pointing out, " Germany had won air superiority, and was bombing England, and particularly London, by day and by night, whilst the British were at most sending a few planes over Germany at night, in order to drop bombs at random. During the day no British planes dared to fly over German territory. Germany, however, was carrying out strong reprisal attacks by day as well as by night. On one occasion—it was as early as August—the German Luftwaffe had been ready for a large-scale attack, but this attack had to be called off because of bad weather. A really large-scale attack had not taken place since, as the Führer wished to assume responsibility for this only when it was certain that such an attack would mean the beginning of England's destruction. Although Germany had merely carried out reprisal attacks from the air, their results for England had already been extraordinarily serious. With a continuation of these attacks London would be in ruins within a short time. The British armament factories had been seriously affected, and important ports, such as Portland, had been entirely crippled. Moreover, all aerodromes from the South Coast to London had been made unusable."

As so often with Ribbentrop, it is not easy to determine what precisely he is talking about. One thing, however, he clearly wishes to convey to the Duce, and that is, that there is not going to be any invasion of Britain just yet. There is air superiority, there is bombing by day and by night, London is in ruins, all British aerodromes in the coastal areas are out of commission—but what it is all for, if anything, he does not say. Later on when the discussion turns to Greece and Yugoslavia, Ribbentrop assures Mussolini that these are an Italian preserve and that Italy could be certain of Germany's sympathetic assistance, " but it seemed to us to be better not to touch on these problems for the time being but to concentrate instead all our forces on the destruction of England."

Has " Operation Sea-Lion " been called off for good, or is it only postponed ?

Postponement or Cancellation ?

The next reference to " Operation Sea-Lion " we find two months later, in Hitler's War Directive No. 18 which was issued on November 12th, 1940. It deals mainly with France, Spain and Portugal, and the Italian position in Egypt, but at its very end has a single small paragraph dealing with Britain. Under the heading " Landing in England," Article Six of the Directive says :

" Owing to a change in the general situation it may yet be possible or necessary to start ' Operation Sea-Lion ' in the spring of 1941. The three services of the Armed Forces must therefore earnestly endeavour to improve conditions for such an operation in every respect."

Just that, and no more. The Directive is signed by Hitler and initialled by Jodl. Translated into normal language, the first sentence would mean : " If the general situation changes, it may yet become possible or necessary to start etc. . . . " In other words : " as long as the present situation lasts, it is neither necessary nor possible to start etc. . . ." But there seems to be more in the sentence than even that. Actually, Hitler seems to envisage two ways in which the situation may change. It may change in such a way as to make the invasion possible without its being absolutely necessary ; but it may also change in such a manner as to make its execution vitally necessary, although it would at the same time have to be possible, i.e., feasible. The first case would envisage a situation where Hitler might wish to take advantage of a particularly favourable tactical constellation in order to effect a swift surprise coup ; the second rather indicates a Hitler placed in a tactical dilemma whence he has no other way out but to dare the invasion. One wonders what these various military and political constellations may have been that crossed the Führer's mind at this time when, as we know, he was up to his ears in the preparations for the invasion of the Soviet Union. It is at this time, on November 14th, 1940, that following a discussion between Hitler and Raeder, the latter's Chief of Staff notes in his war diary : " Führer is still inclined to instigate the conflict with Russia. Naval Supreme Commander recommends putting it off until the time after the victory over England since there is heavy strain on German forces and the end of warfare not in sight." But we know by now that Hitler did not always tell his Naval Supreme Commander all he ought to know, and on occasion even fooled him.

Clearly, then, in the middle of November, 1940, Hitler considered " Operation Sea-Lion " merely as postponed (and not necessarily postponed until after the invasion of Russia, since he talks of it as being either possible or necessary in the spring of 1941), and not as cancelled for good. He even orders his three services to make the best possible preparations for the operation. But on December 3rd, 1940, an important decision was made in Berlin. We learn about it from a long memorandum, entitled " Basic Facts for a History of German War and Armaments Economy " which was compiled in 1944 by Maj.-Gen. Thomas, Chief of the War Industry Department under Goering. In this memoradum Gen. Thomas states :

" As both the Army and Minister Todt were urging the high priority of the Panzer and ' Axis ' programme (code name for the African campaign), the Navy demanded its ' Sea-Lion ' measures accelerated, and aerial armaments were being even more intensified, the Chief of the War Industry Department (Gen. Thomas himself), at a conference of chiefs of departments presided over by Field Marshal Keitel, pointed out the difficulties of accelerating everything at the same time, particularly in view of the bad situation as regards manpower. He demanded once more a clarification of the organization which was really the most important thing. Resulting from this the following decision was made on December 3rd, 1940, (enclosed as Appendix XX, 35) which affected future measures as follows :

(1) There is no longer any mention of an Invasion of Britain but only of a siege of Britain ;

(2) Aerial defence of the homeland was placed at the top of the list for the first time ;

(3) The prospective big action (Russia) is mentioned for the first time, and its postponement to some later date date admitted as possible.

" At the beginning of December, instructions were received that for the time being there was no question of an invasion of Britain, and that preparations for ' Sea-Lion ' should merely be concluded."

If this is not yet the final cancellation, it comes very near it.

But Raeder has not yet given up his fight to keep Britain at the top of the list of operational priorities. On December 20th, 1940, the war diary of his Chief of Staff notes : " The strengthening of the British position through unfavourable developments of the situation in the Eastern Mediterranean and help from the U.S.A. demands absolute concentration against Britain. Therefore, serious doubts concerning ' Barbarossa ' before the defeat of England." On December 27th, 1940, he has an interview with Hitler in which he emphasizes these points and maintains that " strict concentration of our entire war effort against Britain as our main enemy is the most urgent need of the hour." He does not advocate the launching of " Sea-Lion " at this time of year, but he insists that " what is being done for submarine and naval-air force construction is much too little. Our entire war potential must work for the conduct of the war against Britain ; thus for the Navy and Air Force every fissure of strength prolongs the war and endangers final success." Once again he asks for postponement of " Barbarossa " until after Britain has been defeated. But he is pleading a lost cause. Hitler's eyes are on Russia. (See Chapter V, Case Barbarossa).

But Hitler has not forgotten " Sea-Lion." He has not forgotten that " Britain is the main driving force against Germany " and that he has pledged himself to " force her to her knees." Yet several months after the defeat in the Battle of Britain and only a few more months to go until his greatest military venture begins, the whole proposition appears to him in a somewhat different light. When Mussolini, Ciano, and the Italian Service chiefs visit him at his headquarters on January 19th, 1941, and he reviews the world situation for their benefit, he has a brief but very instructive reference to Britain.

" The general situation in the East," says Hitler on this occasion, " can be judged correctly only from the situation in the West. The attack against the British Isles is our ultimate aim.

" In this respect, we are in the position of a man with only one round left in his rifle ; if he misses, the situation is worse than before. The landing cannot be repeated, since too much equipment would be lost in the event of failure. Britain would then have no need to worry any more and could employ the bulk of her forces at the periphery wherever she pleases. As long as the attack has not taken place, the British must always reckon with the possibility.

" A landing can only be made under certain conditions which, however, did not exist last autumn—there were no three consecutive days of good weather."

The last statement may or may not be correct—one is inclined to distrust it. Its chief purpose was presumably to placate the worried Italians who during this winter were feeling the main weight of British pressure and probably reflected that they would have been spared all these anxieties if only Hitler had launched " Sea-Lion " in the autumn of 1940 and finished with Britain once and for all.

But Hitler's comparison with the man who has only one round left in his rifle, sums up his position with compelling aptness. He understands the situation perfectly ; he knows or guesses that Britain looks at it in the same way, and he draws the correct conclusion : nothing would be worse than giving Britain the certainty that the danger of invasion has finally passed. The longer he can leave the British in doubt as to whether " Sea-Lion " is still to come or not, the better.

The truth is, however, that " Operation Sea-Lion " is dead. On February 3rd, 1941, Hitler holds a secret briefing meeting with his Service chiefs, in which preparations for the campaigns in Russia and Tripolitania are discussed. (See Chapter III, Otto to Alaric). A great reshuffle and redeployment of troops on the European continent is ordered, to meet the demands for the new offensives. A number of planned operations, such as the seizure of French North Africa and the invasion of Spain which had been held in readiness, are scrapped because troops and equipment are needed elsewhere. And almost in passing the conference record notes a casual remark from the Chief of the Army General Staff :

" Sea-Lion can no longer be carried out."

The operation that was to have won the war is dead. From now on, as we have seen from Hitler's remark, it is to play the part of a useful stake in the poker game with Britain, but not for long ; soon " Sea-Lion " is reduced to a ghost, occasionally conjured up by Ribbentrop to deceive satellite diplomats ; and it ends its day as a cheap and ineffective deception trick in the bag of German Counter-Intelligence propaganda.

The Ghost of " Sea-Lion "

On February 13th, 1941, ten days after the secret conference at which it had been decided that " Sea-Lion " could no longer be carried out, Ribbentrop had a meeting with the Japanese Ambassador Oshima at Fuschl near Salzburg. Its obvious purpose was to convince the Japanese that the moment had come for them to strike at Britain and thus help Germany to bring the war to a rapid conclusion. In order to make the proposition palatable to Oshima, Ribbentrop painted a glowing picture of German measures against Britain, culminating in this remark :

" We now have air supremacy over the whole continent. How soon we can win air supremacy over Britain will depend on further developments. The landing in England is prepared. Its execution, however, depends on various factors, above all on weather conditions. Every eventuality has been provided for. The war has been won today militarily, economically and politically. We have the desire to end the war quickly and to force England to sue for peace soon."

In support of this thesis, particularly with regard to Britain Ribbentrop cites a number of factors. He points out that in the war against Britain it was true that the Germans had had poor weather for their bombers during the autumn and winter, " but in spite of this, heavy damage has been done which has had a strongly retarding effect on British war production. The bombings would continue in increasing measure so that we hoped to destroy very much more than America was able to replace. At sea the commitment of the U-boat weapon had so far been comparatively slight ; after the end of March it would multiply in a short time. Then, with the combined Air Force and U-boat weapons we would deal Britain terrible blows. The loss of tonnage was already creating considerable difficulties for Britain's food supply. Meat and fats were already scarce. It was now a matter of reducing imports by sinkings to a definite level below the absolute minimum of British existence. Thereby Britain's situation would take catastrophic shape overnight."

It was at this stage, given suitable weather conditions, that an actual landing operation was envisaged. " In an air duel," Ribbentrop went on, " Germany would always be superior. The Führer would beat England wherever he would encounter her. Besides our strength was not only equal but superior to a combined British-American air force at any time. The number of pilots at our disposal was unlimited. The same was true of our aircraft production capacity. As far as quality was concerned, Germany's was always superior to the British (to say nothing about the American), and we were on the way even to enlarge this lead."

So he rambles on. The Japanese Ambassador is not convinced.

It is amusing to see that only a few days after this interview, on February 18th, 1941, Raeder's Chief of Staff notes in his war diary with reference to the " Barbarossa " preparation, certain deception and camouflage measures which have been ordered for the purpose of screening the large-scale troop movements which are taking place at this time across the European continent. He records these instructions which have been received from OKW (Supreme Command of the Armed Forces) :

" Aim of the deception is to conceal the preparations for operation ' Barbarossa '. The important point is that in the first period, *i.e.*, up to about the middle of April the now prevailing uncertainty concerning our intentions should be maintained. Later, those preparations for ' Barbarossa ' which can no longer be camouflaged, must be represented as a deception diversion from the invasion of Britain. The following directions for this deception are given :

    (a) for the first period—to increase the already existing impression of an impending invasion of Britain.

Estimate of new weapons and transport equipment. Exaggeration of the importance of minor operations and the troops employed therefor, *i.e.*, 'Marita' (Greece), and 'Sunflower' (Tripolitania).

(b) during the second period the deployment for 'Barbarossa' is to be made the greatest deception in the history of warfare the purpose of which is to camouflage the last preparations for the invasion of Britain.

" In spite of the far-reaching disintegration of the operation 'Sea-Lion' everything possible should be done to maintain the impression amongst our own troops that the invasion against Britain is being further prepared. In order to create further uncertainty about our plans, the Army High Command has to prepare the sudden 'blocking' of certain territories along the English Channel and in Norway. The code-word for this action is 'Albion'."

On June 1st, 1941, the time-table for the invasion of the Soviet Union is issued by Hitler. It states briefly that " Air Fleet II has been withdrawn from action and transferred to the East " while " Air Fleet III has taken over sole command in the conduct of air warfare against Britain," and then confirms the camouflage measures already mentioned :

" Second phase of deception of the enemy (code-names : 'Shark' and 'Harpoon') in operation with the aim of giving the impression that landings are being prepared from Norway, the Channel Coast, and Brittany. Troop Concentration East will be represented as a deception exercise for the landing in Britain."

Thereafter the ghost of " Operation Sea-Lion " went east and stayed there. No more was heard of it.

IV

Felix and Isabella

German-Spanish Relations 1937-43

In his secret speech before an assembly of Gauleiters at Munich on November 7th, 1943, General Jodl attributes the fact that " the palm of victory has eluded us " to Germany's failure to attain three specific objectives.   These were :

The impossibility of a landing in Britain ;

The failure to bring the war against the Soviet Union to a victorious conclusion during the first winter ;

The failure to draw Spain into the war at some time during the first two years of fighting.

It is noteworthy that the German Chief of Staff should have attached such importance to Spain. It is even more remarkable that he should attribute Spanish resistance to a man who was always regarded as Ribbentrop's understrapper, namely, Franco's Foreign Minister Serrano Suñer. " Our third objective," says Jodl, " that of drawing Spain into the war on our side and thereby creating the possibility of seizing Gibraltar, was wrecked by the resistance of the Spanish, or better, Jesuit Foreign Minister Serrano Suñer."

Jodl does not explain this remark. Does it mean that Franco was ready and willing to resist a German entry into Spain with what arms and troops he had ? The Nuremberg Documents as well as the collection of captured German documents which was issued by the U.S. State Department on March 4th, 1946, fail to clarify this specific point. But they do reveal that in June, 1940, Franco promised both Hitler and Mussolini to enter the war on the side of the Axis. They make clear, furthermore, that the Nazis had achieved a peaceful penetration of Spain with the help of their agents, and that an operational plan existed to carry out a military campaign on Spanish soil.

This plan, which in certain contingencies also envisaged the occupation of Portugal, has the code-name " Felix and Isabella." It makes a particularly interesting study in the light of the publication, in December, 1945, of a memorandum prepared by Mr. Sumner Welles in 1941, in which he states that Mr. Churchill informed President Roosevelt in August, 1941, of an impending highly secret operation—the occupation of the

P

Canary Islands about September 15th, at the risk of war with Spain. Hitler's Directive No. 18, we now know, envisaged precisely the same operation, from the German side. But the date of his Directive is November 12th, 1940.

Case Richard

What happened to " Felix and Isabella ? " What happened to relations between Hitler and Franco ? The Nuremberg documents provide at least part of the answer, and some of the gaps are filled in by the documents issued by the Washington State Department on March 4th, 1946. Together they give a reasonably complete picture. Hitler had his own ideas about the Caudillo. Already the Blomberg Directive " for all war eventualities " of June 24th, 1937, mentions under " special preparations " an operation code-named " Case Richard " and covering " warlike entanglements with Red Spain." The Spanish Civil War, this Directive points out, " contains the danger that, through accidental or provoked incidents, a conflict may arise between Germany and Red Spain which can lead to a state of war between the two governments."

The Directive lays down that " for this case preparatory plans are to be made only by the Navy. For the Army and Air Force it will remain a matter of assistance to White Spain with material and personnel, as has been the procedure heretofore. Subordination of parts of the Air Force under the command of the Navy may have to be considered."

It seems clear from this that, in case a state of open war should be declared between the governments of Republican Spain and Nazi Germany, Hitler did not contemplate more than what would have amounted to a blockade of Republican Spain and naval bombardments of its main ports. For the rest it was apparently intended merely to " legalize " and declare official such armed intervention as was already going on. The reason for this hesitation to bring too much weight to bear on the Republican side and thereby hasten Franco's progress, becomes soon apparent. Four months later, on November 5th, 1937, the record of a conference between Hitler and his Service Chiefs, (known as the " Hossbach Minutes "), reveals Hitler as stating :

" From the German point of view a hundred per cent. victory by Franco is not desirable. We are more interested in a continuation of the civil war and preservation of the tensions in the Mediterranean. Franco in sole possession of the Spanish

Peninsula would mean the end of Italian intervention and of the presence of Italy on the Balearics. As our interests are directed towards continuing the war in Spain, it must be the task of our future policy to strengthen Italy in her fight to hold on to the Balearics. However, a consolidation of Italian positions on the Balearics cannot be tolerated either by France or England, and could lead to war by France and England against Italy, in which case Spain, if entirely in Franco's hands, might participate on the side of Italy's enemies."

Shadows of the non-intervention committee ! Before he has even won his civil war, Franco is already to be a pawn in Hitler's game. How does he manage to get out of it ?

Benevolent Neutrality Only

Once the Spanish civil war is over and Hitler's plans against Poland are nearing fruition, Franco appears in a somewhat different, although still rather dim light.

On August 12th, 1939, Hitler has a conference with Ciano, the Italian Foreign Minister, who explains why Italy is not yet ready to join in a general European conflict. Pointing to Spain Ciano declares that it had " just secured a government friendly to the Axis and needed a period of rest after the civil war. But in two or three years' time, Spain would be in fact a considerable factor on the side of the Axis. Within two years Spain proposed to build four battleships of 35,000 tons, the plans for which having recently been taken to Spain by an Italian General." These constructions, incidentally, were to take place at Ferrol.

In his speech to the Commanders-in-Chief on August 22nd, 1939, Hitler went no further than saying that " Franco is a factor favourable to us. However, we can ask only benevolent neutrality from Spain. But this depends on Franco's personality. He guarantees a certain uniformity and steadiness of the present system in Spain. But we must take into account the fact that Spain does not as yet have a Fascist party of our internal unity." In other words, Hitler doesn't trust his pupil and looks for no support from him.

Gibraltar

After the conclusion of the campaign in the West and the defeat of the German Air Force over Britain, the question of strangling Britain by shutting the Mediterranean becomes an urgent strategic consideration. Gibraltar moves into the fore-ground. The Washington Documents reveal that already in June, 1940, Franco had promised both Hitler and Mussolini to enter the war on the side of the Axis. This promise was made on two conditions—(a) that Gibraltar, French Morocco, and the part of Algeria colonized and predominantly inhabited by Spaniards be handed over to Spain ; (b) that military and general economic and material assistance required for carrying on the war be made available to Spain.

Franco's promise is recalled in a memorandum, dated August 8th, 1940, by Dr. Eberhard von Stohrer, German Ambassador in Madrid, which declares : " The Spanish Foreign Minister and the Minister of the Interior have, up to the last few days, repeatedly pointed out this Spanish offer to me. It may therefore be assumed that Spain even today will keep the promise made in June." A letter from Franco to Mussolini, written at about this time and also contained in the Washington Documents, after hailing the German victories in France, contains this reference : "From this moment our horizon became brighter, and our operation became possible and could become very effective once the difficulties of provisioning have been removed."

On September 17th, 1940, Serrano Suñer is in Berlin and has a conversation with Hitler. The minutes of this conversation, which are among the Washington Documents, show that the Gibraltar operation was discussed in detail. Suñer expressed fear of a British landing on the Cantabrian coast where Communist elements were strong. Hitler replied that a group of dive-bombers could halt such an operation just as they had destroyed Britain's landing in Norway.

The question of the capture of Gibraltar, Hitler said, had been studied most carefully by the Germans, and a commission of front-line officers who had taken a leading part in the destruction of the Maginot Line had gone to Spain to examine the matter on the spot. Hitler told Suñer, according to these minutes, that Germany's part in the attack on Gibraltar would be, first to expel enemy warships from the straits, and secondly, to make available a small contingent of specialist troops with special weapons to overwhelm the fortress without great sacrifice. This contingent would consist of assault engineers equipped with armour-destroying guns, called " pillbox crackers."

At this time, Ribbentrop, the German Foreign Minister, was

in Rome. On September 19th, 1940, he had a conversation with Mussolini the minutes of which reveal the following :

"The Reich Foreign Minister further announced a statement by the Führer regarding the military part of the Spanish problem, *i.e.*, the conquest of Gibraltar. The Spaniards wanted to conquer Gibraltar by themselves. But in order to prevent failure, Germany would provide Spain with special troops equipped with special weapons, and a few squadrons of aeroplanes. The Führer had carefully examined the Gibraltar problem from the military point of view and had come to the conclusion that the conquest of the rock was absolutely possible, but only if the Spaniards were given assistance.

"The Reich Foreign Minister then showed the Duce the German map regarding the Spanish territorial demands, and this was duly noted by the Italians. A question which was put to the Duce by the Reich Foreign Minister showed that Spanish ambitions did not clash in any way with those of Italy. In this connection the Reich Foreign Minister announced that Serrano Suñer intended to make also a visit to Rome.

"On his return to Berlin, the Reich Foreign Minister intended to sign a secret protocol with Serrano Suñer, dealing with Spain's entry into the war, as well as the supplying of Spain with the aforementioned materials, recognizing Spanish ambitions, and providing an attack against Gibraltar as a declaration of war. The protocol would also state that Spain's entry into the war would be left to the judgment of that country. It had been verbally provided that Spain would come into the war as soon as Franco had completed his preparations and particularly after the German special weapons as well as aeroplanes had arrived at their destinations in Spain."

This was on September 19th, 1940. Only a few days after the interview between Hitler and Suñer, Franco wrote personally to Hitler regarding the plans for the attack on Gibraltar, stating : "We have been preparing operations in secret for a long time, since the area in which the operation is to take place has no suitable network of communications. Points of resistance can withstand even the strongest action from the air, so that they will have to be destroyed by good, accurate artillery fire." In the same letter Franco conveyed to Hitler his "assurance of my unchangeable and sincere adherence to you personally and to the German people and the cause for which you fight."

Up to this point agreement on principles seems to have prevailed between Hitler and Franco. Whether or not the secret protocol between Ribbentrop and Suñer was signed, the documents fail to state. But it is clear that Germany had agreed to Spanish territorial ambitions in North Africa and obtained Mussolini's consent ; it is also clear that it had been left to Franco to decide when the time was ripe for the assault on Gibraltar. But details of the bargain apparently still remained to be cleared up, and it was on these that Franco seems to have remained non-committal. Early in October, 1940, there is a letter from Suñer to Ribbentrop in which the Spanish Foreign Minister, apparently under pressure from the Germans, promises " a concrete counter-proposal to the offer of economic aid received from the German Government," and expresses the wish that negotiations should be continued " through our personal contacts and through secret correspondence between the Führer and Caudillo." Suñer disclosed in the same letter that two additional Spanish divisions had just been sent to Morocco.

Directive No. 18

Meantime German plans for operation " Felix and Isabella " had been going forward. On October 23rd, 1940, Hitler and Franco met at Hendaye, and the notes on the conversations say that Franco began by declaring : " Spain will gladly fight at Germany's side." The date for the attack was apparently fixed at this meeting, although very little else seems to have been clarified. Later documents indicate that January 10th, 1941 was envisaged for the opening of the assault.

On November 12th, 1940, Hitler issued War Directive No. 18 which stated that " political steps to bring about an early Spanish entry into the war have been taken." This is clearly a reference to the Ribbentrop-Suñer negotiations, and their outcome does not seem to have been altogether unsatisfactory. " The aim of German intervention in the Iberian Peninsula," the Directive continues, " will be to drive the British out of the Western Mediterranean. For this purpose Gibraltar will be taken and the Straits closed, and the British will be prevented from gaining a foothold at another point of the Iberian Peninsula, or the Atlantic Islands."

Preparation and execution of this operation envisaged the following :

" Reconnaissance troops (officers in civilian clothes) make the necessary preparations for the action against Gibraltar and for taking over aerodromes. Regarding disguise and co-operation with the Spaniards they will comply with the security measures of the Chief of Foreign Intelligence." This was Admiral Canaris, who reveals himself, from the Nuremberg documents, as one of the key men in all Hitler's planning. "Special units of the Foreign Intelligence Bureau are to take over the protection of the Gibraltar area, in secret co-operation with the Spaniards, against British attempts to widen the terrain in front and against premature discovery and frustration of our preparations.

"The units intended for this operation will be kept in readiness away from the Spanish border, and information will be withheld from the troops at this early stage. In order to start operations, a warning order will be given three weeks before the troops cross the Spanish-French border, but only after the conclusion of the preparations regarding the Atlantic Islands. In view of the low capacity of the Spanish railways, the army will detail mainly motorized units for this operation, leaving the railways available for reinforcements.

"Units of the Air Force, directed by observation at Algeciras, will, at a favourable moment, carry out an air attack from French soil on the units of the British fleet lying in the port of Gibraltar, and will force a landing on Spanish aerodromes after the attack. Shortly after this, units intended for use in Spain will cross the Spanish-French frontier on land or in the air.

"The attack for the seizure of Gibraltar is to be carried out by German troops. Troops should be mobilized to march into Portugal should the British gain a foothold there. The units intended for this operation will march into Spain immediately after the units intended for Gibraltar. Support from the Spaniards in closing the Straits after the seizure of the Rock from the Spanish-Moroccan side as well, should be enlisted if required."

The plan now reads somewhat differently from what Ribbentrop told Mussolini two months earlier. The part to be played by Franco's troops has dwindled to insignificance. They are permitted to help in the storming of the Rock, but no more. The attack proper is to be carried out by German troops. If necessary, they may also help in the closing of the Straits from the African side, but it seems that Hitler would prefer to avoid this necessity. Intelligence personnel are to prepare, together with Franco's men, the taking over of Spanish aerodromes, but little faith is apparently placed in their reliability, for the Luftwaffe is instructed to force landings on these aerodromes, and resistance is apparently not excluded. The detailed instructions to the three Services which follow, make this even clearer. The Directive continues :

" The units intended for Gibraltar must be in sufficient strength to seize the Rock even without Spanish assistance. Apart from this, a smaller group must be available to aid the Spaniards in the unlikely event of the British attempting landings at a different point on the coast. The units to be kept in readiness for a possible invasion of Portugal are to be predominantly of a mobile nature. Sufficient air forces will be detailed for the air attack on Gibraltar to guarantee substantial success. For subsequent operations against naval objectives and for the support of the attack on the Rock mainly dive-bomber units are to be transferred to Spain. Provision is to be made for U-boats to attack the British Gibraltar Squadron, particularly when they leave harbour, which they are expected to do after the air raid. To support the Spaniards in the closing of the Straits, preparations are to be made in co-operation with the Army for the transfer of single coastal batteries. An Italian participation is not envisaged."

This is clearly not what had been envisaged during the Ribbentrop-Mussolini talks. But what went wrong ? Did Mussolini ask for Italian participation in this operation in which he must have been vitally interested ? If he did, why was he denied it ? Where and when did the difference with Suñer arise to which Jodl makes reference ? The documents so far available do not make this clear. In the light of the correspondence between Hitler and Franco which took place some months later, it seems that Jodl blamed Suñer for rather more than the Spanish Foreign Minister was responsible for. As the weeks go by it becomes increasingly evident that it is Franco himself who is stalling and trying to avoid a definite commitment.

Directive No. 18 concludes with Hitler's instructions.

" As a result of the Gibraltar operation, the Canaries and Cape Verde Islands will gain increased importance for the British conduct of the war at sea, as well as for our own. The Commanders-in-Chief of Navy and Air Force are to examine how the Spanish defence of the Canaries can be supported and how the Cape Verde Islands can be occupied. The question of an occupation of Madeira and the Azores is also to be examined, and the advantages and disadvantages that would arise from this."

This is where Mr. Sumner Welles' memorandum comes in. But where did Franco finally get out ? Did Hitler refrain from his action for reasons similar to those that made Mr. Churchill drop his plan ? Did the disadvantages outweigh the advantages ? Would Franco and Salazar have fought, and how much of a serious nuisance would they have been ? Again we must wait for the full answer.

Two Months Lost

Spain's entry into the war, we now know from the Washington Documents, was fixed for January 10th, 1941.

But in reply to a telegram from Stohrer, the German Ambassador in Madrid, dated December 12th, 1940, we find Franco declaring that " it is impossible for Spain to enter the war on the suggested date." He cites as reasons the " continued menace of the British fleet, incompleteness of Spain's own military preparations, and absolute inadequacy of Spain's provisioning."

Almost two months later, on February 6th, 1941, Hitler writes to Franco, declaring that " two months have been lost," and the opportunity to have Gibraltar safe in Axis hands missed because of " Franco's refusal to enter the war on January 10th."

Franco does not reply until February 26th, 1941. He now suddenly recalls that Hitler had described Spanish territorial demands as excessive compared with those of Italy and Germany, and complains roundly of the " vagueness and lack of precision of the Hendaye protocol in this respect." In conclusion, Franco writes : " I want to dispel all shadow of doubt and declare that I stand today ready at your side, entirely and decidedly at your disposal, united in a common historical destiny, desertion from which would mean my suicide and that of the cause which I represent in Spain."

Felix no longer Possible

But nothing happens. In Hitler's military plans, operation " Felix and Isabella " has already begun to recede into the background. Other operations, such as "Attila" (the seizure of French North Africa), are planned and dropped again. By February 3rd, 1941, the date of Hitler's operational conference with his Service Chiefs on "Case Barbarossa" (the invasion of the Soviet Union), the Chief of the Army General Staff points out that in view of the impending operation in the East, " Attila " can be carried out only with difficulty, and " Sea-Lion " (the invasion of Britain) can no longer be executed. " Felix " is now " no longer possible as the main part of the artillery is being entrained."

Five days later, on February 8th, 1941, the Commander-in-Chief of the German Army, after an interview with Hitler, notes in a memorandum : " It becomes clear that with regard to the imminent " Marita-Barbarossa " operations (the attacks on Greece and Russia), the troops held in reserve for operation " Felix " will have to be utilized for the new undertaking."

At the time, therefore, when Hitler complained to Franco about the " two months lost," he had already silently written off his expedition to Spain.

" Isabella "—the precautionary invasion of Portugal—had meanwhile also disappeared from the plans. But still Hitler hates to abandon the idea altogether. In the general instructions accompanying the time-table for " Barbarossa," issued on June 1st, 1941, there occurs this curious reference : " Attila or Isabella can be executed at ten days' notice." The Rock had been given up. But not the Azores or French North Africa. Hitler, it seems, knew very well whence danger was fast approaching. But it was too late for him to do anything decisive about it.

There is a large gap in Franco's negotiations with the Axis between his letter of February 26th, 1941, and the signing of a secret protocol pledging Spain to resist any Anglo-American entry into Spanish territory, on February 10th, 1943. Two months have passed, the Azores have, after all, become an Anglo-American base, and the Axis is about to be expelled completely from the whole of the North African seaboard. So far from offering assistance to Franco for the conquest of The Rock, Hitler is now anxious to ensure that his defective ally does not make common cause with his enemies.

In the last document of the series issued by the U.S. State Department—notes of a conversation between Franco and the then German Ambassador Dieckhoff, in December, 1943—it is stated that Dieckhoff conveyed to Franco German complaints about several of his actions, particularly the withdrawal of the Blue Division from the eastern front, and the " unjustified internment " of German U-boat crews.

Franco has discovered on which side his bread is buttered.

In his reply he says that his country is recovering slowly from the effects of the civil war and could not do without imports of petrol and cotton which he can get only from the Americans with

British navicerts. The Anglo-Saxons were demanding in return, however, "that Spain assume a not too outspoken pro-Axis attitude." But Franco repeats that there is no question of a change in his foreign policy. "Of course, Spain will not go beyond the comparatively trivial concessions mentioned above."

In the view of Gen. Jodl these concessions were anything but trivial, at any rate in their effect upon Germany. The failure of Spain to come into the war at some time during the first two years of fighting is, in his view, one of the three major causes responsible for Germany's defeat. In his Munich speech, he makes the funeral oration on this phase of the war :

"Spain and Portugal have decided to remain neutral. They have not the necessary strength to defend themselves against Britain and America. Everything depends, therefore, on the goodwill of our Western opponents as to the measure in which they recognise this neutrality. Latest events in Portugal have shown this. I do not believe, however, that it is in the interest of the Anglo-Saxons, either for political or military reasons, to unleash a war on the Iberian Peninsula, and that is undoubtedly what would happen were Spain to be attacked. Whether simpler methods of political disintegration, which are at present being employed, will be successful, is doubtful, at all events in the case of Spain."

V

Case Barbarossa

German-Soviet Relations 1939-41

Two weeks before the German attack on Poland, on August 12th, 1939, Hitler had a conference with Ciano at Berchtesgaden. Ciano informed him that Italy was not ready for war, and that Mussolini would like to see the invasion of Poland which he was certain would lead to a general European conflict, postponed. Instead the Duce had in mind a proposal for an international conference. To this Hitler replied that " if a conference were held, the Soviet Union could no longer be excluded from future meetings of the Powers. In the German-Soviet conversations the Soviets had made it clear with reference to Munich and other occasions when they were excluded, that in future they would not submit to such treatment. In addition to the four great powers and apart from the Soviet Union, Poland and Spain must also be summoned to a conference. That would mean, however, that Italy and Spain would be ranged against Britain, France, the Soviet Union and Poland, *i.e.* an unfavourable position."

Towards the end of the conversation Hitler was handed a telegram from Moscow. After a short interruption he told Ciano what it contained. " The Soviets agreed to the despatch of German political negotiators to Moscow." Ribbentrop added that the Soviets were fully informed of the intentions of Germany with regard to Poland. He himself, at the Führer's order, had informed the Soviet *Chargé d'Affaires*. The Führer added that according to his opinion the Soviet Union would not be ready to take the chestnuts out of the fire for the Western Powers. Stalin's position would be endangered as much by a victorious as by a defeated Soviet army. Soviet interests were directed towards the extension of Russia's access to the Balkans. Germany had nothing against this. On the other hand, the Soviet Union would never interfere on behalf of Poland whom she hated whole-heartedly.

Thus the official German record of the Berchtesgaden conversation. It shows the strange mixture of shrewd judgment and hopeless delusion in Hitler's mind which one encounters so frequently in secret Nazi state papers. Apparently Ribbentrop told the Soviets something with regard to German intentions in Poland, but that he gave them a full and correct version one need not too readily assume. On the other hand Hitler then knew something which the Chamberlain Government either did not perceive or refused to believe—that Munich finally determined the attitude of the Soviet Union towards Western Europe and drove her into an understanding with Nazi Germany. Within a week from the conversation with Ciano the German-Soviet accord was signed.

It is possible to retrace with the help of the Nuremberg Documents the development of German-Soviet relations as they lead up to the Moscow agreement and beyond it, to end up finally with " Case Barbarossa " which was the code-word for the invasion of the Soviet Union. It is, of course, only half the story and seen with Nazi eyes. The other half has to come from Moscow. But if it is a Nazi story it is at least not told for public consumption and propaganda purposes, but shows Hitler and his associates amongst themselves, guessing and planning behind their closed doors.

The Soviet Union before Munich

From the very start of his régime, the Soviet Union was never absent from Hitler's political and military calculations. The " Directive 1937–38 " for " all war eventualities " issued by Blomberg, then German War Minister and Commander-in-Chief of the Armed Forces, on June 24th, 1937, opens with this paragraph : " The general political situation justifies the assumption that Germany need not fear an attack from any side. Chief grounds for this are, in addition to the lack of desire for war in almost all nations, particularly the Western Powers, the deficiencies in the preparedness for war of a number of states and of the Soviet Union in particular."

Four months later, on November 5th, 1937, Hitler held a conference with his Service Chiefs. The record, known as the " Hossbach Minutes," reveals that Hitler was hoping for " a development in the situation which would lead to a planned attack on our part in the years 1943-45 " but that he was planning at the same time against an earlier outbreak of the war. Munich, in fact, is now seen to have forced his hand. The suspicions of the world had been aroused, and he had to act quickly if he was to preserve and exploit his superiority. Under the more favourable alternative, however, " the measure and speed of our action would decide Poland's attitude (towards a conquest of Austria and Czechoslovakia). Poland will have little inclination to enter the

war against a victorious Germany, with the Soviet Union in her
rear. Military participation by the Soviet Union must be
countered by the speed of our operations. It is a question whether
this need be taken into account at all in view of Japan's attitude."
The tendency here is obviously to have as little to do with the
Soviet Union as possible. Living space is to be conquered, in the
first instance, in the South-East, not the East.

By the summer of 1938, the situation had changed. Austria
had fallen into Hitler's lap, and " Case Green " (the invasion of
Czechoslovakia) was being prepared. On August 25th, 1938, the
General Staff of the German Air Force issued a secret directive
covering " Extended Case Green," namely war with other
powers resulting from the attack on Czechoslovakia. " The
basic assumption," says this directive, " is that France will
declare war during ' Case Green '. The Soviet Union will
probably side immediately with the Western Powers." Munich
had not yet happened and Hitler took for granted a proximity
of views or even an understanding between the Soviet Union
and the Western Democracies which, in fact, did not then exist.
But, continues the directive, " thanks to the expected neutrality
of Poland the active participation of Soviet Russia will be largely
restricted to the prosecution of the war in the Baltic. Air attacks
against East Prussia and the Baltic coast are to be expected and
occasional raids on Berlin are regarded as possible." The
assumption here was obviously that there would be no direct
Soviet help for Czechoslovakia but that Stalin, apart from
seizing the Baltic republics, would not hesitate to violate Polish
air space in order to bomb Berlin.

Keitel's draft for a new overall directive of June 18th, 1938,
states in Part III, which is dated July 7th, 1938, a similar view.
" Among the Eastern Powers," it says, " the Soviet Union is the
most likely to intervene. This, in the beginning at any rate, will
probably consist of reinforcements of the Czech Air Force and
Armament. However, a decision must not be neglected concerning what measures are to be taken if the Soviet Union were to
come to the point of starting a naval and air war against us or of
wishing to penetrate into East Prussia through the Border States."

But Mussolini tricked Hitler into Munich and that, in a way,
spoiled the game. Czechoslovakia had to be absorbed in instalments, and the German Army was prevented from showing the
world what it could do. But on January 5th, 1939, Colonel
Beck, the Polish Foreign Minister, appeared in Berchtesgaden,

and the record of his converation with Hitler contains a significant reference to the Soviet Union.

" In his (Hitler's) opinion the community of interests between Germany and Poland, so far as Russia was concerned, was complete. For the Reich, Russia, whether Tsarist or Bolshevist, was equally dangerous. The latter was perhaps a greater danger because of Communist propaganda, but the former was more dangerous in the military and even more so in the imperialist sense. For these reasons, a strong Poland was an absolute necessity for Germany. At this point the Chancellor remarked that every Polish division engaged against Russia was a corresponding saving of a German division. The Chancellor further declared that he was interested in the Ukraine from the economic viewpoint but he had no interest in it politically."

Although at this stage Hitler put some Russian cards on the table, they were not the cards he intended to play. What he was going to play was " Case White," the invasion and crushing of Poland, for which operational plans were at that moment already in Keitel's desk. However, his intention to make war on the Soviet Union is clearly indicated. Had not Goering said, before a Council of Ministers on September 4th, 1936, that Hitler's instructions for the execution of the German rearmament programme started " from the basic thought that the showdown with Russia is inevitable ? " What is surprising is the amount of confidence Hitler must have had in Polish-Soviet ill-feeling not to fear that Beck would pass on his remarks to Moscow. But perhaps Beck did ? And perhaps Hitler did not care ?

Contact With Stalin

The latter is not likely in the light of the briefing speech which Hitler gave his assembled Service Chiefs, including Goering, Keitel and Raeder, on May 23rd, 1939. The Polish situation had matured considerably. Hitler declared roundly that it is " inseparable from a conflict with the West." But he still believed that " the isolation of Poland is a matter of skilful politics " and he was not at all clear how Russia felt in the matter. " Poland's internal power of resistance to Bolshevism is doubtful," the minutes continue. " Thus Poland is of doubtful value as a barrier against Russia. The Polish Government will not resist pressure from Russia." The Soviet Union must therefore be induced to co-operate, directly or indirectly, in the isolation of Poland or this isolation will not be achieved.

Immediately Japan entered Hitler's calculations. "Japan is a weighty problem," he went on. "Even if at first for various reasons her collaboration with us appears to be somewhat cool and restricted, it is nevertheless in Japan's own interest to take the initiative in attacking Russia in good time." But that was for the future. In the meantime contact must somehow be established with Moscow. "Economic relations with Russia," Hitler explained to his Service Chiefs, "are possible only if political relations have improved. A cautious trend is appearing in (Soviet) press comment. It is not impossible that Russia will show herself to be disinterested in the destruction of Poland. Should Russia, on the other hand, take steps to oppose us, our relations with Japan may become closer."

This is the first indication, from the documents available, that Hitler considered a political approach to Moscow even a possibility. The date was May 23rd, 1939. The attack on Poland was scheduled for the second half of August. But the essential condition for its success was still missing. Hitler had to work fast. On August 12th he was able to inform Ciano that he had been successful in establishing contact. Ten days later, on August 23rd, 1939, the Non-Aggression Pact with the Soviet Union was published, and Hitler held another briefing conference with his Commanders-in-Chief at Berchtesgaden. The record of this conference was found among the archives of the German Supreme Command at Flensburg. In it Hitler said :

"The enemy had another hope—that Russia would become our enemy after the conquest of Poland. The enemy did not reckon with my great power of resolution. Our enemies are little worms. I saw them at Munich.

"I was convinced that Stalin would never accept the British offer. Russia has no interest in maintaining Poland, and Stalin knows that it is the end of his régime no matter whether his soldiers come out of a war victorious or beaten. Litvinov's replacement was decisive. I brought about the change towards Russia gradually. In connection with the commercial treaty we got into political conversations. A proposal was made for a non-aggression pact. Then came a general proposal from Russia. Four days ago I took a special step which resulted in Russia answering yesterday that she is ready to sign. The personal contact with Stalin is established. The day after tomorrow Ribbentrop will conclude the treaty. Now Poland is in the position in which I want her. I am only afraid that at the last moment some *Schweinhund* (dirty swine) will make a proposal for mediation."

In the event, the "dirty swine" turned out to be Mussolini who canvassed once more his idea of a conference. This aspect is discussed fully elsewhere in these studies (Chapter II, Otto to Alaric). Hitler, as we know, brushed Mussolini aside with some impatience.

Some Obscure Points

Hitler's *exposé* to his Commanders-in-Chief, although it gives a few hints of how he proceeded in Moscow, leaves a number of points unelucidated. He does not say who made the first proposal for a non-aggression pact, but it may be assumed that it came from the German side. Nor does he explain the precise nature of the "general proposal" which he says came from Moscow. Finally he says that "four days ago"—which would be August 18th, 1939—he took a "special step" which resulted in the Soviet Union answering on August 21st, 1939, that she was ready to sign. What this "special step" could have been is not clear since, as has been seen, Moscow agreed to the despatch of German political negotiators already on August 12th, 1939. By August 18th, 1939, Hitler's sands were undoubtedly beginning to run out. "Case·White" was scheduled for August 26th, 1939. Was Hitler able to put Stalin under special pressure to achieve a speedy conclusion of the agreement and if so, how did he blackmail him? The answer to this can only be given by Moscow. But it remains a fact that even so, Hitler got his pact signed only in the nick of time.

For the rest, some of Hitler's peculiar delusions continue to prevail. He was convinced that Stalin's régime could not survive a war, whether it emerged victorious or not. He was persuaded that Russia had no interest in maintaining Poland. On both counts Stalin and Russia have corrected his estimate, although Stalin was probably right in placing no reliance on Colonel Beck's Poland, and Hitler was right in assuming that he wouldn't. But in order to know that one need not have been Hitler.

It is not necessary here to inquire into the motives which prompted the Soviet Union to seek an understanding with Hitler Germany. There is today little doubt that Stalin never considered it a genuine and permanent accord. Part of the explanation has been given by Hitler himself. It is, of course,

Q

Munich. One wonders how good Soviet intelligence about Hitler's plans was. It is unlikely that it had not gained at least an approximate idea of the sequence of events as planned by Hitler, and knew that the Soviet Union was not scheduled to be attacked until at any rate the Western Democracies were beaten. In the event it seemed imperative for the Soviet Union to make sure that her continued isolation after Munich did not deteriorate into a direct temptation for Hitler to tackle her even before her time had come on the Nazi time-table. The only way, it seems, of ending this isolation and to gain the necessary breathing space, was to make a pact with Hitler and see how long it could be made to last. If this interpretation is incomplete or lacks plausibility, it is for the Soviet Union to correct it.

But assuming that this was Stalin's calculation, its correctness is borne out by another secret briefing speech which Hitler made before his Commanders-in-Chief, after the conclusion of the Polish campaign, on November 23rd, 1939. In it he said .

" What has been desired since 1870 and considered as impossible of achievement has come to pass. For the first time in history we have to fight on only one front. The other front is at present free. But no one can know how long that will remain so. At present Russia is not dangerous. She is weakened by many incidents today. Moreover, we have a pact with Russia. Pacts, however, are only kept as long as they serve their purpose. Russia will hold herself to it only as long as she considers it to be to her advantage. Even Bismarck thought so. Let us, therefore, think of the pact as securing our rear. Now Russia has far-reaching goals, above all the strengthening of her position in the Baltic. We can oppose Russia only when we are free in the West. Further, Russia is striving to increase her influence in the Balkans and towards the Persian Gulf. That is also the goal of our foreign policy. Russia will do that which she considers to benefit her. At the present moment she has retired from inter-nationalism. In case she renounces this, she will proceed to Pan-Slavism. It is difficult to see into the future. It is a fact that at the present time the Russian Army is of little worth. For the next year or two the present situation will remain."

To this Hitler added two incidental observations. Explaining that Italy could not be asked to join in the battle before Germany had gone over to the offensive in the West, he said : " Just so Russia did not attack until we marched into Poland." And further : " As long as Italy maintains this position, no danger from Yugoslavia is to be feared. Just so is the neutrality of Rumania achieved by the position of Russia." He concluded with the remark that " just as the death of Stalin, so the death of the Duce can bring danger to us."

Twenty-one Months

Hitler thus counted on the Non-Aggression Pact holding good for one or two years. In the event, it held for 21 months. During this period the German-Soviet economic agreement, the conclusion of which had preceded the non-aggression pact on August 19th, 1939, and had provided the basis for the political accord, dominated the field of German-Soviet relations. Both parties seem to have considered the economic agreement as the price they had to pay for obtaining the political accord which both felt they required, although obviously for different reasons—one in order to protect himself, the other in order to prepare his attack. This does not mean that both did not draw substantial material benefits from the economic agreement. That they did the Nuremberg Documents indicate beyond doubt. But they also indicate that Stalin played this political-economic see-saw game with great sagacity, and almost from the start had Hitler worrying. Considering the uncomfortable position in which he found himself, this was no small achievement for the Soviet leader. On the other hand his shrewd and circumspect tactics did not go unperceived in Berlin and undoubtedly in turn hastened Hitler on to what both must have recognized to be the inevitable end—the armed clash.

One of the most striking and informative documents issued at Nuremberg is the War Diary of General Jodl, believed to cover in a most detailed manner the entire period from about 1936 until nearly the end of the war. Unfortunately, only those sections of this unique document that were directly relevant to the prosecution's case were released, and these do not include the period here under review. But the gap is filled in the meantime by another War Diary, kept officially for the Chief of Staff of Raeder, the Supreme Commander of the German Navy. Its authenticity has been vouched for by Raeder, and although written largely from the Navy's point of view it serves to answer most of the questions which must now arise.

Once the Polish issue was largely settled—the Russian entry into Poland is valued by the Chief of Naval Operations as an event of the most far-reaching importance the resulting possible

effect of which " must be estimated as especially favourable "—
Germany lost no time in trying to see what she could get out of
Russia. On September 23rd, 1939, the Supreme Commander of
the Navy (Raeder) for the first time discussed with Hitler the
question of Russia ceding submarines to Germany and providing
facilities for the outfitting of auxiliary cruisers at Murmansk,
and Hitler asked the Foreign Office to put out feelers in Moscow.
Two days later the German Naval Attaché in Moscow reported
that " there is no doubt about Russia's honest attitude. The
Soviet Government is convinced of the necessity of co-
operation with Germany."

Naval Co-operation

On October 3rd, 1939, Raeder, who already then had his
eyes on Norway, forwarded to the German Foreign Office
suggestions on how Russia could support German naval warfare,
and Ribbentrop told him that in his opinion far-reaching support
might be expected. He believed that with Russian help naval
bases in Norway could be obtained. On October 5th, 1939,
however, Raeder's Chief of Staff noted that " a threatening
situation has arisen for Germans living in Estonia and Latvia
because of Russian demands " but he records that " the increase
of Russian influence in the Baltic States is happening with full
German accord." The evacuation of Germans, mismanaged by
the Foreign Office, caused anxiety because " the impression of
misunderstandings between Russia and Germany must be
avoided under all circumstances." The following week Russia
offered a well-situated base near Murmansk, but Raeder
insisted on obtaining in addition Norwegian bases, chiefly
Trondheim, with the help of Russian pressure. Hitler promised
examination but " refused the earlier request to build or buy
submarines in Russia, for political reasons."

When the British-Soviet trade agreement was announced,
providing for an exchange of timber for rubber and zinc, Berlin
was far from displeased. " Rubber and zinc via Russia " were
considered " just as important for Germany as timber for
Britain." Export of Russian timber would take place on
British or neutral ships from Murmansk " so that German
interference remains possible." Berlin was convinced that no
damage at all was intended by Russia against German economic
warfare. But on October 17th, 1939, the Chief of Naval
Operations, after a conference with the Naval Attaché in Moscow,

had to give up his plan for enlisting far-reaching Soviet support in matters of repair of warships, outfitting of auxiliary cruisers in Soviet yards, etc. This turned out to be " impossible for political and technical reasons." What was more, at the request of the Attaché, espionage and intelligence work against the Soviet Union through neutral countries had to be stopped immediately " to prevent Russian distrust."

The overall atmosphere, however, remained good. Ambassador Ritter reported on October 24th, 1939, that " Russia will, fulfil in full accord with Germany's policy all treaty obligations. She will not permit an actively hostile attitude on the part of Turkey against us or the passage of British and French warships through the Dardanelles." The Kremlin also issued a sharp note against British blockade warfare which was noted with satisfaction in Berlin. Assessing Russian wishes for the delivery of war materials which had become very pressing, Raeder's Chief of Staff came to the conclusion that " Russian economic help is of decisive importance for us. The offer was made in such generous terms that a success of the British blockade appears impossible. Accordingly, generous reciprocation is required from the German side as well." One begins to wonder which of the partners is squeezing the other harder.

But something was brewing in or around Finland, and the Germans did not like it. On October 26th, 1939, Molotov, mentioning political apprehension concerning the appearance of German warships in the Finnish Gulf, requested that " German economic warfare be restricted in the Baltic to West of 20 degrees East." The request was complied with but Raeder's Chief of Staff noted angrily that he " does not consider himself bound by this for the entire future." But Molotov made up for this somewhat rude notice with a speech on foreign policy in which he talked of " permanent friendship between the Soviet Union and Germany " while sharply attacking the British blockade for " violating international law."

Was Moscow playing a double game ? If it was the purpose of these periodical outbursts against the Western Democracies to please the Germans and lull their suspicions at the expense of Britain and France then engaged in the " phoney war "—which annoyed Hitler who would have liked to see them come out of their Maginot Line, but feared they might in the process invade Holland and Belgium before he himself could get there, and thereby threaten the Ruhr—then this purpose seemed fully

achieved in Berlin.   But as autumn drew into winter, Soviet
demands became uncomfortably heavy.   On November 4th,
1939, a Soviet economic delegation requested the delivery of
the hulls of the warships *Seydlitz* and *Lützow,* and although
Raeder was anxious to be co-operative, he rejected the delivery
of the *Seydlitz* and " a decrease of our own building programme
in favour of assistance to Russia."   The *Lützow,* however,
was to be handed over.   A week later, Hitler once more
rejected the purchase of Russian submarines for which
Raeder had been pressing, since he was convinced that " the
Russian ships are in bad condition and that the Russians should
not see any weakness with us."

Russia Is Not Able To Act

On November 23rd, 1939, Hitler talked to his Commanders-
in-Chief and Russia, as has been seen, on that occasion was
uppermost in his mind.   " The opponent in the West lies behind
his fortifications.   There is no possibility of coming to grips with
him.   The decisive question is : how long can we endure this
situation ? "   He reached the conclusion, already quoted, that
" we can oppose Russia only when we are free in the West."
Two days later, on November 25th, 1939, Raeder held a briefing
meeting with the heads of his department, presumably as a
sequel to the Hitler conference, and he summed up the situation
as follows :

" Russia is not able to act at the present time.   As long as
Stalin is in the government, a positive attitude is certain.   Changes
are possible after years of inner consolidation, especially in the
event of the overthrow or death of Stalin.   The expansion of
Russian interests in the direction of the Persian Gulf is supported
by Germany.   The Northern States, under joint German-Soviet
pressure, will stay neutral.   The South-eastern States, under
Soviet pressure, will equally remain neutral.   Germany in the
East has no military commitments.   For the first time in fifty
years a one-front war is possible."

Clearly this was a reflection of what Raeder had heard from
Hitler.   Once again the surprising thing is the curious notion Hitler
had of internal conditions in the Soviet Union.   Pinning his entire
faith in the person of Stalin whose overthrow he nevertheless
considered possible, he insisted on measuring Nazi and Soviet
authoritarianism with the same yardstick.   There is not one
among his confidential speeches in which he does not draw

attention to the irreplaceability of his own person. He is consistently preoccupied with the possibility of his own sudden death and the catastrophe it might bring in its train for Germany. Just so does he judge Stalin and the Soviet régime. It never occurred to him that the few outward similiarities might weigh rather light against the profound differences in spirit and structure. His ambassador in Moscow, Schulenburg, was a shrewd man who knew Russia well. Was he unable to dispel this delusion, or was he himself a victim of it ? Or did Ribbentrop dilute the ambassador's reports for the Führer's consumption ? It would not be unlike this very stupid man. On the other hand, it is true, and has been confirmed many times, that Hitler had a poor opinion of career diplomats and did not care much for the opinions of his accredited ambassadors. Yet one cannot help feeling that, faced with hard and well-substantiated advice, Hitler might have revised and corrected his estimate of Stalin and the Soviet Union. He was a stubborn man, undoubtedly, but if these documents show anything at all, it is that he was open to expert advice, and the neglect of important detail, despite his reliance on his " intuition," was not among his glaring defects. As it was, and as further study will show, his entire conduct of the Russian affair was based on these misconceptions. They are a vital component in the whole picture of the war.

The Finnish War

When the Soviet-Finnish war broke out, Molotov hastened to assure the Germans that " the primary goals of Russia lie in South-Eastern Europe and on the Black Sea. Russia will attempt a rapid olution of the Finnish problem to free her forces for other missions." In the same breath Moscow made further " high armament demands in return for economic aid." The German Navy was now to be asked to hand over not only the *Lützow* and *Seydlitz* but also the *Prinz Eugen*, besides the plans for *Bismarck* and *Tirpitz*, and the gun turrets for even bigger battleships in the yards. It almost looked as if the Soviet Union were trying to take a friendly hand in relieving potential pressure on the British Navy, but she was certainly working hard towards establishing some sort of naval balance between herself and Germany. Hitler, however, stiffened and refused to play. " According to the Führer's decision, our own naval armament may not be retarded under any circumstances." The sale of *Seydlitz* and *Prinz Eugen* was vetoed as well as the heavy gun turrets. Raeder added the worried sentence that there was now " a moral burden for Germany as a result of the Soviet-Finnish conflict."

A clear line of policy in this conflict was required for the German Navy. Raeder suggested to Hitler " a correct stand, no support for Finland which might become an unreliable burden." He advocated favouring Russia and pointed out the advantages offered by the Soviet Union. At the same time he drew Hitler's attention to increasing anti-German and pro-British feeling in Norway as a result of the Soviet-Finnish conflict and noted, with his tongue in his cheek, having told Hitler that " in several circles the opinion exists that the partition of Norway between Russia and Germany has already been agreed upon." When the invasion of Norway did occur several months later, Stalin refused to have anything to do with it.

The Fundamental Mistake

It was at this stage that Germany made what was perhaps her fundamental mistake. Hitler's Service Chiefs are seen to be drawing—along with much of the rest of the world—entirely erroneous conclusions about the weakness of Russian fighting power as revealed in Finland. Raeder's Chief of Staff noted on December 17th, 1939 : " It is important for our own attitude towards Russia not to over-estimate in German actions and decisions the still noticeable impact of the colossus Soviet Russia— an impact that is noticeable despite the existence of the pact of friendship ; but on the contrary to throw into the scales in all negotiations the military and political strength of Germany— perhaps even more so than has been done in the past." A fortnight later, on December 31st, 1939, the diarist quotes an official evaluation of the Red Army by the German General Staff. It runs :

" In quantity a gigantic military instrument. Commitment of the ' mass '. Organization, equipment, and leadership unsatisfactory. Principles of leadership good. Leaders themselves, however, too young and inexperienced. Communications system bad, transport bad. Troops not very uniform. No personalities. Simple soldier good-natured, quite satisfied with very little. Fighting qualities of the troops in heavy fighting dubious. The Russian ' mass ' is no match for an army with modern equipment and superior leadership."

Four years later, on November 7th, 1943, Gen. Jodl, in his confidential review of the war before a meeting of Gauleiters in Munich, stated : " If today, in view of the repeated and prolonged setbacks of the year 1943, the question arises again and again whether we had not thoroughly under-estimated the strength of the Bolshevist opponent, the answer to this question in regard to the execution of individual part-operations may certainly be said to be Yes."

And so into 1940. The Finnish war was still on, and so was the " phoney war " in the West. German-Soviet economic negotiations continued satisfactorily, but the Soviets were pressing for further naval deliveries. Hitler hedged, and the trade negotiations immediately got into difficulties " because the Soviet Government demands reciprocal assistance, that is to say, no performance without simultaneous corresponding German performance." But Hitler ordered that delivery of the *Lützow* and the construction plans for *Bismarck* should be delayed as long as possible. " He hopes, with a favourable course of the war, to get out of it altogether," notes the diarist. Evidently Hitler estimated that the Russians were in a bad way in Finland.

Apprehension in Berlin

On February 11th, 1940, the new German-Soviet trade agreement was concluded, and Raeder immediately urged Hitler to authorize a change in the annoying 20 degrees East limitation for German naval warfare in the Baltic. Hitler thought it over, and on April 1st, 1940, told Raeder, " for political reasons " not to press the matter any further. On February 12th, 1940, peace was concluded between the Soviet Union and Finland, and Raeder and Rosenberg had at last sold the Führer their idea of invading Norway with the help of Quisling. Preparations were going forward when Raeder had a new idea. On March 9th, 1940, he suggested to Hitler to inform the Russians during the occupation of Norway that the Germans did not intend to occupy Tromsö which the Russians would consider a recognition of their interests. " Better the Russians sit in Tromsö than the British." But Hitler " prefers to have the Russians not sit so close. He believes that Tromsö should also be occupied by us."

On March 29th, 1940, Molotov made another speech containing sharp criticisms of Anglo-French war policy and an affirmation of friendly relations between the Soviet Union and

Germany, but on April 5th, 1940, the German Naval Attaché in Moscow reported " an attitude of refusal " on the part of Molotov in the question of " use of a Far-Eastern base," and " temporary limitations on the use of Base North " have to be accepted.   Both disappointments the Attaché traces back to " the present Russian nervousness because of the future position of Britain and France toward Russia."   Meantime Norway is invaded, and Russia " declares herself disinterested in the action " ; she even " shows understanding for the German measures."   The German Ambassador in Moscow reports a very positive attitude of the Soviet press towards German military successes, and states that he can find no signs of uneasiness because of German victories.

But there was uneasiness in Berlin.   Hitler believed he had recognized " Russian intentions for the incorporation of the Baltic States,"   and was uncomfortable over the Russian entry into Bessarabia.   In the opinion of the German Foreign Office, Russia " is prepared to take a hand in the Balkans, but for the time being no action is expected."   On June 4th, 1940, Hitler described to Raeder his next objectives.   They were : after the defeat of France, reduction in the Army, discharge of the older age classes, especially skilled workers, emphasis on Air Force and Navy.   Raeder added : " No talk about Russia yet."   The planned strengthening of the Navy and Air Force seemed to indicate that Hitler's immediate pre-occupation was " Operation Sea-Lion "—the invasion of Britain.

On June 5th, 1940, Raeder's Chief of Staff evaluated the situation thus :

" Russia keenly appreciates Germany's military successes but she fears, after a decisive victory by Germany, a German attack against herself.   An allied victory, however, is not desired either.   Active participation of Russia in the war is entirely out of the question because of her military weakness and the lack of internal stability.   Stalin is definitely determind not to sacrifice himself for the Allies.   Official Russian policy is still absolutely correct.   However, the possibility of an attempt slowly to sabotage our economic co-operation is not out of the question. Owing to her apprehensions regarding the further development of her relations with Germany, Russia considers that further expansion of her bases in the Baltic is indicated.   The pressure on Lithuania and Estonia points to an attempt to obtain full domination over that area."

This clear analysis betrays no illusions on the part of its author as to the real causes and motives of the beginning Soviet-German tension. Soviet moves are recognized for what they are— protective measures, while the writer discerns no indication of Russian inclinations or preparations to attack. Coinciding with this the German Naval Attaché in Moscow reports on June 10th, 1940, a "noticeable cooling off and technical difficulties on the part of the Russians," and sees the reason for it in " Russian apprehension about the British attitude in case of too strong Russian leanings toward Germany and over a German attack on Russia after victory over the Western Powers."

With Tears in Her Eyes

On June 15th 1940, the Soviet Union absorbed Lithuania, Estonia, and Latvia. Raeder's Chief of Staff gave it as his opinion that this " was to be expected for some time," as indeed it apparently was. But it may be remarked in passing that in the German note to the Soviet Union of June 22nd, 1941, it is said that " the German Ambassador in Moscow declared to the Soviet Government that the decision came to the Reich Government ' entirely unexpectedly '." Molotov, however, notified Germany that the purpose of the operations in the Baltic was " to end all intrigues by which the Western Powers had attempted in the Baltic to sow distrust between the Soviet Union and Germany "—a statement which cost him nothing, but which, in the circumstances, does not seem to have made a very deep impression in Berlin.

Berlin was now beginning to worry seriously lest Moscow should " cool off " faster than desired, and before Hitler was ready to tackle the Red Army. The Battle of Britain had begun, and Hitler's eyes were on " Sea-Lion." Russian entry into Bessarabia is recorded as being imminent, and a crisis in the South-East is averted only by Hitler making a handsome concession. " By intervention of the Reich Government and through German pressure on Rumania, a peaceful settlement was reached ceding Bessarabia and Northern Bukovina to Russia." On July 8th, 1940, the diarist notes that " contrary to foreign reports the Foreign Office emphasizes the correct behaviour of the Soviet Government toward Germany." Preparations were made for the despatch of " Ship 45," in co-operation with the Russians, by the Siberian sea-lane, but at the same time the diary notes, on July 10th, 1940, that " Russia desires closer relationship with Bulgaria and further advances in the Balkans with Bulgarian help. Bulgaria and Rumania are remaining reserved and are looking to Germany for support. There is increasing Russian influence in Yugoslavia, and Russia is penetrating into Persia."

On July 21st, 1940, Raeder had another interview with Hitler who lectured him on America and Russia. " Even though Russia views Germany's great successes with tears in her eyes, she herself has no intention of entering the war against Germany. It is naturally a duty to weigh the American and Russian question seriously. It is in the German interest to wage war rapidly, but there is no urgent need for it. War material is plentiful, and the food supply is secure. The fuel situation is the most difficult part, but as long as Rumania and Russia deliver and hydro-electric works can be safeguarded against air attacks, it is not critical."

Finland, meanwhile, becomes a fresh worry. Rumours about a Russian ultimatum to Finland at the end of July, 1940, are untrue according to Ribbentrop's Foreign Office, but according to the German Naval Attaché in Helsinki, there is a depressed mood in Finland and a hope that one day Germany will bring help to Finland after all. On August 13th, 1940, Hitler instructs Raeder to strengthen the fortifications of the North Norwegian fjords against possible Russian attacks in case of a renewed Russo-Finnish conflict. A week later the naval diary records another estimate of Soviet long-term aims by Raeder's Chief of Staff. They are an ice-free port in the North Atlantic, an advance through the Balkans for the annexation of the Dardanelles and domination of the Black Sea, an advance through Persia to the Persian Gulf, strong pressure in Rumania, Bulgaria and Yugoslavia through pan-Slav Communist propaganda which is partly successful, strong activities by agents in Greece but demands on Turkey unknown. " Force of arms," concludes the appreciation, " is not expected at present. Russian behaviour is strongly dependent on the further development of the war. The political weight of the Axis should be able to keep the peace in the Balkans. Economic deliveries by Russia are good beyond expectation."

In Case of Rapid Action

The " further development of the war " was, of course, that by the end of August 1940 it had become clear that the Battle of Britain had ended in a German defeat, and that " Operation

Sea-Lion " was not immediately feasible. The first transfers of German troops from the West to the Eastern border were carried out. According to Hitler's Directive for " Sea-Lion " which is dated August 17th, 1940, and quoted by Raeder's Chief of Staff, ten infantry and two armoured divisions were sent to the Government-General (Poland) " in case rapid action should become necessary in the interest of a protection of the Rumanian oil-fields." The documents unfortunately do not make it possible to establish here beyond all doubt what was cause and what effect. Was it anxiety about Rumanian oil (undoubtedly genuine) which crippled the preparations for " Sea-Lion " or was it the impossibility of launching " Sea-Lion " with a beaten Air Force as protection which caused Hitler to begin thinking, for the first time, of a move against Russia with unconquered Britain at his back ?

Gen. Jodl, in his Munich speech, apparently favours the second interpretation. He says that " the Führer himself has always kept this danger (of an approaching Bolshevist East) steadily in view, and even as far back as during the Western campaign informed me of his fundamental decision to take steps against this danger the moment our military position made it at all possible." Raeder's memorandum to Admiral Assmann of January 10th, 1944, which has already been quoted elsewhere in these studies, in referring to this same period, makes a similar point. " The Führer very clearly had the idea of one day settling accounts with Russia," the memorandum says. " Doubtless his general ideological attitude played an essential part in this. In 1937-38 he once stated that he intended to eliminate the Russians as a Baltic Power. They would then have to be diverted in the direction of the Persian Gulf. The Russian measures against Finland and the Baltic States in 1939-40 probably further strengthened him in this idea. During the campaign in France and also during the beginning of the preparations for ' Sea-Lion,' while the Führer still had hopes of gaining control of the air (which he too recognized as being an essential pre-requisite for ' Sea-Lion '), it was doubtless his intention after France's fall to concentrate on the Navy and Air Force. The Führer described the moving of troops to the Eastern front in August (1940) to me as a large-scale camouflage measure for ' Sea-Lion '. A statement from the Supreme Command of the Army would have to be obtained on this point." Apart from the fact that Hitler is here seen to have blandly deceived his own

Naval Supreme Commander (whom he knew to be in opposition to an attack against the Soviet Union before Britain had been decisively beaten) Raeder's statement largely confirms Jodl's story.

It can, therefore, truthfully be said, that Germany's preparations for an attack on the Soviet Union began in August 1940, that is, they took nearly a year. Indeed, during his cross-examination as a witness before the Nuremberg Tribunal, Gen. Paulus stated that " he first heard of the proposed attack on Russia on September 3rd, 1940 " when he became quarter-master-general of the General Staff. The Chief of the General Staff at that time was Gen. Halder, who, said Paulus " handed over to me the plan for the attack, in so far as it had already been prepared, and told me to examine the possibilities of the attack. The forces required were between 130 and 140 divisions." From that moment then, when troops were tied down though not committed, in both East and West, Germany actually faced the position of a two-front war. The fact that there was no land fighting in either West or East did not relieve her of the necessity of thinking and planning, henceforth, in terms of a two-front war. The " ideal state of affairs " was no more and the new situation did not take long to assert itself and impose its strain. From now on German strategic planning becomes increasingly complicated and involved until in the end the multiplicity of planned operations strangles everything.

On September 6th, 1940, Jodl issued from Hitler's Head-quarters an interesting document. It was addressed to the Counter-Intelligence Service whose head was Admiral Canaris. It states :

" The Eastern territory will be manned more strongly in the weeks to come. By the end of October the status shown on the enclosed map is supposed to be reached. These regroupings must not create the impression in Russia that we are preparing an offensive in the East. On the other hand Russia will realize that strong and highly-trained German troops are stationed in the Government-General, in the Eastern provinces, and in the Protectorate. She should draw the conclusion that we can at any time protect our interests, especially in the Balkans, with strong forces against any seizures by her.

" For the work of our own Intelligence Service as well as for the answer to questions from the Soviet Intelligence Service, the following instructions apply :

(1) The respective total strength of the German troops in the East is to be veiled as far as possible by giving news about a frequent change of army units there. This change is to be explained by movements into training camps, regroupings, etc.

(2) The impression is to be created that the centre of the troop concentrations is in the Southern part of the Government-General, in the Protectorate, and in Austria, and that the concentrations in the North are relatively unimportant.

(3) Regarding the question of equipment of these units, especially of the armoured division, things are to be exaggerated, if possible.

(4) By disseminating suitable news the impression is to be created that the anti-aircraft protection in the East has been increased considerably since the conclusion of the campaign in the West and that it continues to be increased with captured French material on all important targets.

(5) Concerning improvements on railroads, roads, airfields, etc., it is to be stated that the work is kept within normal limits, is needed for the improvement of the newly won Eastern territories, and serves primarily economic traffic.

" The Supreme Command of the Army decides to what extent correct details, *i.e.*, numbers of regiments, manning of garrisons etc., will be made available to Counter-Intelligence for purposes of counter-espionage."

Who is Setting the Pace?

From now on things begin to show signs of tightening up, the inevitable result of each move acting and reacting upon the other. The question is : who is setting the pace, Hitler or Stalin? From the documents available it is impossible to answer it. The impression one gains, at any rate from the German side, is that the inherent dynamics of the constellation are driving matters forward almost under their own steam. To which, of course, must always be added the important qualification that we know that Germany intended to attack, sooner or later, whereas we possess no such knowledge from the Soviet side but a good deal of evidence to the contrary.

September 1940 was a month of worry for the Germans, with all manner of conflicting reports and advice coming in. On September 8th, 1940, the Russians were noted as being annoyed by the Vienna arbititration award which they regarded as being pointed against the Soviet Union (which it was), and the diarist

recorded a " deterioration in the relations with Germany."
But official quarters regarded this as merely temporary. On
September 12th, 1940, the Naval Attaché in Moscow said that
" the Russian attitude, which was very reserved in the beginning,
is now markedly friendly," and remarked that " the reason for
this change is not clearly understandable." On September 14th,
1940, the German Naval Attaché in Tokyo had a conversation
with Toshio Shiratori, former Japanese Ambassador in Rome,
who told him bluntly that he did not believe in a long duration
of the German-Russian understanding and hoped that Germany
would join up with Japan " for the destruction of Russia."

On September 18th, 1940, information was received about
anti-German propaganda in the Red Army. The Germans
were in no doubt about the reason for this : the Red Army
was assuming German intentions to attack and based its work on
this assumption. The following week an article in the official
Soviet press emphasized that the Soviet Union stood " outside
the present fight for the Balkan peninsula, true to its peace and
neutrality policy " but in Berlin this was scarcely believed, and the
Ambassador in Moscow reported that " there is no doubt about
the very strong Russian interest in the Balkans where nothing
can be decided without Russia." On September 26th, 1940,
Raeder told Hitler that something had to be done in Libya.
" The Suez Canal must be captured with German assistance.
From Suez we must advance through Palestine and Syria.
Then Turkey is in our power. The Russian problem will then
assume a different appearance. Russia is fundamentally fright-
ened of Germany. It is questionable whether action from the
North will then still be necessary."

It seems obvious from this last remark that some such action
must have been considered in the meantime. What it was we
can only guess. But Hitler's hope of deflecting Russian pressure
towards the South-East and into Asia is clearly discernible.
He agreed to Raeder's suggestion. " Russia will be induced to
advance in the direction of Persia and India in order to find
there an outlet to the ocean. That could be more important
for Russia than the position in the Baltic." Both Hitler and
Raeder were of the opinion that Russia was seriously afraid of
Germany's strength, and considered " fresh Russo-Finnish
entanglements this year improbable." The Baltic and the
Rumanian oilfields were Hitler's two main worries. As long as
he could see his way to get the Russians off the Baltic hinge

where they clustered much too thickly for his liking, and keep' them at a fair distance from his oil, he did not really care very much in what direction they were going.

The Three Power Pact between Germany, Italy and Japan is concluded next, and the Russians declare that they see in it " a recognition of Russian neutrality and peace policy." The Germans march into Rumania and expect the Russians to be annoyed but "there are no signs of change in the Russian attitude." Nor does the Russian attitude with regard to the Italian-Greek conflict which breaks out on October 28th, 1940, give rise to any anxiety. " Russia will continue to form the rear protection of the European bloc " notes Raeder's Chief of Staff. " Economic deliveries are running according to schedule. Increasing relaxation of the tension between Russia and Japan." Ill-feeling is caused in Moscow as a result of the transit of German troops through Finland, but it is smoothed out. The Ambassador reports that " renunciation by Moscow of interference in Balkan interests permits very well the possibility of compensation in other areas."

Case East Appears

Under the date of October 30th, 1940, the code-word "Ostfall" (Case East) appears for the first time in the documents. But we can find no precise explanation of its meaning, at any rate in the documents so far available. One may presume that it is a fore-runner of " Case Barbarossa," which was the final operational plan for the invasion of the Soviet Union, possibly in a modified form with its main emphasis on either the Baltic or the Balkans. The naval diarist noted that " in view of the present development of the situation ' Ostfall ' is no longer considered likely. Nevertheless, readiness for defence and preparations in armaments continue at an increased speed." It is possible that Hitler, at this stage, was reckoning with a locally isolated incident which would not involve the entire Russian front ; it is equally possible that he wished to safeguard his preparations in case of a flare-up caused by the Russians. On November 4th, 1940, he told Raeder that in case of a German advance in the Balkans in support of Italy, he expected Russia to remain neutral, but that the whole question would be talked over with Molotov in the near future. " Preparations for an Eastern Incident (Ostfall) are, however, to be continued."

The conversations with Molotov begin in Berlin on November

R

10th, 1940, and on November 12th, 1940, Hitler issues from his headquarters "War Directive No. 18" which, after dealing mainly with France, Spain and the Italian position in Libya, states in reference to Russia :

" Political discussions have been initiated with the aim of clarifying Russia's attitude for the time being. Irrespective of the results of these discussions, all preparations for the East which have already been verbally ordered, will be continued. Instructions on this will follow as soon as the general outline of the Army's operational plans has been submitted to, and approved by, me."

Raeder doesn't like it. He has a conference with Hitler on November 14th, 1940, from which he gathers that " the Führer is still inclined to instigate the conflict with Russia." Raeder recommends " putting it off until the time after the victory over Britain since there is a heavy strain on the German forces and the end of warfare in the West not in sight." In his opinion Russia will not press for a conflict within the next year since she is in the process of building up her Navy with Germany's help and for the time being continues to be dependent upon German assistance. But Hitler is either bored or disgusted with the West and keeps his eyes on the East.

The Molotov Conversations

The course of the negotiations with Molotov was regarded as satisfactory in Berlin. On November 16th, 1940, the naval diarist recorded the following conclusions :

" For the time being there will be no fixed treaty. Russia is apparently ready to join the Three Power Pact after several further questions have been clarified. Regarding the Finnish problem, Molotov put a ' careful ' question in respect of an annexation of Finland by Russia. Germany is unwilling to consider this but is ready for concessions in respect of the exploitation of the Petsamo nickel mines. The Polish problem was not discussed. Molotov was notified of contemplated German action in the Balkans in support of Italy and raised no objections. He suggested the creation of conditions suitable for Russian influence in Bulgaria, similar to German influence in Rumania, but this suggestion was not entered into by the Germans. However, Germany disclosed her disinterestedness in the Turkish domination of the Dardanelles, and sympathy with Russian desires for bases there, as well as for the regaining of the Kars and Ardahan areas from Turkey. Molotov agreed to examine the suggestion of joint pressure on Turkey. Regarding Persia Germany declared to have no interests there, but the Russians remained very reserved on this question. Japan was discussed, and Molotov was ready for an understanding. He insisted, however, on first having a thorough discussion of all problems affecting both countries."

One has little reason to doubt that this was the truth about the Molotov visit as the Germans knew it. The purpose of the conversations, from the German point of view, becomes clear. While Hitler was talking to Molotov, Jodl and his staff officers were busy working on the details of the operational plan for "Barbarossa." Hitler wished merely to "clarify Russia's attitude for the time being," that is, until he was ready to strike. He wanted to know "where he was" and to safeguard himself, as far as possible, against surprises arising from his insufficient familiarity with the Russian frame of mind. He got what he wanted, or at any rate most of it. From his point of view the conversations were indeed satisfactory. Yet it is clear from these meagre notes, that the talks were conducted on both sides with infinite care, circumspection and fox-like caution.

The account given of them by Hitler in his Note to Russia of June 22nd, 1941, and in his public speech on the same day, bears no resemblance to what we now know actually went on. The only point where some similarity can be detected is the question of Bulgaria, while the Turkish issue is completely distorted. According to Hitler's public speech, Molotov demanded "unconditional free access to the Dardanelles and occupation of a number of important bases along the Dardanelles and the Bosphorus" which Germany was "unwilling to agree to." In actual fact, as we see now, Hitler gave Molotov a free hand against Turkey and even suggested helping him attain his aims by putting Turkey under joint pressure—a suggestion from which Molotov wisely shied away. Finally it appears now that the Soviet claim to Kars and Ardahan and other Turkish regions bordering on Georgia and Soviet Armenia, raised officially by Moscow in December 1945, is not a new one but figured, whatever its merits or demerits, among the long-term objectives of Soviet Foreign policy already five years earlier.

Case "Barbarossa"

With Molotov departed and the world wondering whether

Moscow would really join the Three Power Pact, the Chief of the General Staff of the German Army, on December 5th, 1940, reported to Hitler on the planned operation in the East. The Führer declared his agreement with the plans as submitted and added this:

" The most important goal is to prevent the Russians from withdrawing on a closed front. The eastward advance should be combined until the Red Air Force is no longer able to attack Reich territory, and, on the other hand, the German Air Force is enabled to conduct raids to destroy Soviet war industrial territories. In this way we should be able to achieve the annihilation of the Soviet Army and prevent its regeneration. The first commitment of forces should take place in such a way as to make possible the annihilation of strong enemy units. It is essential that the Russians should not take up positions in the rear again. The number of 130-140 divisions as planned for the entire operation is sufficient."

This is apparently the conference to which Gen. Paulus referred when testifying as a witness for the prosecution at the Nuremberg Tribunal on February 11th, 1946. Paulus went on to say that the Supreme Command Directive No. 20, issued on December 13th, 1940, was " the basis of all military and economic preparations for the invasion of the Soviet Union." This Directive is not among the documents made available at Nuremberg. But we possess Directive No. 21, issued from Hitler's Headquarters only a week later, on December 18th, 1940, and marked " Case Barbarossa." This bears the signature of Hitler and is initialled by Jodl, Keitel and Warlimont. It is possible although not very likely that Gen. Paulus confused the two directives and their dates and in his testimony was actually referring to Directive No. 21. On the other hand it is quite possible that Hitler issued two directives on the same subject at only a week's interval, the second being a modification of the first after discussion. We know this to have occurred on several other occasions. Whatever the explanation, the point is not of vital importance, and Directive No. 21 of December 18th, 1940, which is before us, certainly appears as a very final and definite document. It opens with this sentence :

"The German Armed Forces must be prepared to crush Soviet Russia in a quick campaign before the end of the war against Britain."

It then goes on to outline the specific tasks of Army, Navy and Air Force.

The Army " will have to employ all available units with the reservation that the occupied territories will have to be safeguarded against surprise attacks." The Air Force " will have to free such strong forces for the support of the Army that a rapid completion of the ground operations may be expected and damage to the eastern German territories avoided as far as possible." But this concentration of the main effort in the East is limited by the following reservation : " The entire battle and armament area dominated by us must remain sufficiently protected against enemy air attacks and the attacks against Britain and especially the supply for them must not be permitted to break down ! " The Navy is instructed to continue concentrating its main effort " unequivocally against Britain also during the Eastern campaign."

The Directive continues :

" If occasion arises I shall order the concentration of troops for action against Soviet Russia eight weeks before the intended beginning of operations. Preparations requiring more time are— if this has not yet been done—to begin presently and are to be completed by May 15th, 1941. Great caution has to be exercised lest the intention to attack be recognized."

More detailed instructions follow.

" The mass of the Russian Army in Western Russia is to be destroyed in daring operations by driving forward deep wedges with tanks. The retreat of intact battle-ready troops into the wide open spaces of Russia is to be prevented. In quick pursuit a given line is to be reached from which the Red Air Force will no longer be able to attack German Reich territory. The first goal of operations is the protection from Asiatic Russia along the general line Volga-Archangel. In case of necessity the last industrial areas in the Urals left to Russia could be eliminated by the Air Force."

The task of Rumania " together with the forces concentrating there " is defined as " pinning down the opponent on the other side and, in addition, rendering auxiliary services in the rear areas."

The Directive concludes :

" It must be clearly understood that all orders to be given by the Commanders-in-Chief on the basis of this directive are precautionary measures, in case Russia should change her present attitude toward us. The number of officers to be drafted for the preparations in the early stages is to be kept as small
S

as possible. Otherwise the danger exists that our preparations—the time for their execution has not yet been fixed—will become known and grave political and military disadvantages would result from this."

The date has not yet been fixed. But May 15th, 1941, is envisaged. Hitler reckons with having another clear six months in hand.

" Sea-lion " Shelved

But Raeder still does not like it. On December 20th, 1940, the naval diarist records it as the opinion of his chief that the " strengthening of the British position through an unfavourable development of the situation in the Eastern Mediterranean and the help from the U.S.A. demand absolute concentration against Britain," and he has therefore " serious doubts concerning ' Barbarossa ' before the defeat of Britain."

A week later Raeder goes to argue it out with Hitler. Again he " voices serious objections against the Russian campaign before the defeat of Britain." Hitler on his part desires all possible advancement of submarine construction—the present construction figures (12-18 per month) are much too low—but he insists that " the last continental enemy must be removed under all circumstances because of the present political development (Russia's tendency to interfere in Balkan affairs) before he can come to grips with Britain. Therefore the Army must acquire the necessary strength. After that, full concentration on Air Force and Navy can follow."

Raeder has to give in. He notes the next day, December 28th, 1940, that " the political situation is changed by Russia's unreliability, as evident in the Balkan states. Consequently strengthening of the Army is necessary. But the emphasis on Navy and Air Force against Britain is not to be impaired." In his memorandum to Admiral Assmann, already quoted, he says very much the same thing. " At this time," he writes there, " the Führer had made known his ' unalterable decision ' to conduct the Eastern campaign in spite of all remonstrances. Experience had shown that, after this, further warnings, unless entirely new situations arose, were completely useless. As Chief of Naval War Staff I was never convinced of the ' compelling necessity ' for ' Barbarossa.'."

Raeder knew his Führer. Operation " Sea-Lion " was thus shelved, and the all-out effort against the Soviet Union began.

The Economic Balance Sheet

Meanwhile, how does the Soviet-German economic balance-sheet stand at the turn of the year? Much of the answer is contained in a manuscript entitled "Basic Facts for a History of German War and Armaments Economy," compiled by Major-General Thomas, Chief of the War Industry Department. In this long and detailed account, General Thomas writes :

"As reported previously in 1939, according to the German-Soviet treaty of August 19th, 1939, German deliveries on credit were to attain during the next two years the sum of 200 million Reichsmarks of which 120 million during the first year. It was indicated that German deliveries of material to the value of 500 million were desired during the first year alone. As such quantities of machines, vehicles, apparatus, etc., could not be obtained, from the production point of view, in such a short time and as the Russians had also included war material in their requests, the preponderant desire, from the beginning, at the Foreign Office and the Reich Ministry of Economy was to place at the disposal of the Russians as much finished war material as possible.

"As reported previously, the Russians had made ready for their first reciprocal delivery valuable foodstuffs and raw materials—one million tons cereals, 500,000 tons wheat, 900,000 tons oil by-products, 100,000 tons cotton, 500,000 tons phosphates, 80 million Reichsmarks' worth of timber, 10,000 tons of flax, manganese, platinium, and the transit of one million tons of soya beans—and in consideration of the importance of these quantities to German war economy and the importance which the Supreme Command attached to the maintenance of friendly relations with Soviet Russia, the question of immediate reciprocal deliveries became steadily more pressing.

"The desire to produce war material became stronger from week to week, so strong, in fact, that the Supreme Command created a special section at the 'Wirtschafts-Rüstungs-Amt' (War Industry Department) charged with working on these Russian requests and arranging them in accordance with the German production programme. As the Russians delivered quickly and well, it was imperative to accelerate German deliveries. Consequently the German Supreme Command decided to offer the Russians even more war material which was either already manufactured or under construction and the monetary value of which was high. The cruiser *Lützow* especially came into this category, other ordnance installations for ships, patterns for heavy artillery and tanks and important patents for war materials. As the contracts for these materials did not satisfy the Russian requests, the Führer ordered on March 30th, 1940, that—as far as necessary—the delivery of war material to the Russians should have priority over the delivery to the German Armed Forces.

" This order placed some of the Army departments in a difficult position as the Supreme Command also desired production for German requirements stepped up and demanded punctual delivery. On August 14th, 1940, the Chief of the War Industry Department (General Thomas himself) during a conference with Reich Marshal Goering was informed that the Führer desired punctual delivery to the Russians only until spring 1941. Later on we would have no further interest in completely satisfying Russian demands. This allusion prompted the Chief of the War Industry Department to allot priority to matters concerning Russian War Economy. By the end of October, 1940, Reich Marshal Goering insisted once more on pressure being exerted for accelerated deliveries to the Russians according to schedule. Later on the urgency of the Russian deliveries diminished as preparations for the campaign in the East were already under way.

" The Russians carried out their deliveries as planned, right up to the start of the attack. Even during the last few days, transports of Indiarubber from the Far East were completed by express transit trains."

In a later section of his voluminous memorandum, General Thomas adds this :

" Until June, 1941, the negotiations with Russia were accorded a great deal of attention. The Führer issued a directive that, in order to camouflage German troop movements, the orders Russia had placed in Germany must be filled as promptly as possible. Since the Russians only made grain deliveries when the Germans delivered orders placed by the Russians, and since in the case of individual firms these deliveries to Russia made it impossible for them to fill orders for the German Armed Forces, it was necessary for the War Industry Department to enter into numerous individual negotiations with German firms in order to co-ordinate Russian orders with our own and to establish priorities. In accordance with the wishes of the Foreign Office, German industry was instructed to accept all Russian orders, even if it were impossible to fill them within the limits of time set for manufacture and delivery. Since, especially in May, large deliveries had to be made to the Navy, the firms were instructed to allow the equipment to go through the Russian Acceptance Commission, then, however, to make such a detour during its transport as to make it impossible for it to be delivered over the frontier prior to the beginning of the German attack."

General Thomas's Forecast

General Thomas's memorandum contains a number of other points of considerable interest with regard to Soviet Russia. He states that in November, 1940—that is, before the issue of the first " Barbarossa " Directive—he and a number of Under-Secretaries of State were informed by Goering of the action planned in the East and received instructions for the preliminary preparations of the campaign. Work on these began in his department toward the end of 1940. It included the following :

" Obtaining a detailed survey of Soviet armaments industry, its location, capacity, and associate industries ; investigation of the capacity of the various big armament centres and their dependence upon each other ; determination of the power and transport system for these industries in the Soviet Union ; investigation of sources of raw materials and crude oil ; preparation of a survey of industries other than armament industries in the Soviet Union."

After insisting that his department had taken great pains " to give a completely objective picture of the situation regarding defence and armament economy in the Soviet Union, and had held it necessary to draw attention to the points which might cause difficulties to a military operation," General Thomas sums up his conclusions " on the basis of safely proved facts."

Any operation, he says, which leads to the occupation of the European part of the Soviet Union excluding the Urals, should result in the following : during the first few months Germany would be relieved in the field of nutrition and raw materials if a rapid seizure should succeed in preventing the destruction of stocks, capturing the mineral oil fields of the Caucasus undestroyed, and solving the transport problem. Should the campaign last longer, effective relief would be dependent on the solution of the transport problem ; the staying-put of the population and winning them over to collaboration ; preventing destruction of motor transport and the possibility of replacing the

Russian pool of tractors and agricultural machines by resuming production in the U.S.S.R. ; the possibilities of fuel supply ; the capture of power stations undestroyed or their fast restoration ; securing the delivery of raw materials not existing in the European part of the Soviet Union. Further, the supply of Germany with Indiarubber, tungsten, copper, platinum, tin, asbestos, and manila hemp would remain unsolved until communication with the Far East can be established.

General Thomas adds that " the territory south of the mouth of the Volga and Don including the Caucasus must be included in the operation. The Caucasian fuel supply is indispensable for the exploitation of the occupied territories." He concludes his survey by forecasting that " in the field of mere armament industries the campaign will lead to taking possession of about 75 per cent. of the total Russian armament industry and almost 100 per cent. of the industries manufacturing precision tools and optical instruments."

It appears that General Thomas had a shrewd and precise idea of what a war against the Soviet Union involved, and it cannot be said that he did not tell Hitler so in good time. Read together in the light of what occurred later, Hitler's Directive No. 21 and General Thomas's memorandum pin-point with almost uncanny exactitude all the major danger points on which the campaign ultimately broke down. All the German foresight and technical thoroughness were unable to prevent this. As Hitler (according to Gen. Paulus) told his staff in Poltava on June 1st, 1942, when the war against Russia was nearly a year old : " If I do not get the Grozny and Maikop oilfields I shall have to wind up the war."

An Ice-cold Blackmailer

On January 11th, 1941, new and far-reaching agreements were signed between Germany and the Soviet Union covering economic, resettlement and frontier questions, but the atmosphere grew increasingly uncomfortable. More disturbing reports reached Berlin from the Balkans, especially from Rumania and Bulgaria, and the naval diarist noted " much Russian interference." At the same time British diplomatic moves in Moscow were for the first time noted as being of a possibly serious character. By now Hitler is calling Stalin an " ice-cold black-mailer " and tells Raeder that it is hope in the U.S.A. and Russia which keeps Britain together. " With an American and Russian entry into the war a very great burden would be placed on our conduct of the war. Therefore, every possibility of such a threat must be excluded from the very beginning. If the Russian threat can be removed, we can continue to fight against Britain under very tolerable conditions. Russia's collapse would mean considerable relief of the burden for the Japanese and increased danger for the U.S.A."

On January 19th, 1941, Mussolini accompanied by Ciano and the Italian Service Chiefs visited Hitler at his headquarters. This meeting is fully discussed elsewhere in these studies (Chapter II, Otto to Alaric). The Italians were in a bad way in Albania and in Libya. Hitler gave them his appreciation of the situation.

" Finland," he pointed out, " is of great importance to us owing to her nickel deposits which are unique in Europe. The Russians promise to supply us with the quantities of nickel required but only as long as they see fit to do so. Therefore Finland must not be interfered with any more."

He revealed that there had been a Russian *démarche* " on account of our troop concentrations in Rumania " and stated that it would be duly rejected. " The Russians always become insolent at a time when they cannot be harmed, namely in winter." Contrary to what he had just told Raeder, Hitler assured Mussolini that he didn't see " great danger coming from America, even if she should enter the war. The much greater danger is the gigantic block of Russia."

He proceeded to impart to the Duce some of his worries. " Although we have very favourable political and economic agreements with Russia, I prefer to rely on powerful means at my disposal. Very considerable parts of these are therefore tied down on the Russian frontier, thus preventing me from supplying the armament industry with sufficient man-power to bring the armament of the Air Force and Navy to the highest possible pitch. As long as Stalin lives, there is probably no danger. He is intelligent and careful. But should he cease to be there, the Jews who at present only occupy second and third-rank positions, might move up again into the first rank."

It may be noted, in passing, that this is the first and only time in all the secret documents now available, that Hitler refers in one of his confidential high-level conferences to the Jews and their alleged role in world politics. In all his briefing conferences with his Service Chiefs he never once even mentions them—

not even in his most rabid dissertations on "living space" although he could have conveniently fitted them in—obviously because he knows and his associates know that at bottom there is no substance to the story and that the Jews, although a useful scapegoat, are not a "military reality." Why he should have wished to revive this propaganda line in talking to Mussolini, is not clear. Possibly he felt that a little propaganda could do the Duce no harm.

"It therefore behoves us to be careful," Hitler continued. "The Russians are continually trying to work out new demands which they read into the agreements. That is why they do not like explicit and precise formulas in these agreements. It is therefore necessary to keep a constant eye on the Russian factor and to be on guard, by means of strength and clever diplomacy. Formerly Russia would have been no danger at all, for on land she cannot imperil us in the least, but now, in the era of the air force, the Rumanian oil-fields can be turned into an expanse of smoking débris from Russia and from the Mediterranean, and the life of the Axis depends on these oil-fields."

Even while Hitler and Mussolini were conferring, Stalin made a speech in which he stated bluntly that he was working untiringly for the strengthening of the Soviet Navy and Army. "The international situation is complicated and confused," he said (and the naval diarist noted it), "and even Russia is threatened by the danger of war." Apparently Stalin suspected Germany of making preliminary military contacts in Finland and warned Finland, as the diarist noted, that "going together with any state other than the Soviet Union is causing concern."

As a result of the conference with Mussolini fresh plans were rapidly worked out to help the Italians in Greece and in Libya. The Greek operation received the code-name "Marita" while the support action in North Africa becomes known as "Operation Sunflower." In the upshot, a third operation had to be planned, namely "Operation 25," the invasion of Yugoslavia. One after the other these began to get in the way of "Barbarossa." At the beginning of February, 1941, "Barbarossa" and "Marita" were being treated almost as a joint undertaking, so interdependent had they become.

"Barbarossa" and "Sunflower"

On February 3rd, 1941, Hitler held an operational conference with his Army Chiefs only in which "Barbarossa" and

" Sunflower " were considered jointly. The Chief of Staff of the Army gave his estimate of the Russian situation.

" Enemy strength approximately 100 infantry divisions, 25 cavalry divisions, approximately 30 mechanized divisions. Our own strength about the same but far superior in quality. Among leading Soviet military personalities, Timoshenko is the only outstanding figure."

Details of the strength and organization of Soviet divisions, he continued, were important only in that even the infantry divisions included a comparatively large number of tanks although the material was bad and " merely thrown together." As regards mechanized divisions the Germans had superiority in tanks and artillery. "The Russians are superior in numbers, we in quality." The Russians were normally equipped in artillery but material was likewise inferior. Command of the artillery was inadequate. Russian operational intentions were unknown. There were no strong forces at the frontier. Any retreat could only be on a small scale since the Baltic States and the Ukraine were vital to the Russians for supply reasons. Fortification work was in progress especially on the Northern and Southern flanks.

Operational orders for the three German Army Groups— North, Centre and South—were then outlined by the Chief of Staff who stated that Army Group South required 6 armoured divisions from " Marita " and a further 2 from Rumania itself. But this would depend on the Balkan situation and Turkey's attitude. Hitler interjected that " when the die has been cast, the Turks will not make any further moves. No special protection of the Balkans is therefore necessary. One dangerous moment would arise should North Africa be cleared by the British, thus enabling them to operate in Syria with unhampered forces." The Chief of Staff went on to explain that in the North the Falkenhorst Army could advance on Petsamo with $1\frac{1}{2}$ divisions by using Swedish railways and Hitler added that it could be assumed " that Sweden would join us at a price. This price might be the Aaland Islands although these are not our possessions." The Chief of Staff stressed the uncertainty of Hungary's attitude and insisted that agreements with all states taking part, with the exception of Rumania, should be made only at the eleventh hour. With Rumania, however, " it is a matter of life and death." In the end Hitler ordered that agreements with participating states must not be concluded until there was no longer any necessity for camouflage.

Turning to " Marita " the Chief of Staff stresses the difficulties of transporting back those forces urgently needed for "Barbarossa." A complicated shuffle plan is worked out. But it turns out that " from now on ' Attila ' (the seizure of French North Africa) can be carried out only under difficulties ; ' Felix ' (the march through Spain on Gibraltar) is now no longer possible because the artillery set aside for it is needed in Russia ; and ' Sea-Lion ' (the invasion of Britain) can no longer be carried out." Hitler asks whether the Army can spare an armoured division to stem the British advance in Libya but the Commander-in-Chief replies " most unwillingly from ' Marita,' " adding that " if it comes to that, ' Barbarossa ' is also in need."

This undoubtedly is the conference which Gen. Paulus, according to his statement at Nuremberg, attended in Berchtesgaden, although he gave the date as one day later, February 3rd, 1941.

" Sea-lion " as a Deception

A few days later Raeder submitted the naval plans for " Barbarossa " and emphasized especially the necessity for the seizure of Murmansk " so that Britain cannot take a foothold there." But Hitler, who evidently failed to foresee that Murmansk was destined to become the chief port through which British and American supplies were to pour into Russia during the campaign, told Raeder that his main mission was " the rapid organization of the supply line to Leningrad." Raeder's Chief of Staff insisted on the occupation of Malta even before " Barbarossa " but was told by the Supreme Command that this was contemplated only after the execution of " Barbarossa." On February 18th, 1941, the naval diarist noted " measures for the covering up of the preparations for ' Barbarossa.' " Concentration movements against Russia are to be put forth as the " greatest undertaking of deception in the history of the war, designed to distract attention from the last preparations of the invasion against Britain. Even in the Armed Forces the impression is to be maintained that the invasion is being further prepared."

This fiction was kept up although it seems that it deluded hardly anyone except possibly the Germans themselves. While on February 2nd, 1941, the diarist noted that " it is intended to leave 31 divisions in France during ' Barbarossa,' " it was recorded on February 18th, 1941, that " in spite of the far-reaching disintegration of the operation ' Sea-Lion ' everything possible should be done to maintain the impression among our own troops that the invasion of Britain is being further prepared." In order to create additional uncertainty about German plans, the Army High Command prepared the sudden " blocking " of certain areas on the Channel coast and in Norway for which the code-word was " Albion." Whom did Hitler hope to deceive ? The British ? The Russians ? Both ? One wonders whether it was not all just a trifle over-sophisticated. On February 24th, 1941, Marshal Timoshenko, calling a spade a spade, issued a proclamation saying that " the entire Soviet nation, despite the success of the neutrality policy, must keep itself in constant readiness for the danger of an enemy surprise attack." This does not sound as if Stalin was allowing himself to be confused by " Albion."

The war of nerves is growing in intensity.

On March 1st, 1941, Germany marches into Bulgaria, and Bulgaria's consent to this is " disapproved in Moscow." The naval diarist says that " other reports also point to a stiffening of the Russian attitude because of events in the Balkans. However, a basic change of the Russian attitude is not anticipated." There is no doubt that the Soviet leaders, while taking all necessary precautions, are anxious to do everything in their power to avoid war and are not allowing the slightest provocation to occur on their part.

At this time, on February 13th, 1941, Ribbentrop had a conversation with the Japanese Ambassador Oshima, in Fuschl. After telling him that " the landing in Britain is prepared, its execution however depends on various factors, above all on weather conditions," he hinted at the coming campaign. " If an unwanted conflict with Russia should arise, we should have to carry the main burden also in this case." The time had come, he indicated, for Japan to stab either Britain or Russia in the back and assist Germany. " A defeat of Germany would also mean the end of the Japanese imperialist idea." But Oshima failed to react.

General Thomas Completes His Plan

On March 1st, 1941, General Thomas had completed his plans for the activities of the War Economy Staff in conjunction with " Barbarossa " and called a meeting with his section chiefs in which they were acquainted with the Russian operation. At the same time he ordered a complete reorganization of his department on a broader and more comprehensive basis, making it independent of the military or civil administration in the occupied areas. The chief mission of the organization was stated to be " the seizing of raw materials and taking over of all important concerns."

A fortnight later Keitel issued an important document. Called " Directives for Special Areas," it is an amplification of Directive No. 21 (" Barbarossa ") and regulates the administration of the areas about to be invaded.

" The Russian territory," it says, " which is to be occupied, shall be divided up into individual states with governments of their own, according to special orders, as soon as military operations are concluded. In the area of operations the Reichsführer S.S. (Himmler) is entrusted with special tasks for the preparation of the political administration, tasks which result from the struggle which has to be fought out between two opposing political systems. Within the scope of these tasks, the Reichsführer S.S. shall act independently and under his own responsibility."

As military operations were never concluded, this plan was never put fully into operation. But it shows that it was intended to leave the political " cleaning up " of the occupied areas to the S.S. under Himmler and that the Army was anxious to have no part in it. The Keitel memorandum continues :

" As soon as the area of operations has reached sufficient depth, it is to be limited in the rear. The newly occupied territory in the rear is to be given its own political administration. For the present it is to be divided, according to its genealogic basis and the positions of the Army Groups, into North (Baltic Countries), Centre (White Russia), and South (Ukraine). In these territories the political administration is taken care of by Commissioners who receive their orders from the Führer. As soon as operations begin the German-Russian frontier, and at a later stage the border at the rear of the area of operations will be closed to any and all non-military ·traffic with the exception of the police organizations to be deployed by the Reichsführer S.S. The Führer has entrusted the uniform direction of economy in the areas of operation and in the territories of political administration to the Reich Marshal (Goering) who has delegated the Chief of the War Economy Department (General Thomas) with the execution of the task."

The Postponement

It is difficult to understand how, at this stage, Hitler could still believe that Stalin did not know what Germany was up to. Perhaps he really did no longer believe it but simply carried on his camouflage manoeuvres because he could not very well drop them. The bubble is inflated to bursting point, and there remains only the question how soon Hitler is going to prick it. That Stalin will not fire the first shot is a certainty. May 15th, 1941, had been set as a tentative date for the attack. In all probability it was meant to be the definite date. A note in the naval diary states that "the extension of operations into Yugoslavia delayed 'Barbarossa' for about five weeks." This, in fact, would bring "Barbarossa" up to June 22nd, 1941, the date on which the attack actually started, and it agrees with General Paulus' statement in his testimony at Nuremberg on February 11th, 1946, that the "Barbarossa" plan was postponed on April 1st, 1941, for about five weeks until the second half of June. It had originally been fixed, according to Paulus, for the middle of May, as this was the earliest possible date in view of the weather in Russia. Paulus added that on March 27th or 28th, 1941, Hitler summoned him to Berlin and informed him of his intention to attack Yugoslavia. The objective, according to Paulus, was to "free the German right shoulder for the attack on Russia."

One may thus assume as correct that up to April 1st, 1941, the attack had been scheduled for May 15th, 1941, and that on April 1st, 1941, a five weeks' postponement was decided upon and the new date fixed for June 22nd, 1941. One interesting point, however, remains. On April 24th, 1941, the German Naval Attaché in Moscow, reporting widespread rumours about the danger of war between Germany and the Soviet Union, fed by transient travellers from Germany, quoted the British Ambassador in Moscow as predicting June 22nd as the day of outbreak of the German-Soviet war—the accurate date. The secret of the date was therefore discovered by British Intelligence some time between April 1st and 24th, 1941, the day the date was fixed by Hitler and the day the British Ambassador gave it away (according to the Germans). We know from Mr. Churchill that the British Government, was, in fact, in the possession of information showing that a German attack on the Soviet Union was in preparation, and that some time during the spring Mr. Churchill warned Stalin of what was coming. The puzzling thing in all this is that Mr. Churchill, possessing this information as he did, apparently nevertheless thought a German attempt at invasion of Britain possible at the same time. For in his speech during the secret session of the House of Commons on June 25th, 1941 (three days after the German attack against Russia) he warned the House that " in a few months or even less we may be exposed to the most frightful invasion the world has ever seen." What made Mr. Churchill think so ? Was it, after all, " Albion," the German deception scheme in Norway and along the Channel coast ? It does not seem likely since " Albion " (whose existence was confirmed by Paulus) was intended to operate only until the start of the attack on Russia, and Mr. Churchill spoke in secret session three days after the beginning of the attack. Did he then think that Russia was likely to collapse so utterly and in time for Hitler to start an invasion of Britain " in a few months or even earlier " ? Or did he think it possible or at all probable—in view of the vast German commitment in Russia which had already then become apparent—that Hitler had enough forces and equipment left to start on the journey across the Channel before he had arrived in Moscow ? This would seem too gross an over-estimate of German potentialities for Mr. Churchill to make. What, then, was the reason for Mr. Churchill making this estimate ? One hesitates to think that it was "Albion," after all. Nor is it credible that he should have seen through the " Albion " smoke-screen but nevertheless pretended to the House that he accepted it as real. There would have been a point in this poker move if his speech had been made in public session. It might have confused Hitler and kept sections of the British people from sitting back and thinking that now that Hitler had attacked Russia all was well and the invasion danger over. But in secret session ? One wonders what the answer is.

Japan is no help

Whatever the date on which Mr. Churchill passed on his information to Stalin, the German naval diarist recorded already on March 15th, 1941, a report from diplomatic circles speaking of an " improvement of relations between Russia and Britain." The following day the diarist noted " Russian preparations for mobilization on the Baltic front," and the next day " signs of Russian partial mobilization are noticeable on the Western border." On March 18th, 1941, Raeder had a communication from Admiral Nomura who told him that the Japanese Foreign Minister Matsuoka had grave doubts about the Russian problem and Japan's entry into the war, and recommended that Matsuoka be informed of Germany's intentions towards the Soviet Union. The Soviet-Turkish Non-Aggression Pact was signed, providing against an attack by a third power, and Berlin considered that it was pointed at Germany—a disappointing fruit of the conversations with Molotov. Matsuoka arrived in Berlin, and on March 29th, 1941, saw Ribbentrop and on April 4th, 1941, Hitler.

A first attempt was apparently made to get Japan to drop her neutrality and turn the Anti-Comintern Pact into a military alliance. Before the interviews with Matsuoka Keitel had already issued, on March 5th, 1941, " Basic Order No. 24 regarding collaboration with Japan " which stated : " It must be the aim of collaboration based on the Three Power Pact to induce Japan as soon as possible to take active measures in the Far East so that the centre of gravity and interests of the United States may be diverted to the Pacific." Ribbentrop did not let Matsuoka in on Germany's secret, as Raeder had suggested. He promised that Germany would attack Russia if she intervened after Japan had gone to war with Britain over Singapore. This apparently was not good enough for Matsuoka. Hitler assured the Japanese Foreign Minister that " he would not hesitate for a moment to reply instantaneously to any widening of the war, be it by Russia, be it by America," and, according to Raeder, informed Matsuoka " that Russia will not be touched if she behaves in a friendly way according to the treaty. Otherwise he reserves action for himself."

Matsuoka returned home by way of Moscow and there concluded a neutrality pact with Russia. Raeder was informed by Hitler that " the Japan-Russia Pact has been concluded in agreement with Germany. It is designed to prevent Japan from advancing against Vladivostok and to cause her to attack Singapore. This stand on the part of Germany has affected Russia's position favourably. Russia is now behaving very correctly and does not expect an attack."

Two and a half years later General Jodl in his Munich speech remarked mournfully : " We ourselves, from the purely military point of view, would be glad to see the Manchurian Army cross the Amur or advance against Vladivostok. But on this point both Asiatic powers stop their ears to the siren songs of the West."

Stalin continued to keep his temper. On April 6th, 1941, the naval diarist stated that " the position of Russia at the moment is one of quietness and waiting. Apparently Russia has firmly decided on neutrality towards Germany." Two days later he adds that "fear of Germany is still a decisive factor in Soviet policy, and a change in her neutrality is anticipated only in case of a serious German weakening. An increasing coolness, however, is unmistakable." In Moscow, at this time, a war council is held under Timoshenko and a state of emergency and increased military preparations are ordered for all units on the Western border. But economically Russia is as co-operative as before. A new oil agreement is signed on April 12th, 1941.

Economic Staff Oldenburg

On April 29th, 1941, a conference is held in General Thomas's office with all branches of the Armed Forces. It is announced that for the purposes of " Barbarossa " a new and entirely separate economic general staff has been formed which bears the code-name " Economic Staff Oldenburg " and is under the command of Major-General Schubert. The area of its operation is to be divided up into 5 economic inspectorates, 23 economic commands, and 12 sub-offices at the most important places within the areas of the economic commands. General Thomas explains that " Economic Staff Oldenburg " will deal not only with military industry but comprises the entire economic field. Its organization falls into three groups. Group M will deal with troop requirements, armaments, and industrial transport organization ; Group L with all questions relating to food and agriculture ; Group W with the entire field of trade and industry including raw materials, as well as forestry, finance and banking, enemy property, commerce and exchange of commodities, and manpower allocation. Of the 5 planned inspectorates, 4 are already determined while the fifth is held in reserve.

Inspectorate I with the code-name " Holstein " is at Leningrad with economic commands at Vilna, Riga, Reval, Leningrad and Murmansk, and sub-offices at Vologda and Archangel.

Inspectorate II with the code-name " Saxony " is at Moscow with economic commands at Minsk, Moscow, Tula and Gorki and sub-offices at Briansk, Yaroslavl and Rybinsk.

Inspectorate III with the code-name " Baden " is at Kiev with economic commands at Lodz, Kiev, Kishinev, Odessa, Kharkov, Dniepopetrovsk, Stalino, Rostov and Stalingrad, and sub-offices at Sevastopol, Kerch, Voronezh and Kursk.

Inspectorate IV with the code-name "Westphalia" is at Baku with economic commands at Krasnodar, Grozny, Tiflis and Baku and one sub-office at Batum.

Inspectorate V, held in reserve, was to have the code-name "Hesse."

General Thomas declares that "the whole organization requires a gigantic staff apparatus and that in view of the general shortage and lack of qualified personnel, only such posts can be filled with army personnel as are justified by practical necessity." Announcing that the establishment has to be completed by May 15th, 1941, he requests notification of the wishes of the Armed Forces not later than May 2nd, 1941.

The stage is almost set. On May 1st, 1941, proclamations by Stalin and Timoshenko show, according to the naval diarist, that "Russia is striving with all her means at her disposal to keep out of the war and, on account of the fluid international situation, to prepare for any eventuality."

On May 2nd, 1941, "Economic Staff Oldenburg" sends a memorandum to General Schubert on the "result of today's discussions with the Under-Secretaries of State regarding 'Barbarossa'" which opens with this sentence :

"The war can only be continued if all armed forces are fed by Russia in the third year of the war. There is no doubt that many millions of people will starve to death in Russia if we take out of the country the things necessary for us."

Having made this clear, the memorandum continues :

"The seizure and transfer of oil seeds and oil cakes are most important ; grain is only a second priority. The Armed Forces will probably consume the fat and meat which are on hand. Only those branches of industry are allowed to resume work which are engaged in the production of goods where shortages exist, such as factories manufacturing transport vehicles, textile works and such armament factories in whose fields shortages exist in Germany."

On May 6th, 1941, Stalin's appointment as Chairman of the Council of People's Commissars is announced. It signifies, in the opinion of Raeder's Chief of Staff, "concentration of the entire executive power, strengthening of the government authority and desire to continue the present foreign policy, that is, avoidance of a conflict with Germany."

On May 22nd, 1941, the day on which "the time-table for the maximum concentration of troops in the East is put into

T

operation," Raeder has a conference with Hitler and informs him that all preparations for the holding back of war materials consigned to Russia have been made. "In the near future it will be explained to the Russian Navy that, because of our own needs, there may be slight delays in deliveries without endangering the whole." Hitler agrees. A week later preparatory warship movements for " Barbarossa " begin.

The Time-table for "Barbarossa"

On June 1st, 1941, the time-table for " Barbarossa " is issued from Hitler's Headquarters. It opens with a survey of the " state of preparations as on June 1st, 1941."

Necessary measures in satellite states are shown to have been taken. Bulgaria has been requested not to reduce materially her units protecting the Turkish frontier. The Rumanians have begun a camouflaged part mobilization. Use of Hungarian territory for concentrating part of Army Group South is considered only should it be necessary to push a German unit between Hungarian and Rumanian troops. But this question will not be put to the Hungarian authorities until the middle of June. Two German divisions are drawn up in the Eastern part of Slovakia. Negotiations for preparations with the Finnish General Staff are shown to have been under way since May 25th, 1941. It is added that " Sweden has not been consulted. Negotiations will be started after the beginning of operations."

In the West altogether 42 divisions have been left plus one armoured brigade. Operations "Attila " (seizure of French North Africa) and " Isabella " (prevention of a British coup in Portugal) can still be executed at ten days' notice, but not simultaneously. Air Fleet II has been withdrawn from action and transferred to the East, while Air Fleet III has taken over sole command in the conduct of air warfare against Britain. The " Second Phase of Deception of the Enemy " is in operation under the code-names " Shark " and " Harpoon," with the aim of giving the impression that landings in Britain are being prepared from Norway, the Channel Coast and Brittany. (See also Chapter III, Operation Sea-Lion). Troop Concentration " East " will be represented as a deception exercise for the landing in Britain.

The time-table itself schedules the first landing in Finland of transports from Germany and Norway for June 8th and 9th. But these units are instructed immediately to withdraw from the

Petsamo area in the event of Russian offensive action against Finland.

On June 15th the Rumanians are to be informed of the final " Barbarossa " decisions. On June 16th a hint is to be given to the Hungarians to reinforce their safeguards on the border against Soviet Russia. From the same date " Russian ships are to be kept, by disguising measures, from entering the Kiel Canal and Gdynia harbour."

On June 17th and 18th all schools in the Eastern area are to be closed. German merchant shipping is to withdraw inconspicuously from Soviet ports. Further outward sailings to Soviet ports are to be suspended. Aerial reconnaissance of the Baltic begins.

As from June 18th " the intention to attack need no longer be camouflaged."

June 21st, 13.00 hours is given as the latest time at which the operation can still be cancelled. The code-word for cancellation is " Altona," for the start of the attack " Dortmund."

For the night from June 21st to 22nd it is ordered that " in the event of an encounter with the enemy the use of firearms is authorized."

H-hour for the start of the invasion by the Army and crossing of the frontier by the Air Force is June 22nd, 1941, 03.30 hours.

Still Stalin makes no move. On June 4th, 1941, Raeder's Chief of Staff notes in his war diary that there is " outwardly no change in German-Soviet relations. Russian deliveries continue to full satisfaction. The Soviet Government is endeavouring to do everything to prevent a conflict with Germany." The German Ambassador in Moscow reports on June 6th, 1941, that " Russia will only fight if attacked by Germany. The situation is considered in Moscow much more serious than up to now. All military preparations have been made quietly, and—as far as can be recognized—only defensively. Russian policy still strives as before to maintain the best possible relations with Germany."

The following day the Ambassador reports again. " All observations show that Stalin and Molotov who alone are responsible for Soviet foreign policy, are doing everything to avoid a conflict with Germany. The entire behaviour of the government as well as the attitude of the press, which reports all events concerning Germany in a factual, indisputable manner, support this view. The loyal fulfilment of the economic treaty with Germany proves the same-thing."

" The Eastern Campaign is Inevitable "

On June 14th, 1941, Hitler makes a speech lasting one hour and a half before all Commanders of Army Groups, Armies, and Naval and Air Commanders of equal rank at the Reich Chancery. Final reports on " Barbarossa " by all those ordered to attend, are submitted. Hitler gives the background for " Barbarossa " and outlines the plan of execution. The text of this speech is not among the documents so far available. According to a note made by the Chief, First Naval District and contained in the diary of Raeder's Chief of Staff, Hitler declared that " the Eastern campaign is inevitable, and we therefore must conduct it in a preventive and offensive manner to avoid the Russians overrunning us at a later date, after long appropriate preparations, when we are tied down in other sectors."

Among those present at this meeting one recognizes many well-known names. Keitel, Jodl and Warlimont are there for the Supreme Command. The Finnish front, code-named " Silver Fox," is represented by Falkenhorst and General Stumpff of Air Fleet V. Army Group South is represented by Rundstedt, Reichenau, Stülpnagel, Kleist and Schubert with General Löhr for Air Fleet IV. Army Group Centre has sent Field Marshals Bock and Kluge and Generals Strauss, Guderian and Hoth with Kesselring for Air Fleet II. Army Group North, finally, shows Leeb, Busch, Küchler and Höppner as commanders with General Keller in charge of Air Fleet I. Goering, Milch, Brauchitsch, Halder, Paulus, Jeschonnek and Bodenschatz are also there.

On the same day the Soviet Tass Agency issues an official communiqué discrediting rumours of a coming German-Russian war and emphasizing the conscientious fulfilment of the pact by both parties. Characteristically the naval diarist notes :

" This declaration is evaluated on the German side as an attempt to brand Germany as the aggressor in case of a possible attack."

Some Conclusions

What conclusions can be drawn from this summary of events ?

Once again it must be emphasized that this is only half the story—the Nazi half. A full and objective view of this crucial period of European affairs can only be gained after the Soviet Union has contributed her own version which, no doubt, will amplify and correct much that remains obscure in the German story. Moreover, it must be remembered that here as elsewhere in these studies, only part of the German documentary evidence now in Allied hands was available—that part which was released at Nuremberg for the purposes of the Allied prosecution. The remainder still awaits official publication.

Nevertheless, certain points stand out clearly from the story as told by the Nazi documents. The Munich conference appears as the true turning point. Having been excluded from it, the Soviet Union decided that she could not assume joint responsibility for consequences arising from a situation upon which she had been denied influence. She concluded that she could not rely on concerted action with the Western Democracies in case of an armed conflict with Germany. Driven into political isolation, Stalin apparently decided that, in self-protection, the Soviet Union must sup with the Devil, but he determined to take the longest spoon he could find and draw the meal out as long as possible.

For Hitler, who had always intended to drive East, it was a question of deciding at what stage of the war he should tackle the Soviet Union, before or after the invasion of Britain. We now see that the final decision to abandon the invasion plan in favour of an attack in the East was made immediately after Molotov's visit to Berlin in November, 1940, although tentative preparations were begun several months earlier.

Hitler's purpose in concluding the Pact with Russia was to keep his rear free while dealing with the West and to obtain at the same time those foodstuffs and raw materials which were essential for his conduct of the war and which he was bent on getting in any case—eventually by force of arms and outright conquest. He was ready to do this at the price of building up and steadily strengthening the Red Army through delivery of German war material, at one point even to the detriment of his own forces, but he was apparently convinced that, even so, he would win this " race with himself." For Stalin, who seems to have had few doubts about Hitler's ultimate intentions, it was a question of buying time and arms at the price of assisting his eventual enemy with precious raw materials which he had to deny to his own people.

Thus the vicious circle rounded itself.

Appendix.

A List of the Principal Captured German Documents Quoted or Referred to in this Book.

1. Secret briefing speech made by Hitler to the Commanders-in-Chief on November 5th, 1937, known as the "Hossbach Minutes."

2. Secret briefing speech made by Hitler to the Commanders-in-Chief on May 23rd, 1939.

3. Secret briefing speech made by Hitler to the Commanders-in-Chief on August 22nd, 1939.

4. Second briefing speech made by Hitler on August 22nd, 1939.

5. Secret briefing speech made by Hitler to the Commanders-in-Chief on November 23rd, 1939.

6. Directive for the Unified Preparation for War of the Armed Forces (Blomberg Directive) of June 24th, 1937.

7. Directive No. 1 (Operation "Case Otto"), signed by Hitler, dated March 11th, 1938.

8. Directive No. 2 (Operation "Case Otto"), dated March 11th, 1938, 20.24 hours.

9. Draft for Directive "Case Green," signed by Keitel, dated, May 20th, 1938.

10. Final Directive "Case Green," signed by Hitler, dated May 30th 1938.

11. Draft for Amended Directive "Case Green," dated June 18th, 1938.

12. Directive No. 1 "Occupation of Territory Separated from Czechoslovakia," signed by Keitel, dated September 30th, 1938.

13. Interim Directive on "Future Tasks of the Armed Forces," signed by Hitler, dated October 21st, 1938.

14. First Supplement to Interim Directive of October 21st, 1938, dated November 24th, 1938.

15. Letter of Instructions from Hitler to Supreme Command, Armed Forces, relative to "Liquidation of Rest of Czechoslovakia," dated December 17th, 1938.

16. Directive for the Armed Forces 1939-40 ("Case White"), dated April 3rd, 1939.

17. Directive for the Uniform Preparation of War by the Armed Forces, signed by Hitler, dated April 11th, 1939.

18. Directive No. 1 for the Conduct of the War, signed by Hitler, dated August 31st, 1939.

19. Directive No. 6 for the Conduct of the War, relative to the invasion of the Low Countries, signed by Hitler, dated October 9th, 1939.

20. Directive No. 8 for the Conduct of the War, relative to the invasion of the Low Countries, signed by Keitel, dated November 20th, 1939.

21. Directive for the Conduct of the War (serial number unstated), relative to the invasion of Norway and Denmark, signed by Hitler, dated March 1st, 1940.

22. Directive for the Conduct of the War (serial number unstated), relative to the invasion of Great Britain, dated August 17th, 1940.

23. Directive for the Conduct of the War No. 18, signed by Hitler, dated November 12th, 1940.

24. Directive No. 21 for the Conduct of the War, relative to the invasion of the Soviet Union, signed by Hitler, dated December 18th, 1940.

25. Directive No. 22 for the Conduct of the War, relative to the participation of the German Armed Forces in the Mediterranean Theatre of war, signed by Hitler, dated January 11th, 1941.

26. Directive for the Conduct of the War (serial number unstated). relative to the invasion of Yugoslavia, dated March 30th, 1941,

27. Time-table for " Case Barbarossa " (invasion of the Soviet Union), dated June 1st, 1941.

28. The War Diary of General Alfred Jodl, Chief of Staff of the Supreme Command of the German Armed Forces.

29. Confidential speech on " The Strategic Position at the beginning of the Fifth Year of War," made by General Jodl to an assembly of Nazi Party Gauleiters in Munich on November 7th, 1943.

30. War Diary kept by the Chief of Staff of Admiral Raeder, Commander-in-Chief of the German Navy.

31. Minutes of an operational conference between Hitler, Keitel and Brauchitsch at Berchtesgaden on September 3rd, 1938.

32. Minutes of an operational conference between Hitler, Keitel, Brauchitsch and Halder at Nuremberg on September 9th, 1938.

33. Minutes of an operational conference between Hitler, Mussolini and the German and Italian Chiefs of Staff at Hitler's Headquarters on January 19th and 20th, 1941.

34. Minutes of an operational conference between Hitler, Keitel, Jodl and Brauchitsch on February 2nd, 1941.

35. Minutes of a conference between Hitler, Ribbentrop, Keitel, Jodl and Brauchitsch on March 27th, 1941.

36. Secret Report by Schacht to Hitler on the " State of Preparations for War—Economic Mobilization," dated September 30th, 1934.

37. Plan Study, 1938 (Instructions for Deployment and Combat during " Case Red "), issued by the High Command of the German Air Force, dated June 2nd, 1938.

38. Memorandum on " Extended Case Green," issued by the General Staff of the German Air Force, dated August 25th, 1938.

39. Memorandum on the " Joint Preparation for the Refutation of Our Own Violations of International Law and the Exploitation of its Violation by the Enemy " prepared by the Supreme Command of the Armed Forces and the Propaganda Ministry, dated October 1st, 1938.

40. Minutes of a conference between Goering and his Economic Planning Staff, dated October 14th, 1938.

41. Confidential speech made by Major-General Thomas, Chief of the War Economy Department, on the state of German War Industries, made before officials of the German Foreign Office, dated March 24th, 1939.

42. " Basic Facts for a History of German War and Armament Economy," a memorandum compiled by Major-General Thomas, dated 1944.

43. Memorandum from Alfred Rosenberg to Hitler on " The Political Preparations of the Norway Action," dated June 17th, 1940.

44. Memorandum from Admiral Raeder to Admiral Assmann, dated January 10th, 1944.

45. Minutes of a conference between Major-General Thomas and all branches of the Armed Forces on " Economic Staff Oldenberg," dated April 29th, 1941.

46. Memorandum from the German Embassy in London to Hitler on " Future Anglo-German Relations," dated January 2nd, 1938.

47. Transcripts of telephone conversations between Goering in Berlin and Seyss-Inquart, Keppler, Muff, Dombrowski and others in Vienna, prepared by the staff of the German Air Ministry, dated March 11th, 1938.

48. Transcript of a telephone conversation between Hitler and Prince Philip of Hesse in Rome, dated March 11th, 1938.

49. Transcript of a telephone conversation between Goering in Berlin and Ribbentrop in London, prepared by the staff of the German Air Ministry, dated March 13th, 1938.

INDEX

For Product Safety Concerns and Information please contact our EU
representative GPSR@taylorandfrancis.com
Taylor & Francis Verlag GmbH, Kaufingerstraße 24, 80331 München, Germany